MW00416329

I'M LAUGHING BECAUSE I'M CRYING

I'M LAUGHING BECAUSE I'M CRYING

A MEMOIR

By Youngmi Mayer

LITTLE, BROWN AND COMPANY

New York Boston London

This memoir reflects the author's life, faithfully rendered. Some chronologies and details have been compressed or altered to aid the narrative. With dialogue, the intention is to convey the essence of conversations rather than verbatim quotes. Some names and identifying characteristics of individuals have been changed.

Copyright © 2024 by Youngmi Mayer

Hachette Book Group supports the right to free expression and the value of copyright. The purpose of copyright is to encourage writers and artists to produce the creative works that enrich our culture.

The scanning, uploading, and distribution of this book without permission is a theft of the author's intellectual property. If you would like permission to use material from the book (other than for review purposes), please contact permissions@hbgusa.com. Thank you for your support of the author's rights.

Little, Brown and Company
Hachette Book Group
1290 Avenue of the Americas, New York, NY 10104
littlebrown.com

First Edition: November 2024

Little, Brown and Company is a division of Hachette Book Group, Inc. The Little, Brown name and logo are trademarks of Hachette Book Group, Inc.

The publisher is not responsible for websites (or their content) that are not owned by the publisher.

The Hachette Speakers Bureau provides a wide range of authors for speaking events. To find out more, go to hachettespeakersbureau.com or call (866) 376-6591.

Little, Brown and Company books may be purchased in bulk for business, educational, or promotional use. For information, please contact your local bookseller or the Hachette Book Group Special Markets Department at special.markets@hbgusa.com.

Print book interior design by Taylor Navis

ISBN 9780316569231
LCCN 2024931058

Printing 1, 2024

MRQ-T

Printed in Canada

To Mom and Dad
(Don't be mad at me)

Contents

Author's Note

This is true to what I believe happened, faithfully rendered to the best of my ability. I have changed names and some descriptions to protect the privacy of others. While the events are true, they may not be entirely factual. They reflect my recollections of experiences over time, and these memories can be flawed. I have also reconstructed dialogue to the best of my recollection and reordered or combined the sequence of some events to assist the narrative. Where dialogue appears, the intention was to re-create the essence of conversations rather than verbatim quotes. Others who were present might recall things differently. But this is my story.

This memoir reflects the author's life faithfully rendered to the best of her ability. Some names and identifying details have been changed, some events have been compressed, and some conversations have been reconstructed. This is a work of creative nonfiction.

Korean romanization was chosen by the author based on what she deemed to be the most accurate as a native Korean speaker and may not reflect the official or most up-to-date versions.

I'M LAUGHING BECAUSE I'M CRYING

Prologue

When I initially had an idea to write a book, I kept thinking, *Why should I write a book? I am a dumbass and a loser, and why would anyone read it to begin with? What would the book even be about?* Then I realized, what if *that* was what the book was about? The fact that I call myself a dumbass and a loser all the time? After all, it's what got me here in the first place. It's the thing that seems to separate me from all the other Asian American comedians: the showing of all my cards. The fact that I am a failure and fucking nuts and also constantly bringing it up. Someone online once called me the "mentally ill Ali Wong," which is weird because I would argue that she already comes off as mentally ill (complimentary). But I think what they meant by that was being mentally ill is sort of my *thing*. I literally won't shut up about it. I bring it up every five minutes because I can't rely on actual comedic talent like she can. When I tell a joke, no one laughs, and instead of working on my craft, I spiral and post a bunch of my unhinged inner thoughts. People like that because it's relatable.

It's not really new for an Asian person to come off as a failure or a weirdo. To subvert the stereotypes that we are all perfect, hardworking, and smart. Literally, Ali Wong does that too. But I think there is a level to my realness that still takes people by surprise. I am comfortable saying shit that I truly should not be saying in any situation. Not only am I comfortable with it, but it's where I have found my strength.

3

I realized that I have gained a following because I'm willing to openly admit the things that so many people spend their entire lives trying to cover up. A lot of people find it off-putting, but for others, it's a respite from an endless existence of shame. They see me displaying openly something they've been running away from all their lives and feel relief. I also receive a huge benefit from this relationship with people who relate to my material: it makes me feel like I'm not alone and that I'm not crazy. Well, I am crazy, but so are a bunch of other people.

Another aspect of my work that people seem to enjoy is that I talk about being Asian with an air of confidence that seems to be lacking in other Asian American comedians. I attribute this to being raised in Asia. I am missing the pathological implication that I'm inferior to white people that is injected at the very beginning of the formation of Asian American identities when they're born in Wisconsin. I think this deep imprint is almost impossible to erase in Asian Americans raised here. There's no way for Asian men to undo the fact that half the time they met someone throughout their years in school, that person would make a small penis joke. That sort of psychological terrorism lives in their bodies. It changes the way they stand. The way they walk. Asian women here grew up answering the phone at their mom's nail salon and heard prank callers scream, "Me love you long time!" or "How much for happy ending?" on a daily basis. The trauma of that is seen in their eyes but also on top of their eyes in the form of heavy-handed winged eyeliner, which they never seem to leave home without wearing. Eye makeup so thick it's hard to tell if they're trying to hide the shape of their eyes in shame or wearing it like war paint—a defense. They move the way a caged animal moves. I do not move like that. I do not joke like that. I was allowed to form an idea of myself outside of it. I think Asian Americans sense this, and they are comforted by it and made confident from it. They can trust I will never hurt them for the cheap reward of a white laugh. Or even if I do, I will include something that hurts white people way more at the end.

4

Speaking of shared Asian American experiences, though, there's nothing I can say about my experience as an Asian American that hasn't already been said in Amy Tan's *The Joy Luck Club*. I thought that was a joke until I rewatched the movie version to write this prologue and then spiraled about how I should just throw the whole book away because everything's already in that fucking movie! Based on a book written in, what, the eighties? NOOO. But my story isn't only about all the Asian-y "my mom got thrown into the river" trauma that it shares with *The Joy Luck Club*. My story isn't about the parts of my life that are subversive to the Asian stereotypes, like doing heroin in my twenties or becoming a single mom in my thirties who fucks guys who skateboard. My story isn't even about being mentally ill. My story is about the fact that no one else in the world has lived my life.

All Asian Americans probably have pretty similar background stories. But so do all the white guys who were the only ones allowed to write books for the last twenty-seven thousand years, and Lord knows that's never stopped any of them. Every year, since the invention of papyrus, like ten thousand college professor white guys write a book about how hot sixteen-year-old girls are. But none of them ever seem to think, *Wait, has someone done this before?* None of them ever seem to think that they're dumbass losers who maybe need to shut the fuck up. So why would I think that?

*   *   *

WHEN I WAS A KID growing up in Korea, sometimes my classmates and I would walk by the pet store to ogle the puppies. We would all crowd around the window to choose the puppy we would purchase if our parents actually let us have dogs instead of beating our asses every time we asked. We chose the puppies based on their personalities. Usually, the other kids would all fight over the friendliest ones, but I always chose the sad, pathetic ones with boogers in their eyes because I felt sorry for them. A few other girls would choose the sad, pathetic ones too. Our view of puppy ownership was about caretaking and being sad, not the actual joys of having a puppy. Even in our fantasies, we didn't let ourselves fly high. We grew up to be the teenagers who chose Joey Fatone as our *NSYNC boyfriend.

These dogs were severely inbred "purebred" dogs: pugs, Maltese, Yorkshire terriers. They were bred for physical traits favorable to humans despite the fact that the traits were deformities detrimental to the health and longevity of the dogs themselves. Above all, they were bred to be identical because it was important for a breeder to expect the same thing again and again. But their tiny dog souls rebelled against the fallacy that they were interchangeable objects by having distinct personalities. Like these puppies, Korean girls were expected to be exactly the same. We all had the same hair, same uniform, same bodies, and were trained to have the same behavior. We saw ourselves in the puppies: powerless objects created to appease the selfish and confusing desires of cruel adults. Since we were all the same, we could see that each one of us was different, just like each puppy was different. We could tell all of them apart. But the adults could not.

One day after school, my friends and I stopped by the pet store to see the owner pulling a sick puppy out of the window. We saw him carry it to the back and asked him what he was going to do. He said he was going to throw it away because it was dying (Koreans DGAF). We all screamed and cried. He looked confused. His wife ran out of the heated room in the back with a flimsy plastic flyswatter in her hand, slapping us with it while screaming for us to leave. By the time she shoved all of us out of the store, we were sobbing uncontrollably. Some of the girls started wailing like we saw the old people doing at funerals. We walked like this to the playground, where we continued to cry all afternoon long, together. A litter of Korean girls. All the same thing.

I moved to the US when I was twenty. Part of the reason I moved here was because I no longer wanted to be the same thing. However, upon my arrival, my new Asian friends warned me that white people would not be able to tell me apart from other Asians. I thought it was a joke. Reader, it was not. White people will confuse a fifty-year-old Chinese woman with a twenty-five-year-old Filipina woman just because they work on the same floor. White people are confused as to why this offends Asians so much. It's the same confusion I saw on the face of the pet store owner that day when we started crying because he was throwing the puppy away. Our sadness confused him. He didn't understand why it mattered if one of the puppies died. There were so many more of them we could play with in the window, and they were all the same thing.

We know what it means when white people can't tell us apart. It means that they can throw us away.

The reason I have to write this book is because I know a lot of you reading this have bought this lie that we are all the same. Maybe white people taught it to you or maybe it was an old Korean pet shop owner. Maybe that old Korean pet shop owner was your own father. Maybe you were convinced like I was that Amy Tan said everything you ever wanted to say forty years ago. But even if your name is Waverly and your tiger mom forced you to play chess while growing up in San Francisco's Chinatown, your story would not be the same story. What I realized was that even the dogs bred to be identical never bought into the lie that they were the same and therefore worthless. It never occurred to those puppies in the window that they didn't deserve a voice. They barked whenever they wanted to. Those bitches barked all the time. Just like white guys. White guys never fall for the lie either. Every day, a white guy who looks and acts like every other white guy wakes up and thinks, *My god, I am unique and everything I say is important and probably has never been said before!* and then starts a podcast. Honestly, that guy is right. Good for him. Unfortunately, he thinks that right is reserved only for him and dogs that look like him. How silly.

Here's the thing, though: we are all the same thing. If you look at a yin-yang symbol, at first you think it depicts a binary of white and black, but the symbol isn't split down the middle—it's a circle encompassing both. We aren't one side or the other; we are both sides, forever and ever. There are two wolves inside of you: a white guy who can't shut the fuck up and an Asian woman who feels ashamed every time she talks. You are both. They are you and you are them. The white guy and Asian woman live within each and every one of us. For me, this is quite literal since my dad is white and my mom is Asian.

Because of this, all my life I have been forced to split the circle in two and choose which side I am on. Am I white or Korean? Am I rich or poor? Am I fat or skinny? Am I a girl or a boy pretending to be a girl (which is something my Korean classmates always accused me of because I was 0.5 kilograms heavier than all of them)? I tried to separate the two parts of myself all my life and analyze them to know which side I was supposed to be on. Everything I did, I examined to see if it was a white thing or a Korean thing. But I could never figure it out. Slowly it dawned on me that the reason I couldn't figure it out was because they were both the same thing. White people aren't really different from Koreans. No one is. None of us are all that different. After being forced to see everything in a binary all my life, I realized the binary isn't real.

So, here's my story. Is it going to be like *The Joy Luck Club*? Yes. Parts of it. There are some references to dragons and yin-yang symbols and a lot of Asian mom trauma. There will be many similarities, but that doesn't mean it doesn't deserve to be said. There will be many differences, but that doesn't mean it is not relatable. To read this book is to avenge the death of the puppy who got thrown away. It's to understand that if a dumbass loser like me deserves to be centered, then maybe so do you.

I'm crying because I'm laughing.

CHAPTER 1

Korean

복순 (BOKSOON; FULL OF LUCK)

THERE ARE VERY IMPORTANT THINGS that happened before I was born that shaped the person I am. As I learned more about my past, I realized I'm a literal clone of my recent ancestors, reliving patterns I inherited from them. People say that the dead live on in the memories of their loved ones, but they are actually fully alive in us. People are immortal not because we remember them, but because we are them. There's a scene in *Back to the Future* where Marty McFly goes back in time and meets his father as a teen. He sees his dad get enraged when a bully calls him "chicken." Before then, we were made to think that was Marty McFly's individual quirk. But it wasn't. It was his dad's. If we went further back in time with Marty, we would probably meet the first person in his lineage who hated that. Some ancient Bavarian peasant who hated being called "Chickenslof" or something. All of us do things every day that don't belong to us. We just don't know who they belong to because they might have lived hundreds of years before we were born.

Around one hundred years before I was born, my Korean great-grandmother on my grandfather's side was kidnapped in a blanket in an act referred to as *bossam*, which is also the word for the disgusting gray boiled pork dish made popular in the US by Momofuku. To this day when I hear an American person say they like this dish, I think they're a loser. Liking the one dish that someone hand-delivered to your shitty corner of Manhattan instead of exploring the breadth of Korean cuisine? Embarrassing.

My great-grandmother's kidnapping left my grandfather abandoned as a ten-year-old boy, leaving him to a life of homelessness and panhandling. At around fifteen, he ended up working as an indentured farmhand for the family of a relatively wealthy landowner. That landowner had three daughters, the eldest being my grandmother.

My grandmother was an exceptional child. She was one of the only female children who knew how to read properly in her town because due to her father's relative wealth and lack of a son, he had kept her in middle school, which was a rarity for girls at the time. My grandmother had a talent for spoken word and singing and was sent around to people's homes to read poems and sing songs. She was the niche Internet microcelebrity of her time. She was celebrated for being talented, but she was not beautiful. Her face was small up top and sort of fanned out at the jaw. To make matters worse, the popular hairstyle for schoolgirls of that era was a tightly pulled braid at the base of the neck. The hair on the scalp was pulled so severely that it resembled a glossy black swim cap and, in my grandmother's case, highlighted her candy-corn-ass head shape. A large mole sat on her cheek. My grandmother very unfortunately resembled a character in traditional Korean comedic theater sometimes named 복순이 (Boksoon-i). In plays, the character was played by a man wearing a braided wig, his face painted with faux freckles, a large mole on his cheek, and his front teeth blacked out. The character's name was an ironic, cruel joke because the Chinese character *Bok* meant "luck" and *Soon* meant "full of." In the middle of a play, the comedians on stage would call out, "복순아! 복순아!" (Hey, Boksoon! Boksoon!) She would appear, hilariously hideous in stark contrast to her name, and then one of the comedians would say, "복터졌네!" (Bok ttujeutnae!; Your luck exploded with this one!) It was a joke based on the humiliation of high expectation. There were two parts to this joke: First, the audience laughed at themselves for their high expectations. Then, they laughed at the hubris of her parents for giving her such a grand name and setting themselves up to be humiliated by fate. This was a genius comedic device, and all the jokes written for Boksoon-i were cutting, sophisticated satire about the nuances of Korean society. This tradition still remains in modern Korean comedies, both television shows and movies. When white people come across it, they write Korean comedy off as lowbrow, unsophisticated slapstick. I hear Americans refer to Korean comedy as a knockoff of American vaudeville without realizing that this form of humor existed in Korea thousands of years before the US was even a country. They lack the capacity to realize that all the jokes are intricate satire because they believe theater and comedy were invented by them. Boksoon-i was always played by the most famous comedian and was the main character. If white people didn't assume that Koreans were stupid, they would realize that Boksoon-i stood for one of the most important underlying themes of Korean art: the ugly, seemingly worthless girl was secretly the most important of us all. The one who made us laugh.

Koreans could appreciate the concept of Boksoon-i in comedic theater, but they couldn't see her in their real lives. In the same way my grandmother's value was not seen in her community. No one gave a shit that my grandmother memorized a bunch of poems and was well educated; that bitch was ugly as hell, and no one would want to marry her ass. My grandmother didn't care about any of this because she dreamt of going to school and becoming a poet. She stated that she never wanted to marry.

For ten years, my great-grandfather had been quietly watching the orphaned boy who would later become my grandfather. Although he was without a name and orphaned, therefore the lowliest of classes, he was still a boy. He was also trustworthy and hardworking. Among his attributes was the fact that he was extremely handsome, which was noted by all the female members of my family. He was so attractive that it was difficult for people to make eye contact with him, something he attributed to his low status in society. The reason he was so hardworking was because he had been an abandoned child. He was terrified of letting anyone down and did all his work efficiently and without ever complaining. My great-grandfather had no sons and knew if he married off his daughters to other families, his wealth would leave his family in the form of dowries. He wanted to keep his wealth in his own family by adopting this humble farmhand as a son. So he decided to marry this hot twenty-five-year-old subby guy off to his fifteen-year-old ugly daughter.

This marriage was my grandmother's worst nightmare and my grandfather's greatest dream come true. She had dreamt of the freedom to shine as a star, and he had dreamt of belonging to someone, anyone. Now he was given the gift of not only a wife, but a wife of relatively high birth. Because of this promise of belonging, despite her appearance, he was obsessively in love with my grandmother. To him she *was* Boksoon-i; his luck had exploded with this one. He worked hard every day doing farmwork, what he was expected to do, as my grandmother did what she was expected to do: have a gang of kids and raise them. Just as my great-grandfather anticipated, my grandfather was so hardworking and talented, he quickly amassed land and a small fortune of his own. But my grandmother was so resentful of losing her dream that she mocked and humiliated him daily, which only caused him to work harder and try harder to gain her love. Subby vibes. He would run around endlessly, in a constant, never-ending scramble to keep her happy. The imbalance of power between them meant that unlike other men during this time, he even participated in child-rearing. He would take care of all the children at night after returning from working in the fields all day so that my grandmother could enjoy some free time, which she spent sitting in her room, smoking her pipe, and crying. Legend. She never did love him and told him that every single day. Up to the day he killed himself.

My grandmother told this story to my mother when she was a child: After being married to a *poor, stupid man* (Grandma's words), she refused to sleep in the same room as him. Then my great-grandfather built them a house over a mile away. She would walk home every single night and cry at the gate to be let in. She did that until she became pregnant at the age of sixteen, within a year of being married.

My Korean grandparents had a shit ton of sons. An unheard-of number of sons. Their luck had exploded with the number of healthy, handsome sons they bore. Even my own mother is unsure of the number since some of them died as infants, but it was around seven to ten. Then, after all these sons, finally, my mother 입분 (Ib-Bun). My mother's name literally means "pretty." 입분이 (Ib-Bun-i). The pretty one.

Her name was a mistake.

*　*　*

입분 (立分; IB-BUN; STAND DIVIDED)

In these times when children were born, a family representative had to travel to city hall in Seoul and record their birth in the national book of births. Since my family lived in a small farm town far from Seoul, they asked my grandfather's friend, who was already planning a trip to Seoul, to record her birth for them. The night before, he came to collect payment for the trip and my grandfather convinced him to take payment in the form of homemade 약주 (yakju; rice wine). They ended up drinking all night on a mat placed over dirt in the courtyard under a single lantern drenched in flies. This was in August in Korea, the month where the overripe, suffocating air of summer can simply kill a bug with its wet heaviness. The bugs scrambled over the lantern light, trying to dry their lungs from drowning in the wet air.

The darkness of the Korean countryside consumed everything besides their faces, drunk and red, lit by the bug lantern. The next day, the man and my grandfather woke up and found themselves still on the dirt ground, surrounded by the dead bugs that had drowned in the wet darkness the night before. The man took off to Seoul without having asked my grandfather what he wanted to name his girl child.

At the city hall office in Seoul, the man was asked what the girl's name was by the government official. It had not occurred to him until then that he needed this information. And he was confused why it was important, since it was just a girl. I imagine the poor farm man, ashamed of his dark skin and clothes covered in dirt from my family's yard, surrounded by other pushy, dark, poor Koreans in tattered hanbok and gomushin falling apart on their feet. I imagine him standing in front of the well-dressed government official with pomade in his hair and those round imperial glasses, sitting behind a desk in front of rows and rows of endless bound books that cataloged every Korean who had been born.

There were no lines in these salad days of Korean independence where they were recovering from the trauma of Japanese imperialism and the Korean War. Koreans moved in an anxious, desperate mob everywhere they went, carrying babies and baskets of dried peppers and dates on their backs and heads. The flies clung to their faces and clothes, attracted to the sweet smell of sweat and spit. Seoul was a chaotic swirl of humans who had recently learned that they were indeed humans and had the right to exist. In their hunger to proclaim their humanity, they ascended the steps of city hall to record their little lives in big books. They anxiously pushed into this strange building in the center of their hometown. The city hall was built by Japanese imperialists in the style of European architecture because, like the idea of supremacy, the Japanese weren't even talented enough to come up with this shit on their own. Like the drowning bugs clinging to a lantern, the Koreans were drawn to this alien building made of marble, and their shoes felt slippery on the floors that were not wet.

I imagine the government official behind the desk, barely not a child, maybe the meek second or third son of a medium rich person, watching the pulsating mob enter the doors every day. I imagine the government official being humiliated by the realization that these people were *his* people, their dark hands and faces dotting the sea of beige hanbok, waving pieces of paper. No matter how much he tried to dress and act like a sophisticated Japanese, his face was the same as the faces in the crowd. Faces of people who were meant to die but would not die regardless. Again, like the bugs. Waving the pieces of paper without understanding that they needed to have order, to have manners, that they needed to form a line. Had they not learned anything from the Japanese? But they could not form a line in their desperation. They were drowning and had found this marble life raft. They scrambled up the stairs. They cried out, "Please write this down!" I imagine the people pushing toward the counter, knowing if they didn't write the births down, no one would know they had lived and died. They wanted to prove their oppressors wrong. They were not insects. I imagine the Korean government official—a little boy pretending to be a man in a suit, glasses, and hairstyle borrowed from the Japanese, who had borrowed them from the Europeans—thinking to himself, *Look at these fucking insects.*

Humiliated by insisting on his existence, my grandfather's friend— illiterate, terrified, sweaty, dark skinned—had one fucking job. It was the most important job of all time. To tell them that even a 기집애 (gijibae; girl) from 방게리 (Bangeri; the small farm town my mom is from) deserved to be in the book. She belonged in the fucking book. And then the government official asked, "But what is her name?" I imagine my grandfather's friend's pounding headache from drinking nothing but moonshine yakju, and in that moment, being pushed by a halmoni holding a basket of godungu on her head, I'm imagining he said, "이름? 뭔 이름 두 필요해유?" (in Chungcheongnam-do dialect: Ileum? Mwon ileum du pilyohaeyu?; Name? Why do you need a name?) Then he said, "아이고 이쁘든대... 이쁜이로 져유." (Aigo ippundae ippun-I lo jyeo yu; Well, she's pretty, so call her "pretty one.") Then I imagine the government official looking at him, thinking, 무식한 개자식 (musikan gaejasik; Idiot son of a bitch) and asking him, "What are the Chinese characters?"

Traditionally, Koreans chose names based on the meaning of the Chinese characters and not the phonetic pronunciation. When having a baby, a Korean couple would consult an older relative or a fortune teller/ Chinese character specialist and tell them what traits they wanted in their child. Because their names were chosen by meaning, the sound of the name was not important. Much like astrology, where a lot of people actually seem to have the personality assigned to their signs, people in Korea eerily become like the traits they were named after.

But the word *Ippun* was just a country-bumpkin term for a pretty little girl. It was not something that could be an official name, because there were no Chinese characters. The official wrote my mother's name, 입븐 (Ib-Bun), with the characters 立 (Ib; stand) and 分 (Bun; to divide). A nonsensical collection of important words that means nothing, thus turning a childish and whimsical name into one that fit in the book.

So my mother's name, a mistake, was 입븐. Ib-Bun. To stand. Divided.

* * *

수미 (水美; SU-MI; WATER, BEAUTY)

I THINK A LOT OF white people will read this and not understand why no one cared about my mom's name or cared enough to change it afterward. White people have a pathological attachment to names as important individuality markers. But Koreans see it in a different way. A name means something to them, but only spiritually and for official reasons. Names are rarely used outside of government or workplace situations. I find this part of my Korean upbringing difficult to shake even after years of living in the US. I don't like knowing people's names and using their names. It almost feels rude to know someone's name. Names are treated like secret personal information, much like how Americans think of age, which is interestingly something Koreans give out freely and openly.

For Asian Americans, names are phenomenally important because the mispronunciation of their names is a dehumanizing tactic used to covertly state that individuality belongs only to the whites who would get angry if you spelled it *Jennifer* with two *N*s when it's actually spelled with one! I remember after the Atlanta shootings in 2021, an Asian American comedian made a viral video about how the white news anchors had mispronounced the names of the dead. She made a video correcting them, and then mispronounced the names herself. LOL. Shortly after, the families of the deceased who were Korean politely asked the news channels to remove the victims' names completely, because in Korea, names are private and full of magic and power. In Korea, victims of violent crimes have their identities shielded from the public to protect their living families from bad omens or shame. To this day I am filled with rage against this comedian who put her personal Asian American trauma over the wants and needs of the Korean women who died. She called out their names into the universe, inviting all the demons and ghosts to haunt their souls. 재수없어씨발 (this is hard to translate but it means something like "someone who brings fucking bad luck"). How funny that in her ignorance, she mispronounced their names and shielded them from being haunted. Koreans do not want you to say our names. Our names are ours.

I don't know the names of any of my family members besides my mother and cousins of my own age. I've never known the names of anyone who is older than me. To me they are 외숙모 (whe sook mo; my mother's brother's wife), much different from 이모 (e mo; my mother's sister). My mom's friend is 수빈엄마 (Su-Bin umma; mother of Su-Bin, her eldest child). My neighbor growing up was 진호엄마

(Jin-Ho umma; mother of Jin-Ho). I remember when Jin-Ho died. We still called her Jin-Ho umma. Because she was still Jin-Ho umma. She will be for an eternity. This way of being called is stronger than death; it means so much more than the one *N* in Jenifer. Koreans are not called by the marker of our individuality. We are called by our connection to one another. I've never met a Korean who was upset when someone did not know their name or got their name wrong. Because Koreans are not their names. They are someone else's family member.

So my mother has lived her whole life with the wrong name without caring about it. She used it until she met my white father, who, unlike her Korean friends and family, insisted on using her first name, instead of "so and so's daughter" or "so and so's sister." His pronunciation of Ippun was so coarse and jarring, my mother asked him to call her by the name my grandparents had intended to name her, the name they forgot to tell their drunk friend who went into Seoul that day: 수미 (Su-Mi; water, beauty).

Ib-Bun was born and the whole family adored her because she was the 막내 (mangnae; youngest child) and a girl who came after an endless string of boys. They also loved her because she took after her father and was breathtakingly, excruciatingly beautiful. In a time when female children were routinely thrown away, given away, or made to live outside, my mother was prized. I imagine my grandmother's relief that she would not be hard to marry off. She would not be the comedic relief. Boksoon-i had a beautiful daughter. Unfortunately, my mother was also immensely intelligent.

* * *

DYING LAUGHING

MY FIRST UNCLE WAS MURDERED by the Japanese as they left Korea in a tactic meant to destabilize the nation. They executed anyone with a high level of education or position in government. It was effective, but what they didn't realize was Koreans fucking love being angry and doing shit out of revenge. Korea's recent success on the global stage, I believe, is due to the fact that the Japanese (and then the Americans) fucked them over so bad and the Koreans became great to spite them.

My uncle was considered part of the political gentry because he worked at the post office. I'm sorry, but that's so fucking funny. Imagine feeling threatened by the post office man. After his death, the remainder of the family's wealth went to my second uncle. My second uncle was a drunk gambling addict and not only spent all the money but also accrued significant debt. He was found dead in a lake a few years after my first uncle was murdered. No one is sure if he drowned while drunk, died by suicide out of shame, or was possibly murdered by debt collectors.

My grandfather was allegedly devastated by losing all his money, and not necessarily by the death of his eldest two sons, and killed himself. He did this by swallowing a block of solid bleach, and it took nine days for it to kill him. This chain of events started years before my mother was born and into her early childhood, since she was more than twenty years younger than her oldest sibling. By the time my grandfather killed himself, she was only around four years old, but she still remembers how terrifying he looked in the days before his death. His already skinny body shriveled up into a skeleton wrapped loosely in dark skin. He lay dying on rough white bedding on the floor. The way my mother described his death was beyond painful—he starved as his insides melted. He couldn't even ingest water to alleviate the burning without vomiting it back up. However, telling me this story, she laughed at how skinny his head was, resting on a traditional Korean pillow, which is just a piece of hard wood. She laughed imagining his family members around him, trying to comfort him by pulling up the painfully starchy, rough blanket and adjusting a literal piece of wood under his skinny, raw, crunchy skull. Korean comfort is pain.

He had lived his entire life trying to convince my grandmother that he was worthy of her love, and in the nine days he lay dying, all she did was roast him for being stupid and lazy. She told him while the bleach melted his esophagus and he swallowed spit into his open body cavity that she never loved him and he was worthless. She couldn't give him the acceptance he had wanted all his life from being an orphan because the only thing she had wanted had been denied her. He died while listening to an ugly woman tell him he wasn't good enough. After he died, my grandmother wailed for days. She said she wasn't sad that he died; she was sad that all the money was gone and she no longer had a husband to make more money. In the middle of her crying, she joked about how she knew he had killed himself because he was lazy and wanted to get out of work. She cried hard but insisted it wasn't because she had loved him—she had never loved him.

I know everything she said was a lie. I know she loved this man who had been forced to marry her just as much as she had been forced to marry him. I know she was angry at this world for seeing them, two people with infinite worth, as worthless. I know she loved this gentle, hardworking man who had done everything for her. But she was smart enough to know she had to keep it a secret. Maybe my grandmother might seem cruel to some, but this was how Koreans were taught to show love in times of genocide. You don't show anyone what you love, because if you do, they will take it away from you. My grandmother thought they had killed her first, shining, beautiful son because she was proud of him and loved him so much, and people saw that and destroyed him because of her pride. She learned to pretend the best thing that happened to her was a curse. If she pretended that she hated her husband, he would not be killed. But she had not anticipated that he might kill himself.

She loved him. And hated him. He had saved her from being unwanted but subjected her to the loss of her dreams: of being a bitch who loves attention and goes around reading poems in front of everyone. She never wanted a husband and children. She was forced to do it, and joking and complaining about it was her soft rebellion. My grandfather was a great partner. He was hardworking, trustworthy, and loving. On top of all that, he was not only hot but Korean hot. But to a woman who doesn't want that life, that doesn't matter.

My grandmother constantly complained about her life and her husband. But she always made it funny. People always listened to her complaints because she disguised them as jokes. That in itself is a talent created out of survival, an invisible talent. My family was thrown into poverty and ruin in the years following my grandfather's suicide, but they all survived. I want to say it's because of the jokes, but all of the Korean people from this era were like this. Full of humor and self-deprecation. And a lot of them died. They died while laughing.

Even in their final moments, they would comfort one another by telling them how funny it all was. I know this was how my grandfather left this earth. While making a joke. My Korean family is poor and uneducated. They are ashamed of it, and continually try to hide their shame with endless jokes. At funerals we laugh. As an adult I have had to curb my humor in social situations because other people have told me it's inappropriate. I don't know how to explain to them that I come from the strongest people, who have been through the worst of humanity, and the jokes were what made it possible for us to continue. I would not be here without inappropriate humor.

* * *

A PAINFUL SHIT

WHEN MY MOTHER WAS A CHILD, lepers roamed the Korean country-side. They were exiled from society and had to survive in the forest. A rumor spread saying that if lepers consumed three virgin hearts, they would be cured of the biblical illness. These lepers, terrifying looking with large, gaping holes in their faces and their clothes tattered and soiled from being homeless, would walk up to my mother's home after scoping it out for hours to see if the adults were away. They would come to the gate and call out, "Hello, I'm here to speak with your mother!" anticipating a stupid child's response of "My mom is not home." My mother could see their bloody faces through the cracks in the wooden gate. She would then yell out, "One moment, my mom's taking a shit." The leper would shuffle off quickly, terrified of a confrontation. My mother told me this story while cry-laughing. The violence of a zombie-ass-looking adult eating her heart coupled with the cowardice of said adult being immediately afraid of the presence of a shitting mother seemed comical to her. I laughed while listening as well, both of us forgetting the countless children who met their demise at the hands of the lepers. Both of us forgetting the absolute horror of the lives of the lepers, cut off from society simply for being ill. They could've been our brothers, or mothers, or us ourselves.

My mom also laughed about the woman in her village who was a 바보 (babo; stupid). This term was used for anyone with an intellectual disability, and although it is used as a slur, my mother said it endearingly. This babo was raped constantly all her life, which was how the most vulnerable people in a society are treated after war. She lived in the forests and roamed around freely and would go in and out of the town. When she inevitably became pregnant, the other women in the town tried to care for her and give her food and a place to stay. But she would wander off in fits of rage and could not be traced for days. One day she was back in town. She went up to everyone she saw, telling them that she took a painful shit, and she kept pointing to an outhouse. She kept repeating this over and over until one woman noticed she was no longer pregnant. She grabbed her and frantically ran to the outhouse. But by the time she got there, it was already too late. The baby was dead, face down in shit. My mother always laughed telling this story. She kept repeating over and over, "She thought she was taking a painful shit." She would laugh so hard that tears would roll down her face. And I could no longer tell if they were tears of laughter or sadness.

The young men of my mother's town, including her brother, were all shot to death and they laughed. The female children and women were taken away to be raped to death and they laughed. They were exterminated like cockroaches and they laughed. Barely more than one hundred years ago, our people used to live in mud huts with straw roofs, and they cared for and loved one another by candlelight. There was no war. There was no death. There was no rape. No one cried and no one laughed. The twentieth century came to Koreans as a violent surprise. And we learned how to cry. But then we immediately started to laugh. And we couldn't stop laughing. We couldn't stop laughing while crying.

*   *   *

HAIRY BUTTHOLE

WHEN MY MOTHER BEAT ME as a child, I always felt like there was someone else in the room. The reasons for the beatings were always disproportionate to the severity. I would forget to put the juice back in the fridge or I would be too slow at putting my socks on. Then my mother would beat me, while crying. I would cry with her. My great-grandmother who was *bossamed*, my ugly grandmother, Boksoon-i, the leper, the pregnant babo, the hungover man at city hall who didn't know my mom's name, my dead uncle who worked at the post office, my dead uncle who got drunk and fell into a lake, my hot grandfather who killed himself while getting humiliated by his ugly wife, the dead baby face down in shit—they were all in that room watching me get my ass beat for leaving the Tropicana orange juice on the counter.

I would cry and they would all feel bad. So all of them would take turns telling me jokes. Jokes from one hundred years ago that were told by candlelight. Jokes about watermelons rolling down hills, jokes about disobedient frogs, jokes about Boksoon-i and her missing front tooth, jokes about the stupid things my grandfather used to say in his lazy country accent. They would tell me these jokes when my mom was beating me. Until I realized I was laughing harder than I was crying. I would open my eyes and there would be no one there besides my mother and me. The only trace of these ghosts, the only way we knew they had ever existed, were the tears on our faces from the laughter.

Then my mother would say, "Do you know what happens if you laugh while crying? Hair grows out of your butthole."

CHAPTER 2

White

POTATO FAMINE

I HAVE AN EXTREMELY HAIRY BUTTHOLE. It, like, pokes out of my underwear if I wear anything less than full-coverage granny panties. I'm almost forty and I've yet to figure out how to shave my asshole and I hate getting waxes, so I've just sort of let it go at this point. It has not stopped the people that I fuck from putting their mouths all over that fuzzy motherfucker whenever they get the chance. When I started growing butthole hair in my teens, I had long forgotten the saying "If you laugh while crying, hair will grow out of your butthole." However, most of my friends were Korean at the time and I remember I brought up my hairy butthole once, and they were disgusted, terrified, and confused. I started to believe I was uniquely disgusting as the only woman in the world with a hairy asshole. Then I saw *The NY Friars Club Roast of Hugh Hefner* and a comedian made a joke about all of his blonde girlfriends having to bleach their asshole hairs or something. It dawned on me that I didn't have a hairy asshole because I cried and laughed at the same time; I had a hairy asshole because I was white.

My dad is Irish, German, and French. His mother came to America from Ireland with her parents, who quickly died after their arrival. My father insisted that they moved to America because they were the victims of the potato famine. I didn't know anything

25

about Ireland or the potato famine, so I just took his word for it. Later I found out the potato famine happened in the 1840s through 1850s, and my grandmother was born in 1915. I do not believe my dad knowingly lied about it; my belief is that he was told this by my grandmother and never took the time to look into it. I'm assuming she was traumatized by her childhood and wanted a historically epic story to justify her monumental pain. Also, thinking about the trauma inflicted onto me by my mother, which was directly the result of Japanese imperialism and the Korean War, I think I understand what my grandmother was trying to express by claiming she was a part of this historic event. I assume that her family was thrown into chaos and turmoil following the 1850s, and she was most likely born from people who came from people who suffered directly.

As a child, if I ever did anything well, my mother would immediately react by cutting me down and belittling my accomplishments in order to make sure I didn't loudly boast about it. She would say, "An empty can makes a lot of noise when dropped, while one that is full is silent." Or "Animals eat the arrogant stalk of rice that stands straight up, not knowing that the one that is full of rice is bowed down." Or my personal favorite, "If you don't say anything, no one will know that you're stupid." I believe this to be a direct response to watching her own mother punish her for her accomplishments out of fear that she would be murdered for being great, just like her oldest brother. This happened on a large scale in the entire country of Korea after the years of political unrest—a hatred for conspicuous greatness, born out of fear of having it taken away. Koreans hate people who have pride and are not humble. In Korea a common insult is 잘난척하네 (jallancheokanae; you're pretending to be highborn). Someone who acted this way was considered not only stupid but a liar, because a true 잘난자식 (jallanjasik; highborn child) would be smart enough to hide it in order not to be killed.

* * *

GERMANY, YEAR ZERO

MY IRISH GRANDMOTHER DIDN'T LIVE through the potato famine, but the circumstances of her life came about because her parents' parents lived through it. My grandfather was German. His family came to America while my great-grandmother was pregnant with him. He was the youngest of his siblings and the only child born outside of Germany, a fact that his siblings used against him. They severely abused him physically and emotionally for not being German enough. Also, my grandfather and his siblings were mocked by the American school children who were influenced by anti-German sentiment during the rise of the Nazi Party. So my grandfather essentially got abused at home and school for being both German and not German enough. As teenagers and young adults, my grandfather's siblings opted to move back to Germany to join the Nazis. My grandfather very much wanted to join them but was left behind because he was too young and also because he was an American citizen.

My grandfather spoke of his victimhood—being bullied for being German by American school children—while longingly wishing he had the "privilege" of moving back home and becoming a Nazi. Because he was called a Hun or whatever, he saw his "suffering" as more profound than the suffering of the victims sent to the gas chambers at the hands of his siblings. Although I think this is fucking demented, I understand the confusion he must have felt. The confusion of not being allowed to align with either side. He couldn't figure out which side he belonged to, and because he was villainized by both sides, he sided with the villainy-er side of the two. Instead of denouncing his culture and hating the Nazis for being the cause of his antagonization, he aligned with them and their pathological ideology. He

27

pledged allegiance to his "motherland," the one who had abandoned him and beaten and tortured him since his birth for not being good enough for her. Until the last day my father saw my grandfather before he ran away with all the family money, he spoke fondly of his bitch mother, Germany, even though she and her fucking idiotic ideology had been defeated. He clung to Germany because she had convinced him that no matter how shitty she was, he would never be good enough for her.

Both my grandmother and my grandfather saw themselves as victims. In a lot of ways, they were. They were both the victims of physical and emotional abuse their entire lives. My grandfather perpetuated that abuse in the form of domestic violence onto my grandmother and my dad throughout their lives. I think Americans of my generation can recognize that the horrible old white people of the silent and boomer generations were victims themselves and that's why they continue to perpetuate harm onto other people. However, the disgusting nature of white supremacy is to take the original pain of abuse and amplify it to terrifying degrees onto other people. The entire world is full of people of all backgrounds who are victims of abuse, but we didn't run off and join the Nazi Party like my grandpa's siblings because of it. We didn't cause more destruction from this initial destruction. Or did we?

When I see a video of some old white boomer going absolutely apeshit racist on an innocent bystander at the gas station or on the subway, I see this look in their eyes that is familiar to me. It's the look I've seen in the early moments my mother had while beating me, during the rage of it before she broke with laughter or crying. People who are not white didn't have the option of joining a political party formed around their supremacy to inflict their pain onto someone else who didn't look like them, so they took that harm and inflicted it on themselves and their own people. The victim is the perpetrator in a sense that the energy needs to go somewhere, and sometimes it goes inside rather than outside.

As far as I know, my grandmother was innocent of believing in or perpetuating racist ideology. I did not know her and knew very little about her beliefs. She entered this country through Ellis Island with her parents, who died in a car crash shortly after their arrival. She insisted the reason her parents wanted to come here was because of the potato famine. This is all I know about her. After finding out that her timeline didn't match up, I started reading about the famine. It's a whole fucking long-ass messy story so you can just google it, but basically what happened was that the English did a bunch of shit to fuck with the handling of the catastrophe on purpose. Today there is a movement to try to classify this historical event as a genocide, since the English knowingly did shit to ensure Irish people would die. And here we are again. Back to this shit. Back to not knowing if any of us are the victims or the English.

I made one joke about the potato famine one time on Twitter and was met by an angry mob of Irish people who said it was in poor taste. Which is 100 percent valid and it's unfortunate the word *potato* is so comical. An Irish priest retweeted my tweet and I was met with an immediate flood of American white supremacists threatening my life. For some reason in the US, the word "Irish" is online code for white supremacy, which is sort of funny considering Irish people were victim numerus unus of the brutal imperialism of the English, a disease that went on to infect the entire world. I took down the potato joke, even though I felt like I had a right to it. Because the abuse I received from my father had been passed down from his Irish mother, and it all stemmed from the fucking potato famine. If she could claim it, why can't I? But Irish people would never in a million years accept that I was "one of them," even though I got the same abuse they endured from being from the same people. Biracial people of mixed white heritage understand that as soon as our pure whiteness gets diluted with anything else, the whites will drop us like a sack of potatoes (sorry).

As much as I've been rejected by Koreans for being mixed, it's nothing compared to the absolute exile I've received from the whites. I own no stake in whiteness. I am not allowed any criticism of it. Even though as an insider/outsider with close proximity, I believe I have a powerful and much more accurate assessment of the culture of whites than white people themselves. I'm Vittorio Storaro, and white people are the landscape of China. I can see the shit so clearly that whites can't, and it's baffling to me that they can't see it.

*   *   *

US VS. THEM

EARLY ON IN MY COMEDY CAREER I gained a fair amount of attention for making satire videos about how white people acted. A lot of what I mocked were stereotypes and tropes that have already been dissected and discoursed to death, but a lot of the videos were things people had never considered. I believe the popularity of these videos was due to the fact that I pointed out things people could not see because their faces were pressed up against them their entire lives. I put a camera with a powerful lens onto things that were brutally mundane, illuminating the horror of them. Some of them were baffled by how they had not seen these things before I pointed them out, and others were angry that I had the nerve to come and dissect their disgusting culture as an "outsider." But a lot of them didn't even understand why it was bad.

People ask me all the time why I don't identify as a white person when I am as white as I am Korean. The answer to that is simple: white people will not let me. Some white countries around the world, like most non-white countries, have a separate category for mixed-race people. But in the US, due to anti-Black miscegenation laws and the one-drop rule in particular, anyone who is even a touch not-white is simply just not white. White people see biracials claiming their white heritage as hubris in need of being punished. The fact that we can fly close to the sun without wearing a North Face rash guard or SPF 50+ sunblock and not get a life-threatening sunburn is proof we are not white.

The online hatred I've received from white people is terrifying. Around the same time I was "blowing up," there was a way more successful white female comedian making similar content, mocking the shockingly "acceptable" casual racism white people display in everyday life. I remember reading the comments on her videos. All of the comments from white people were positive. No one had a problem with her making fun of her "own" culture. It sent a clear message to me: You're not white. Shut the fuck up.

This made me want to say it even more. Do you realize how funny it is that I would make cruel and harsh criticisms of Korean culture and Koreans would take it in stride, while the whites were trying to call the police on me because I made fun of them eating kung pao chicken without rice? Hilarious. Even in writing this book, I am afraid of the backlash this chapter will receive compared to the chapter before where I talk about a Korean shitting out a baby in an outhouse. White people being "hurt" by the softball jokes I make about "us" while simultaneously voting for Republicans, banning critical race theory in schools, and perpetuating anti-Asian hatred is EXACTLY what my grandfather was doing when he centered his pain of being mocked and called a sauerkraut in grade school while wanting to become a Nazi and kill Jewish people. It's exactly that. It's bad. And you all should feel bad.

It's funny white people won't let me be white, but they're right to a certain extent. I'm not white, I'm biracial. People hate talking about biracials with white heritage because they can't decide if it's our fault that we are descendants of Nazis, colonizers, and rapists, or the descendants of their victims. This conversation shakes the entire foundation of race for most people who grew up in one society and never had to

31

question "us versus them." Because what if you're from both "us" and "them"? This is the plight of the mixed-race/biracial. We are strung between two branches: on one are the people who did the harm and on the other are the victims. Here's where this shit gets real funny. I did a 23andMe and found out I have a significant percentage of Ashkenazi Jew in me. So the Nazi part of my family is also Jewish. Now what? What does that make me?

The only time a white has called me a white person is when I'm in the middle of making fun of or criticizing white people, and they'll stop me and say in an accusatory tone, "Wait, but aren't you also white?" How fucking convenient that I'm only white when it's time to feel bad about being white. I can't reap any of the benefits of being a white person, but I have to share in the punishment. But yes. I am to blame for the acts of my ancestors. There is no white person alive today who doesn't have blood on their hands. Even if that white person is me, a Korean. And because of this I deeply feel like it's my job to criticize and call out white people, as it is the job of every white person. I am confused why they do not feel the same way. How could they not see it? I see it because I see it in my own father and every white member of my family. I see it in EVERY white person I've ever met to this day. I see it in myself. When they ask me why I'm mocking white people as a white person, I am so confused. The reason I am doing it is BECAUSE I'm white.

* * *

THE MARK OF THE BEAST

MY DAD AND I WERE talking about how his uncles and aunts were allowed to return to the US after some time, even though it was known that they had been active members of the Nazi Party. He said it was fucked up especially in light of the Japanese concentration camps that were imprisoning Japanese Americans. Some of these Japanese Americans had lived in the US for three generations or more. They had no tie to their motherland and many denounced the actions of imperial Japan, unlike my German family members, and they were still punished for it. We all know why Japanese Americans were placed in concentration camps while nothing really happened to German Americans who were known Nazis. We all know why America dropped two fucking atomic bombs on the poor innocent civilians of Japan who had nothing to do with any of this while Germany was spared. We all know why. It's the same reason I can make jokes about Koreans eating dogs and throwing female children in the river, but if I make one fucking joke about white people loving ranch dressing, I'm getting death threats in my DMs.

My Irish grandma hated English people. The English decided, for some reason unknown to the rest of the rational world, that the Irish (a.k.a. freckled gingers that look exactly like them) were less than human. Fuck those assholes. The Irish were right, the potato famine is not funny. Why the fuck did the English do that? But you know what's hilarious? How fucking stupid are the English that they hate the Irish? What the fuck are you even talking about, Nigel? No one can even tell you apart. Jesus fucking Christ. The English insist that God chose their royal family to rule over the rest of us because God saw them as superior. How weak do you have to be to invent a god that says you're better than everyone else? Ireland forever, motherfuckers.

I do not understand why all white people aren't constantly talking about this shit because it's fucking hilarious. White supremacy is fucking hilarious. It is the legacy of white people everywhere and their responsibility to make fun of it. The dead queen of England was fucking her cousin and he was a Nazi. That's fucking hilarious, bro. It's hilarious that white people freely and openly laugh about my jokes mocking Koreans but get mad the second I turn on them. All of a sudden, I'm a "them" and not an "us." It's funny that they think I do not own their thing. Because I do own their thing. It is "our" thing (hammer and sickle). It is my birthright. It is my curse. It is my responsibility. I will never stop making fun of white people, especially the English. And that makes me the most Irish person alive. I am Irish. I am German. And I have the mark of my people. The mark of the beast. A hairy butthole.

CHAPTER 3
Adults

돌아가 (DORAGA; RETURN)

AT FIFTEEN, MY MOTHER DECIDED to kill herself after a "bad thing" happened. This "bad thing" is the only thing she's never wanted to talk about, and to this day I do not know what it is. The same woman who laughed while telling me adults tried to rip her heart out of her chest and eat it as a kid couldn't get herself to tell me what this "bad thing" was, but I knew instinctively that I needed to never ask her about it again. However, I think I have an idea of what it could be, as anyone who has once been a young girl does.

My mother decided to kill herself one day in the dead of winter. She came home from high school and closed all the doors of the kitchen. A traditional Korean kitchen.

A traditional Korean house is shaped like a hollow rectangle, with rooms making up three sides and the main gate making up the fourth. In the hollow in the center is a courtyard, usually populated with a little garden, clay pots full of kimchi and fermented sauces, and a water source for cooking and cleaning. The bedrooms make up the sides of the rectangle and are elevated by stilts except for the kitchen, which sits at the far end of the wall of elevated rooms at the very back corner of the rectangle. To call the kitchen a room is misleading; it is the absence of a room. It sits at ground level and is almost always open to the elements, a gaping hole in the rectangle that makes up the rest of the home. The reason the kitchen sits at dirt level is because the oven used for cooking is dug directly from the earth. Usually, a traditional Korean home kitchen has big wooden doors that are never closed all the way, because of the smoke. A chimney from the earthen oven runs beneath all the bedrooms and expels out the other end, near the main gate. Thus, the heat from the oven keeps the bedrooms in the home warm in temperatures that routinely reach below zero. In the summer, the chimney is closed off. This is how Koreans kept warm throughout the thousands of years before modern technology, from the recycled energy of the fire they used to cook food.

This ancient system of heating homes through a chimney that runs beneath the rooms is called 온돌 (ondol). Modern Korean homes are still heated through the floors by hot water pipes or electricity for this reason. In the traditional home, the rooms on the other end of the rectangle that are not heated by the fire are for storage. The outhouse is sometimes situated outside the rectangle or built into one of the unheated rooms.

In parts of southern Korea and Jeju Island, the outhouse was built over tall stilts above pig pens. Today, only a few of these traditional houses remain on heritage pork ranches, where special pigs are bred, fed with human waste, and prized for their unique and delicious gamey flavor. Korean homes, much like all so-called primitive homes of the past, were built with this idea of recycling waste and using it for sustenance. Unlike heating systems of the West, which threw away the heat in chimneys shooting directly up into the heavens, the Koreans ran it under their homes like hellfire. Unlike shit that was buried in the West, Koreans made it fall down on animals like manna from heaven.

Although the kitchen heated the entire home and kept everyone else comfortable, it was freezing cold in winter because the doors always needed to be open so that the women who cooked wouldn't suffocate. Therefore, the kitchen was a place of extreme temperatures of fire and ice. In the depths of winter, a coal stove was placed in the center to keep the women warm. A kettle and sweet potatoes sat on top of it, and the women would periodically take a sweet potato and a sip of warm tea from the kettle while working. This was the room my mother went to, a hole carved out of the earth where an eternal fire burned, dancing with the frigid free-flowing air, to kill herself. To return.

In Korea, instead of saying people die, we say 돌아갔다 (dollagatta). To return. To go back to the place you came from. My fifteen-year-old mother went into the kitchen and closed the doors that never close, separating the dark pit of fire from the blinding white of the winter-snow-covered courtyard. She threw an enormous amount of coal into the stove, closed the door, and took one of the sweet potatoes sitting on top of it—her favorite food. She peeled the charred purple skin and ate the insides. Then, as the black smoke cascaded out of the smiling grate, she lay down on the dirt in the position she had been in while in her mother's womb. Her hair was cut in a mandatory blunt bob, and she wore her mandatory school uniform. The uniform was stiff and clean, but it was the color of dirt. Korean school uniforms were always dirt brown or stone gray, to signify that, like particles of dirt and pebbles, we are the building blocks of this earth, and although we are all the same and seem worthless on our own, without our collective, nothing would exist. Her uniform made her blend in with the ground. She fell asleep, her fingers blackened by the char of the sweet potato skin, the meat that now sat in her small belly. Her belly had already begun to digest the nutrients, unaware that it would no longer need them to keep its body alive. On her face she felt the warmth and comfort of the fire that never went out, on her side the relentless support of the earth, and on her back the never-ending dance of cold air. She fell asleep waiting for the black smoke to suffocate her.

After some time, a woman yanked open the door and screamed, "기집애!" (Gijibae!; Girl!)

My mother lifted her head, her desire to die not as strong as her desire not to get her ass beat.

The woman screamed, "너 지금 낮잠자는거야? 게으른 기집애!" (Are you taking a nap right now? You lazy girl!)

My mother thought, *Am I dead? Is this heaven?* but quickly realized that whatever the fuck the beautiful, eternal afterlife was, she probably would not be referred to as a "lazy gijibae" there. She got up and dusted dirt off her dirt uniform and walked back out into the snow-white courtyard, bowing apologetically to the woman.

To this day my mom doesn't remember who the woman was who found her. She always laughs while telling this part of the story, that the woman was stupid enough to think that my mother was taking a nap. I laugh too, even though all three of us—the unknown woman, my mother, and I—know that there was no way she didn't know that my mother was trying to return.

* * *

"THE FLOWER THAT GROWS FROM THE DIRT ON THE BATTLEFIELD" OR SOMETHING

A SHORT TIME LATER MY mother left home for Seoul when her oldest living brother (now the patriarch) informed her he could not afford to send her to college. She deeply resents him for this to this day, because in Korea, in exchange for the privilege of owning all the family money, the oldest son also bears the responsibility of financing the education and early lives of his siblings. She got a job as a seamstress in what Americans would call a sweatshop. A sweatshop is the same exact thing as a couture tailor shop in Europe, the difference being the amount of money the workers are paid. She was paid the equivalent of sixty cents a day, and although it was considered a lot of money then, it was not nearly enough to collect and save to send home to her mother. This was in the seventies and the bulk of her clients were cosmopolitan Koreans, but a healthy portion of them were American GIs stationed in Itaewon, who would come in with their wives who had never in their wildest Midwestern dreams thought they could afford hand-tailored clothes. The Americans became tyrannical in their realization that here, twenty dollars made them kings and queens. For twenty dollars, they could buy leather jackets that looked like Gucci or tweed suits that looked like Chanel, and no one would be able to tell that the people who made these beautiful garments were Korean and not European.

My mom worked in the back room and watched these grotesquely large people stomp into the front of the shop, loudly pointing and shouting at clothes on the wall and rolling out Korean words with 느끼한 (neukkihan; greasy) accents. The Americans thought they were being polite by booming their "annyeonghaseyo" and forcing intense, unbroken eye contact. But to Koreans used to bowing and averting eye contact when meeting strangers, their jolly greetings felt like an assault. My mom would watch the GIs come in and put their arms around the tiny Korean owner of the shop while pointing at the brown leather vests and fur coats.

The owner of the shop was a very "traditional" Korean woman in the sense that she had never been touched by a man outside of her family and her husband, and despite the movie theater at the end of the street that constantly played Hollywood propaganda and tried to convince Korean women that these grizzly, hairy-chested men were hot, she found them scary and gross. They smelled like alpine aftershave and their mustaches looked like they were made of the same hair that grew on the tails of cows back home. Because of the modern popularity of K-pop, it's easy now to imagine the ick that Korean women might get from a manly man who looked like Burt Reynolds compared to a hairless, slender Korean man. Westerners can now finally understand the Asian female gaze. But back then, the American GIs assumed Korean women were dying to suck their hairy pink dicks, and the American men probably thought the Korean shop owner was wet in the panties from meeting a man who looked like 존 트라볼타 (Jon Turabolta; John Travolta).

My mother had been taking night classes to learn English, because unlike the owner of the shop, she had fallen for the intoxicating song of the siren (the siren being the lead singer of the Bee Gees). She also had started going to an American Christian church, because she noticed that behind the podium, they had a statue of what to her looked like a shirtless lead singer of the Bee Gees. She went to worship to gawk at this man on Sundays after dancing to his music all night at a nightclub on Saturdays.

One day, an American couple walked into the shop, the man's chest hair displayed in full seventies-button-down-fake-silk-shirt regalia, and the woman with eyes so large and round they looked like they were about to roll out of her sockets when she screamed, "ULMAY-AEYO?" (How much is this?) My mom watched the Korean owner squirm under the oppressive eye contact of the blue round balls surrounded by crispy black Revlon mascara. She ran out from the back room yelling, "Hello! How are you?"

She pushed the owner aside while saying, "언니 나 영어학원 다니는대 영어쫌 연습한깨." (I'm taking English classes, unni. Let me talk to them.)

The owner happily hid behind my mom, relieved that the eye contact could finally be broken. From then on, whenever any American entered the shop, the owner would call for my mom and hide behind her from the evil eye. My mom's English was actually shit, but her dynamic personality and her face, the face of a shocking beauty, endeared her to the Americans. My mother was beautiful in a way that frustrated Koreans, because she had dark skin, full lips, and high cheekbones. All of which are deemed "ugly" traits there. Koreans would ask her questions like, "Why are you so pretty? You're dark but you're still pretty?" Her beauty made them uncomfortable since it shattered the belief that beauty is based on the ancient traditional formula of small chin, small mouth, and white face. But for Americans, whose perception of Asian women was that they were exotic sex creatures from the fields of Vietnam or the opium dens of Chinatown, my mom's severe traits were understood as the reason for her beauty. She had her hair feathered Farrah Fawcett–style and wore flamboyant polyester seventies clothes that clung to her figure. The Americans loved her humor and her confidence. They loved how she didn't wince when they patted her too hard on her back. She quickly learned their sense of humor and rattled off the popular jokes and cool catch phrases of that era. Other Koreans were ashamed of their broken English and clunky accents, but my mother learned that she could use that to her advantage. Americans sensed she was intelligent and attractive, but when they sensed that maybe she was too intelligent or too attractive, she could neutralize the threat by manipulating her accent and purposefully mixing up grammar for humorous effect. This would give them room to laugh at her childish mistakes and assure themselves that they were better than her. The way she manipulated her shortcomings to soothe the arrogant foreigners took a level of comedic talent that was nothing short of genius. If she had been born an American white man, she could have been a great comedian, a celebrated performer. But she was a Korean woman who was doing it in order to survive, so for that skill, she earned sixty cents a day. She did all this masterful manipulation while returning their intense eye contact, with laughing eyes the color of light hazel, way lighter and larger than the eyes of other Koreans. Her eyes read as familiar to them.

Once, I saw a vintage movie poster from around the fifties or sixties hanging on the wall of a soju bar in Korea, and the hand-painted drawing was a rose on a battlefield. The title read, "The flower that grows from the dirt on the battlefield" or something. I've tried googling it but couldn't find it. I did find a Soviet movie with a similar title, and I think maybe it was translated into Korean? I imagine that my mother's face was the flower in this wasteland to these Americans. Americans love foreigners like this. If my mother had been a child, she would've been adopted first. Her life was worthy of saving; her large hazel eyes were worthy. Not the Korean women who conformed to the rules of their own culture of no eye contact and no talking, like the owner of the tailor shop. Americans go around the world looking for this special flower, the one that grows out of the barren battlefield of a war they were responsible for. They find tiny children flowers and adopt them, or tiny women flowers and fuck them. Sometimes they adopt and fuck the same flower. Sometimes these flowers are boys or men. But all of them are rare, beautiful flowers. All of them are in need of being saved, or fucked, or both.

The owner of the shop was married to a Korean man and had Korean children. She went on to save all her money from her shop to buy a thirty-pyeong apartment with her husband. She sent her kids to the best Korean schools and hagwons she could afford, and they grew up, got married, and had Korean children of their own. They visit every weekend to this day. They eat Korean food. They watch Korean TV shows. But for my mother, she was cursed to be the flower that grows on the battlefield. The flower that caught the gaze of the American GI. The flower that got plucked from its home and "saved."

*   *   *

JUICY BAR

AFTER LEARNING ENOUGH ENGLISH, my mom got a job at a "juicy bar" that catered to American GIs. A juicy bar is a type of bar that men go to because the women who work there are forced to sit with them and entertain them. They're called juicy bars because for the company of the women, the male patrons are forced to buy them "shots" that are just juice in order for the women to remain sober. "Juicy" was the American mockery of how Koreans pronounced "juice" and how the women would ask for the shots. Americans are so bad at hearing foreign languages that the actual pronunciation, "주스" (ju seu), was heard as "juicy." These bars catered to GIs but are a form of bar that existed for thousands of years in Korean culture. My mother went to work there with the intention of finding Bee Gees Jesus, so that he could take her to America.

Koreans dislike the juicy-bar girls. In modern times, a lot of the work has been taken up by immigrant workers from the Philippines and Russia. Koreans look down on all these women, but when they are Korean there is an extra layer of shame. What Koreans hate discussing the most is that a large portion of Korean Americans and other Korean expats around the world were saved by the juicy-bar women—they were saved by the whores. These women married American men and were sent away to America like little canaries into darkened coal mines, and if they survived, the men and the rest of their families followed. If they had the "privilege" of being saved, they were sent off to little economically depressed corners of America where their new husbands, men who were so poor they had to join the military, would live. In these barren fields, these wildflowers, the flowers that had the grit to grow despite all odds, lived and died alone. But many others saved enough money to send for their older brothers and sisters and, finally, their parents. Today their hard work and determination can be seen in the form of a random fifteen-thousand-square-foot H Mart in the middle of Texas, or a nail salon called "Beautiful Nail" in some random town in Kentucky, or the simple addition of bibimbap at the bottom of an American diner menu, a little secret signal to other Koreans telling us that there

43

is an 이모 (e mo; aunt, also what Koreans call restaurant workers/owners) there. Many Koreans are ashamed of these women and the work they did, but I cannot think of people who are more worthy of adoration and respect. But many of these women never made it to the US because they died before ever leaving the juicy bars.

From after the Korean War until the late nineties, the GIs would regularly rape, assault, and murder these women. Then they would throw their bodies on the street and go home to the military base, where they rarely faced consequences. The Korean government barely cared because the women were considered worthless whores who brought shame to the nation anyway. However, as the Korean economy grew through the eighties and nineties, nightclubs catering to the new monied Korean class started popping up around the hip neighborhoods bordering Itaewon and surrounding Korean universities. The American GIs started filtering into these much nicer establishments. They continued to assault women they interacted with there. The Koreans became angry because these were not "the whore garbage women" but respectful Korean girls. It was unacceptable that the GIs were not held accountable and were secretly sent back home. A few of these incidents blew up in the news during the nineties and were one of the main arguments used in anti-American occupation movements springing up in universities around the country. With the neutered Korean government failing to react to the brutal crimes committed against their women by the Americans, the owners of these nightclubs took matters into their own hands and started posting signs that read NO AMERICANS.

When I was a child, we never used the word 외국인 (Uegook-in; foreigner). Instead, we called all non-Koreans 미국사람 (Migook saram; American) or 미군 (Mi-Goon; American military), because that was literally the only foreigner in Korea at the time. The NO AMERICANS sign slowly evolved into NO FOREIGNERS in recent years as people from all over the world started living in Korea. Now

Koreans use this as an excuse to not allow Black people into night-clubs, and it's a heated debate in Korea that highlights their horrid anti-Black racism, xenophobia, and nationalism. But it started as a way to keep American men from killing Korean women without repercussions. It's so sad how Koreans turned something that was created to protect their women into something that now harms innocent foreigners.

*   *   *

THE GOLD DIGGER

MY MOTHER MARRIED THE FIRST man who showed interest in her and didn't seem *too* murdery. She moved with him to Fairbanks, Alaska, and quickly had my sister and got a divorce within two years. As a single mom she worked at Baskin-Robbins and KFC. My mom said there seemed to be lots of lonely, desperate men in Alaska, working isolating jobs out in the wilderness. She tells me the story of how men would come into KFC and ask her out. One gold miner would come almost every night and give her gold nuggets covered in dirt. He was an old, gnarled troll because of a lifetime of digging in the dirt with his hands and feet—a literal bridge troll bringing a pouch of shining stones and gems for the human woman, begging her to love him. She was so repulsed by him that she would throw the gold away in the gar-bage as soon as he would leave, wiping her hands on an apron embroi-dered with the face of the Colonel, who probably looked a lot like that man TBH. After a few months of her not accepting his advances, he became enraged and screamed at her that she was a gold digger and demanded that she return his troll gold. The gold digger called my mom a gold digger. Men who use this term against women are always projecting. They are ashamed that they are unlovable and the only way they can even hope to gain love is through a shallow and empty transaction. A scam. The gold digger left after my mother's KFC associates threatened to call the police. He should've known that not even the most precious metal known to man could make a human woman love a troll.

The "bad thing" that happened to the child that was my mother taught her that there was nothing worse than being under the power of a powerless man. Nothing was worth the gold of a troll. Their gifts were curses. She told me she always threw the gold nuggets away no matter what, even though she knew that one piece would be worth the same amount of money she made in a month. She worked at the KFC in the middle of a frozen city, all alone, and she had never been happier in her entire life. She had escaped the kitchen of eternal fire and ice. She had escaped the mandatory uniform that made it impossible to differentiate her from dirt. Her hair was no longer a mandatory black, blunt bob but a wild mane that was permed and surrounded her head in a foot of crispy glory, in a style she had seen before only in the Hollywood movies.

One day after work, she stopped by a bar to pick up a sandwich. While she was waiting for her food, a man came up to her. He was drunk and wore gold-rimmed glasses and had a collared shirt that was open to reveal a hairy chest. He was thin and had long brown hair and a brown beard. He looked exactly like Bee Gees Jesus. They were married within a year because she accidentally got pregnant with me.

What my mom didn't realize in the years that she had waited for Bee Gees Jesus to save her was that she had already saved herself. She saved herself that day as a teenager when she walked out of the kitchen on her own, following the voice of an unknown woman. But she convinced herself that it was a white man who had saved her. A lot of older Koreans are convinced that white men saved them, but it was the juicy-bar girls—who courageously followed these men after watching them kill their sisters—who were the actual saviors of Korea. But

Koreans cannot worship whores. So instead, they worship Bee Gees Jesus. Be'Jesus.

*　*　*

BE'JESUS

MY FATHER GREW UP IN Jersey City with his Irish mom and his German dad. His dad was abusive. He would beat his ass and his mom's ass all day long. My grandfather would get drunk and make my dad hold a lit candle outside in the rain. If the candle went out, he would beat his ass. There was no reason for a candle to be lit in the rain; it was just an arbitrary game that meant nothing but had horrific repercussions. Kind of like the Nazis' idea of eugenics that my grandfather was also a big fan of. My father would go to school after getting his ass kicked by my grandpa all night and then get his ass beat by his classmates and the nuns who taught him in Catholic school. My dad just got his ass beat all the time.

When he was a teenager, he ran away with a girl he was dating. They both turned eighteen on the road and they eloped. After a few weeks it dawned on him that she had schizophrenia, so he returned to Jersey City and I assume she had to be hospitalized. He lived there for a few more years before finally moving out to San Francisco after getting a job flying small airplanes. Then he got a job at Delta or something and was able to fly around the world for free. He moved to Spain with his coworker, a flight attendant or something. They got married, and within a year, she cheated on him with a lawyer or something, so he decided he would move to Nairobi. He said all of his coworkers would use their free flights to go to "regular" places like Hawaii, the Bahamas, cities in Europe—you know, places that Americans felt safe going. He was always trying to convince them to go to the places that

47

were "off the beaten path." Since no one wanted to go and his wife had left him, he went on his own.

He ended up living on the continent of Africa for around ten years. He lived first in Kenya, then other countries like Zambia and Ethiopia before moving to Alaska to fly small planes full of cargo to remote towns. One night he was drinking with his friend who was a forest ranger. At this point in his life, he was wanting a change. He didn't hate flying airplanes, but he had been living a life void of purpose or direction. He was in his late thirties by then and was looking for stability and order. His friend had brought an application form and was trying to convince him that being a forest ranger would provide that order in his life. Then he saw a wild beauty standing awkwardly at the end of the bar. He assumed that she was an Indigenous Alaskan or, in his words, *an Eskimo*. There is nothing a rolling stone loves more than a rock who's never moved. But she wasn't a person indigenous from that land; she was also a rolling stone, and the chances that they bumped into each other on an endless hill were nearly impossible. Two dandelion stems, blown off in two different continents, meeting in the middle of the endless heavens. My mom didn't drink, and she doesn't really eat sandwiches either. To this day she has no idea what drove her to get a sandwich at a dive bar. After meeting my mother, my father woke up the next day with a hangover and reached in his pocket and found my mom's number. He forgot about the park ranger application.

My mom thought my dad was hot and he seemed nice enough to her daughter (my sister). Also, another green flag was when she became pregnant, my dad said, "You can do whatever you want to do," meaning he was down with abortion (a feminist king). My mom decided to keep me since she liked my dad enough. My dad insisted that they move back to Korea because he loved going to "exotic" places. The last thing my mother wanted to do was go back home, because to her it wasn't an exotic place, it was 방계리 (Bangeri). However, she had been scarred by the years of being a struggling single mom and had already seen that the American Dream was bullshit to people who earn minimum wage and speak English with an accent. So at six months pregnant, my mom took her four-year-old daughter and Be'Jesus and she returned.

Whenever people ask how my parents met, I hate explaining their story because it lacks a narrative. None of it makes any sense. There was no reason for it. Every decision that was made that brought them both to that bar that night was made without a purpose. Both of them lived their lives like this. When I ask my dad why he decided to move to Nairobi after his second wife cheated on him, he says he doesn't know. When I ask my mom why she divorced her first husband, she says she doesn't know. I believe them.

* * *

ADULTS

WHEN CHILDREN BECOME ADULTS, everything must be done with a purpose. But somehow neither of my parents knew that. They both moved through the world like permanent children. In the middle of drawing houses and airplanes on the wall with oversized crayons, they opened up the cabinets and started banging the pots and pans. If there was an adult there, they would have stopped them. But there were no adults. So they continued to live like this, all alone and with each other. They would start one project in the middle of another one. None of the projects were ever finished because there was never a goal in mind. If they wanted to move, they moved. It didn't matter that there was no house or no money for a car.

Because they were children, they didn't clean if they didn't want to. Because they were children, sometimes they forgot that they had to buy food or there would be none to eat. Because they were children,

49

when they were playing outside, having fun at a nightclub or a bar, no one told them they would have to go home at suppertime, so sometimes they didn't. When I was born, I was a child born to two children who could not properly take care of me, but I was not upset at them. Because they were children, and children cannot take care of children.

When adults are children, they do heinous things because no one is there to stop them. Some of them drink alcohol and get very angry. Some of them stay out drinking and partying with other children who they're not married to. Some of them starve themselves for days because that's what the people on TV do to look good in swimsuits. Some of them hit each other. Some of them do these things just to hurt the other one, an added bonus to their sociopathic, underdeveloped egos. Some of them get depression and can't get out of bed for days. Then months. Then years. They closed all the curtains and the doors. They laughed. They cried. No—they wailed. They wailed when they were hurt because despite proclaiming that they were happy in their savage independence, deep down inside they knew that there was something very wrong, that there should have been an adult there, but there had never been an adult, so they did not even know what it was they were missing.

When adults who are children have children of their own, they mistake them for their parents who were never there. I was the adult. My parents were the children.

CHAPTER 4
Children

호호 아줌마 (HOHO AJUMMA; MRS. HOHO)

I was born in South Korea on December 8, 1984, at 7:10 p.m. on a Saturday night. When I was born, I had severe jaundice and was kept under a heat lamp for a week. The doctor who delivered me was a born-again Christian Korean man and he told my mother that my condition was caused by my being mixed-race and was a "sign from God" that it was unnatural. My mother had chosen this doctor because he shared her love of Be'Jesus. But like many other hard-line Christians in Korea, he was a staunch Korean nationalist and a misogynist and readily jumped at this new religion because he could hear the dog whistles in the sermons given by the American missionaries. They said Christianity was about loving the Lord, but what they meant, and what the doctor heard, was it was about controlling women and perpetuating a social hierarchy.

My family lived in Songtan, which used to be a tiny farm community that could barely be called a town until the US military built Osan Air Base nearby in 1951. After it was built, Songtan became a makeshift shantytown made up of wooden huts that housed bars and brothels for the US soldiers. Since there had been nothing much there, the residents were almost entirely people who moved there to service the military men: prostitutes, pimps, bar owners, and store owners of tiny shops that sold souvenirs for the Americans to send back home. The shacks were built frantically by Koreans who were on the brink of starvation in a desperate attempt to survive. The chaotic structures, lined with flimsy wood set directly upon the earth with curtains for doors, seemed to appease the American clientele, who had little shame in the acts they performed there and would've done them in front of their god and fellow countrymen anyway. The Koreans built these buildings without realizing they would need to be there for an indeterminate amount of time. Throughout the decades when the structures began falling apart, they just built semipermanent solutions on top of the dilapidated huts. They did this although they were confused as to why the structures still needed to exist. Concrete was poured directly over dirt floors, glass doors were added to rotting wood walls, and linoleum paneling covered counters made of plywood and cardboard. This was the Songtan I knew in the eighties, a permanent town resentfully built over a rotting temporary one.

My father loved this town. Through his eyes, I think it looked like a rowdy outpost in an old Western he might've seen as a kid. The cowboy would ride into town, visit a whore in a whorehouse, and purchase provisions from the merchant at the general store. He saw himself as the cowboy, the main character, and the Koreans as the extras who were shot or run over by a horse with little consequence to the plot. "Whorehouses" and "general stores" were the two establishments that existed in Songtan. He loved the rawness of the whore women and the accommodating nature of the merchant men.

When I was a small child, my father would take me to a bar in Songtan. This bar, like all the others in town, was decorated via a demented game of telephone. The owners of all of these bars decorated them as "American" as they could by listening to what the military men seemed to want. What they wanted was apparently naked chicks and motorcycle stuff. So the bars were decorated with posters of naked chicks and motorcycle stuff. Also, there were posters of bands like the

Doors and Led Zeppelin, whatever seemed to fit the theme. However, the Koreans understood the theme as "America" and not "Rock 'n' Roll Biker Guy." They were not aware that in the US, cultural subgenres were extremely important and adhering to the theme was similar to adhering to the rules of an ancient tribe. So sprinkled in between posters of Playboy centerfolds and a Harley-Davidson Miami shirt nailed to the wall would be a cardboard cutout of Garfield crossing his arms with a thought bubble over his head that said "MONDAYS!" or a movie poster from some random-ass movie like *Breakfast at Tiffany's*, *E.T.*, or *The Wiz*. The music they played fit the theme 45 percent of the time with classic rock and heavy metal, but in between those songs were Donna Summer disco tracks and Barbra Streisand ballads.

Americans didn't seem to mind this mishmash because it was comical to them that the Koreans didn't understand the nuances of their culture. But the Koreans did understand. They knew that anything "American" was bait; they knew they lured in customers who were homesick and desperate to talk about the things they left behind. An Air Force man would walk in, lonely and fearful in this new, exotic land, and he would see a *Star Wars* poster on the wall, while Simon and Garfunkel whispered, "Hello, darkness, my old friend" through a scratchy boom box. His eyes would suddenly light up as he would point at it and say, "DO YOU KNOW THAT MOVIE? VERY GOOD MOVIE. VERY GOOD AMERICA MOVIE!" and the woman working there would give a thumbs-up and say, "Yes. Good! Very good!" The moment the man looked away, she would stop smiling and stare off sadly into nothingness.

All the women who worked there did this. They would face the Americans and smile, and turn around and frown. They kept turning their heads over and over again, their expressions flipping fluidly in between turns. As a child I was convinced these women were the Korean ghost 호호 아줌마 (Hoho Ajumma). Hoho Ajumma was a popular cartoon in these times, but children started sharing horror stories and urban myths centering her as an evil ghost. There were many stories, but in all of them she had merged somehow with the spirit of an evil cat. One of the more popular stories was that Hoho Ajumma was drunk one day and fell and cracked her head open. She lay there dying, but then an evil spirit in the form of a cat entered the hole in her head and kept her alive. She lived among us now, and appeared like every woman, but in the back of her head, hidden by her hair, was the face of the evil cat. If you ever saw the face of the cat, you would immediately die. The lore was that if you ever came across Hoho Ajumma, you would have to stare at her. The moment you looked away, she would turn her head 180 degrees, revealing the cat face, and you would die immediately. I didn't understand how the cat was evil because I loved cats so much as a child, and also I recognized a loophole in the story: How could the cat in her head be evil if it was what was keeping her alive? Because she was already dead.

All the women who worked at these bars were also already dead. The trauma of what their mothers and grandmothers had been through had killed them before they were born. You could tell they were ghosts because of the way they moved. They were dressed in the modern style of the eighties, in bloodred pumps, black pantyhose, and leather miniskirts, with bright makeup and teased hair. But they would squat in front of the bars like an ancient peasant girl squatting at the edge of a river, pounding and washing clothes. They would chew on 오징어 안주 (ojingeo anju; dried squid), sitting atop bar stools with their knees pulled up at their chest, like how an old woman would sit on the landing in front of a farmhouse one hundred years ago while listening to the 매미 (maemi; cicadas). These women came to these small towns surrounding military bases because as dead people, they were the only ones who could bear to work among all the ghosts there. They stared off silently into nothingness in between talking to the drunk Americans, because they were listening to the ghosts.

My father and I walked into the bar, and the woman working

there turned her head and smiled. She ignored me, but I kept staring at her directly in the face. I knew she was Hoho Ajumma, and I wasn't going to let her catch me slippin'. My father pointed at a poster on the wall behind her of Dustin Hoffman, standing behind a skinny, pantyhosed leg. The woman probably thought this poster looked exactly like the advertisement for L'eggs pantyhose on the back of a tabloid magazine she had procured from one of the US military men. This was before I spoke English, but I know my father probably said, "*The Graduate*! Good movie. You know that movie??"

To which the woman probably replied, "That's a movie? I thought that was an ad for pantyhose."

My father probably laughed, and the woman probably fake-laughed. He thought it was humorous that she was too stupid to know the difference between a *film* and a pantyhose ad. But the truth was she was too smart to be fooled into thinking that a movie, no matter how sophisticated, was anything other than an advertisement.

After fake-laughing, she stared off into nothingness. Listening to the ghosts.

* * *

이쁜짓 (IPPUN JIT; [DO A] PRETTY BEHAVIOR)

THE GHOSTS OF SONGTAN WERE not just the prostitutes and the juicy-bar women who'd been killed, but their biracial children. The children born to these women created a huge problem for the Korean government. In 1948, the Nationality Act stated that Korean nationality was gained through paternal lineage. This was hugely influenced by the ideas of racial purity inflicted on them by Japan. I'm not sure if they simply failed to anticipate that foreign forces would be there siring children or if it was one of the reasons for implementing it. After the war, the children left abandoned by the US military were stateless, since they had no Korean fathers. Because they legally did not exist, many of them were killed, kidnapped, or trafficked. This continued for years since many US military men continued to be stationed there and continued producing children. There are accounts of Korean military men routinely combing through Songtan and other towns like this and shooting any biracial child they saw on sight. There were no repercussions because the children didn't exist and were born to mothers who were already dead. Those who weren't killed simply got abandoned or hid among the other Koreans, without an identity.

In Laura Ha Reizman's dissertation, *Conditions of Containment: Mixed-Race Politics in Cold War South Korea, 1940s–1980s*, she explains how the presence of these nonexistent children led to the boom of the foreign adoption industry in postwar South Korea. There were so many orphaned biracial children that an American missionary set up an adoption agency to send them to the US. The Korean government was happy to be rid of these monstrosities who made them question their deep belief of what a Korean was supposed to be, frail after the ethnic annihilation of the imperial Japanese and American forces. Much like the doctor who assisted in my birth, they thought mixed-race children were an act against Be'Jesus's dad, God. Multiple companies popped up, emulating the business model of the first American one, sending children off to all the Western countries in Europe and her colonies. That one adoption company, started by white Christian missionaries as a solution to rid Korea of stateless biracial children, turned into a decades-long exploitative industry that made the white owners of these corporations wealthy beyond belief, and shattered millions of Koreans' lives along the way. Because of the severe social and political stigma surrounding fatherless Korean children, the industry was soon also saturated by full Korean children who were fatherless. There is a slippery slope when a people deem one type of person disposable, because all of a sudden, many others are too. Koreans who were not biracial but poor, from uneducated backgrounds, from unmarried mothers, children of rape and incest—suddenly, they were all seen as worthless and disposable by our own people. A lot of the whites who adopted these children were good people, but many of them were demented, abusive religious fanatics who found the bodies of these tiny Korean children the perfect place to inflict the heinous sins that their god would not allow to be inflicted onto white children.

So, there I sat at this bar next to my father, while the woman who I thought was Hoho Ajumma listened to ghosts that looked exactly like her and exactly like me. Sitting, unfortunately, in front of a Playboy centerfold with a plump, hairy vulva poking out underneath a lacy red teddy. This woman turned her head suddenly, and I realized this was it. I was going to be killed by the evil cat face. I squirmed out of my seat and ran out of the bar, where I was met by a gang of feral cats sitting outside, waiting patiently for someone to notice and throw some 오징어 아주 (ojingeo anju; dried squid) at them. But I thought they were Hoho Ajumma's evil spirit friends, making sure her victims didn't escape. I plopped down on the stoop, defeated. One immediately ran up to me, rubbing my shins with her face, meowing for food. I started petting the cat at my legs, hoping this would endear me to her. The other cats all ran over and I started petting all of them. I forgot they were evil and just enjoyed their company. After some time, I heard the loud cackle of Hoho Ajumma. I jumped up and looked into the bar, half expecting my father to be keeled over on the counter, dead. But he was just sitting there, probably explaining the plot of *M*A*S*H* while Hoho Ajumma fake-laughed. I watched my father, who was oblivious to the fact that he was in the presence of a dead woman. Oblivious that an evil spirit kept her alive. Oblivious that the spirit would kill him at any moment. I do not know if I was afraid of it happening or looking forward to it.

I walked back into the bar, where I'm sure my father said, "이쁜짓!" (Ippun jit!; [Do a] pretty behavior!), to which I would reflexively make an exaggerated cute, smiley face. My father never bothered to learn

Korean, and this was before I learned English. "Ippun jit" was one of the few phrases he ever learned. Until I learned English years later, our dialogue consisted of this one demand from him: do something pretty. I made the pretty face, while the woman working behind the bar continued to not look at me. The reason she didn't look at me was because she in fact was Hoho Ajumma. She didn't look at me because she didn't want me to die. I looked like all of her children, who had all died because she had made the mistake of looking directly at them. She stared off into nothingness, listening to her ghost children as I stood in front of my father, doing something pretty.

* * *

부량품 (BULYANGPOOM; KNOCKOFF)

WE MOVED TO JEJU-DO AT some point in my childhood. Jeju-do is a popular vacation island off the southern coast of South Korea. The majority of my most vivid childhood memories of Korea are from the short time I lived here. I have extremely detailed, well-preserved memories of the early years of my childhood in Korea, even before Jeju. I remember my grandmother. My mother told me that was impossible since she died when I was two, but then I proceeded to explain the layout of her entire house from memory and my mother listened, shocked. I remember being so short that I had to wait at the entrance of her home for an adult to lift me up to the floors that were elevated for the 온돌 (ondol; underfloor heating system). I remember standing there, the floor up to my armpits, holding my arms out for my grandmother. But of my time in Jeju-do, I mostly remember the children who were my elders.

The adults were never around. The children in my neighborhood would band together in a gang every day and roam the streets. At five years old, I was the youngest, and by default the dumbest, slowest, and poorest. I was always losing at all the games and would always be left behind when they would all run off to their next adventure. I became the butt of all the jokes, and they would laugh at how I would do everything so pathetically 열심히 (yulshimi; with a lot of effort). Also, my mother would dress me like a haunted Victorian child for some reason, and I was always in thick white leggings and a burgundy crushed velvet baby doll dress trimmed with lace. My memory of this outfit was that it was so stiff and antiquated that I assumed it was a school uniform until I recently looked through my old yearbook and saw I was the only one wearing it. My hair was pulled into a violently tight ponytail at the top of my head. I wore this royal costume like the dead women in Songtan did, without knowing that my beastly movements betrayed it. My mother probably thought this getup made me look like a sweet, gentle doll, but with my clumsy, boorish nature and my face always covered in melted red popsicle juice, I looked like another child horror main character in Korea at that time, 삐에로 (Pierrot; evil clown).

The children quickly realized that no matter how much they made fun of me, I would never cry. In fact, I would laugh along with them, partially because I was too young to understand that I was the punch line, but also because I inherently understood that making myself the joke was currency. I was a stupid, messy bitch with very little money who loved attention. The children recognized my value as comedic relief and soon became protective of me from kids in other gangs who would try to bully me.

I don't remember the names of any of these children, only their ages, as in Korea that was what was important above everything else. There was a scary eleven-year-old girl who was a year older than even the oldest kid in our gang, and she would always be standing in front of her house. If we ever walked too close to her while walking past, she would attempt to punch our arms while screaming cuss words that not even our rowdy crew had the bravery to say. One day we walked by, and she was eating raw eggs one by one out of an egg carton. She waved over at us. "이리와! 이리와! 씨발 이리오라니까!" (Come here! Come here! I said, fucking come here!)

We all huddled around her as she cracked the top of one, made a small hole in the bottom, lifted her head up, and let it ooze-plop into her mouth. She did this multiple times, pulling egg after egg out of the carton. Years later my mom told me that when she was young, eggs were so expensive that only the rich children would have them, and she would get the chance to eat eggs once a year or so. The Christian churches would give out free hard-boiled eggs on Easter. This was one of her earliest core memories, being in awe that a place would be so wonderful that they would just give eggs away for free. I think maybe this eleven-year-old girl was eating a carton of raw eggs as a flex, even though by the time I was a kid in the late eighties, eggs were pretty affordable, and we all regularly ate them. But the kids in my gang recognized her behavior as some sort of 잘난척 (jallanchuk; pretending to be rich) bullshit. She was always doing this show-offy shit.

I shouted, "징그러워!" (Gross!) after watching her slurp down like maybe the third or fourth raw egg.

She grabbed me by the cheeks, forcing my mouth open. "맛있어 먹어봐!" (It's good. Try it!) She grabbed an egg out of the carton in her other hand and tried to pop the top open with her mouth. The other kids in my gang screamed, and one of the boys grabbed her by the polyester windbreaker and punched her in the face. She fell back onto the bushes in front of her gate, the egg still intact in her hand. Even after she fell over, she had the presence of mind to preserve it. The fragile perception of wealth. We all ran away, and this time the kids all ran at my speed instead of letting me fall behind.

When I say I was poor, I mean poor by the standards of our gang. These children didn't care about the actual wealth of our families, they cared about candy. Every day, all of us were given one hundred won (approximately seven cents) by our parents. I would immediately blow all of it at the corner store on one or two pieces of gum. All the other kids in the gang seemed to have a ton of candy and money left over every day. One day as I was walking to the store after receiving my one-hundred-won allowance, my gang walked by. One of the kids simply said, "따라와." (Follow [us].)

I followed them as they led me to a man standing on a busy street with a cart. There he sold 불량품 (bulyangpoom; knockoff) candy. My mother had warned me about bulyangpoom. It was allegedly made in illegal factories across the countryside with unsafe materials (plastic). I looked into this man's cart, which had a clear plastic lid with dozens of different kinds of sparkly, brightly colored candy. I opened my sweaty palm to show him the hundred-won coin. He snatched it quickly and said, "열개골라." (Pick ten.)

I got a ribbon roll that looked and tasted exactly like pink Scotch Tape, a pack of cocktail straws that were filled with what looked and tasted exactly like pink sweetened baby powder, a bubble pack of what appeared to be indigestion medicine but turned out to be peach-flavored fizzy tabs, and a bunch of other shit. After I ate my fill, the other kids showed me their secret bush in front of our apartment complex where they would hide leftover candy from our parents. They knew we were in on this together. If I got caught, they all would be punished. I had seen most of them getting beaten severely at some point in our short lives, while over at one another's houses on playdates. Our mothers would sit quietly and stare off into nothingness as these children were beaten by their drunk, silent fathers, their catastrophic screams filling the entire apartment. I listened to these children tell me how to hide the candy and did exactly as they told me to do because I didn't want to be the one who ratted out the gang. This was my family. They meant more to me than my mom and dad, the silent woman who spent all day with her back turned to me as she washed dishes and the weird hairy man who was barely home and spoke a language I didn't understand. These children were my parents. I loved them. I felt safe with them. They protected me. And the last thing I wanted to do was fuck up the rules on how to hide illegal candy and cause them to get beaten.

One day the two oldest boys—I'll call them Ten-Year-Old and Nine-Year-Old—asked me if I wanted to go play with all the other boys. These were the "bosses" of the kids, and I was excited that they wanted to play with me. Some of the other girls wanted to come, but they told them not to. There were around six boys, and they took me to a quiet street, behind a large stone wall that blocked off an apartment complex, and surrounded me in front of a high wall. They asked me if I wanted one hundred won. I said yes and stuck my sticky, chubby hand out. My hand was always sticky with sweat because I would run everywhere with balled-up fists while staring at the ground. This was something I was also made fun of for. Ten-Year-Old, whose father was an airline captain for Korean Air, pulled out a shiny hundred-won coin and said, "If you want this you have to show us your butt."

Without any hesitation I turned around and stuck my butt up in the air.

"No. Your naked butt."

Again, without hesitation I pulled down my thick white Victorian-child tights. I remember the crisp, cold air hitting my raw butt. It was in the winter, but the temperature in Jeju rarely dipped below forty-five degrees. Something about the cold air hitting my bare ass felt invigorating, and without even thinking I started rolling my ass around. I did this thing I saw on TV where you spell out your name with your butt. The boys started laughing. They were shocked that I did this not only without hesitation but also without seeming to understand that it was wrong. On top of that, I did a little fucking jig. At this point the boys were in tears with laughter. I also started to laugh because I loved attention and I honestly thought this shit was hilarious. This was the best thing that had ever happened to me, and also I was getting paid.

I am not sure if they had intended to do anything to my naked butt, but the unexpected silly dance unknowingly bought me time because immediately, we heard someone scream, "야!! 지금뭐하는거야??" (Hey!! What are you doing??)

We all turned to see the raw-egg girl standing on the corner. As soon as she saw our eyes, she bolted down the street toward our homes, her windbreaker swish-swashing at the speed of sound. I pulled my tights up and slowly started walking back home with all the rest of the boys. I remember looking at all of them, their heads hanging, shuffling their feet. We knew she would tell our parents, and we all knew what that meant.

Raw-Egg Girl did in fact tell our parents, and everyone else in the neighborhood, what she had caught us doing. Later that night when my dad got home, I could hear a hushed conversation between my parents. They came to me to ask what had happened, and I laughed while telling them the story. Initially they were gentle and soft, but seeing that I was happy about the incident, they became upset. This was the most trouble I'd been in my entire life. I knew it was serious but was confused when my mom didn't beat me like usual. My parents struggled with the fact that I had experienced what they thought was sexual abuse. If I was a normal good girl, I would've been crying, aware of my victimhood. But I was a dumb bitch who loved attention and money. They weren't angry that I did this act, but that I had enjoyed it. If I pretended to cry and act like I was a good, virginal, chaste girl, I would've probably gotten candy and a 미미 (Mimi; Korea's version of Barbie). But I didn't cry.

I was punished by being made to stand in a corner of the kitchen for what felt like years (probably ten minutes). The boys probably all went home and got their asses beat. I am unsure of what they had wanted from me that day. I believe deep down there was no sexual intent, but they just wanted to push me, the village idiot, to see how far I would go. They thought there was humor in my willingness to do anything they wanted of me for acceptance. That act in itself is abusive and exploitative. But what I can't get out of my head was that these boys and I were mimicking the actions of our parents. These boys

63

were raised by fathers who exploited powerless people, and they were beaten by them every night. I was raised by a mother who acted like a dumb bitch who loves attention and money. All of us children were punished for imitating the actions of adults.

* * *

왕따 (WANGTTA; KING LOSER)

It's hard to explain the feeling of brutal comradery I had with children who were bullies in their own right, but one thing that made me feel safe with my neighborhood gang was that they never treated me differently for being a 혼혈 (混血; honhyeol; mixed-blood). Outside of the safety of my neighborhood gang, wherever I went, Koreans would stare at me. In the eighties and early nineties when I lived there, foreigners were rare in Korea outside of the towns surrounding US military bases, and extremely rare on Jeju-do. My father had moved our family to Jeju to teach at the flight training school for Korean Airlines. Outside of my father and a handful of his pilot friends, I don't remember seeing any other foreigners in Jeju. Jeju wasn't Songtan; people didn't know what a honhyul looked like. They thought I was a foreigner. This was years before the first time I heard "혼혈아" (honhyula; slur for mixed-race people) screamed at me on the street in Seoul as a sixteen-year-old. I remember hearing the beautiful singsongy pronunciation of the ancient Chinese characters, a word so ancient it doesn't even sound Korean. Then I remember my mother shouting back at the old man who screamed it, and the shameful fire of the realization that the word that sounded like a song was meant as a slur. Back in Jeju before I knew the word, I remember people would point and stare at me and call their children over to look. But they didn't call me honhyula. They called me 미국사람 (Migook saram; American).

Looking at a class photo of me during this time, I stand out very clearly, but the shocking part isn't how different I look, it's how alike all the other children look. Because the difference between me and the other children is minimal. I am only slightly different. Slightly larger, slightly thicker, slightly lighter in coloring. However, over the backdrop of a sea of children who are identical in size, shape, and hair color—like pebbles that make up the foundation of a building, prized for their likeness to one another, prized for their unity as children of the great new nation of South Korea—I am a mutant. I was large. I wasn't considered overweight at that time, but I remember, as a child, looking at my wrists compared to the wrists of the Korean children in my class and seeing that they were thicker than even the boys. My mother called it "German bones."

"Germans always had meat and milk so their bones are thick." She loved saying this.

I hated being different because I was taught that it was bad. Korean culture is about uniformity and conformity. In Korean school culture, instead of a "bully" tormenting a wide breadth of children, there is someone called a 왕따 (wangtta; king loser). All the children gang up on that one child. Oftentimes, the wangtta will be christened for absolutely no reason, but it's more common that they are neurodivergent or have an intellectual disability and can't understand the social hierarchy, or have some physical disability that visibly differentiates them. Because of my "German bones," I was always teetering on the edge of becoming a wangtta. To have my difference pointed out and stared at was dangerous. I became uncomfortable whenever anyone stared at me, which was a constant, daily occurrence.

This unwarranted attention was the exact reason my father loved living in Jeju. He basked in the same constant stares and pointing that made me fear for my safety. My mom usually picked me up from school, but one time my dad got out of work early and came to pick me up. As he walked up to the entrance, all the Korean children coming out of the school started screaming and running toward him like he was the fucking goddamn Beatles. The kids pushed me out of the way, clamoring for his autograph with their notebooks. I remember watching him be surrounded by a sea of pebbles, their hands in the air, reaching up to him with pencils and notebooks. He smiled as he signed all of them, while I hid in the corner crying. I didn't understand that the thing that I didn't want to be—noticed—was something he was happy about. It was humiliating and scary to be noticed. All the work that I had done to hide myself was undone by his presence. That day I went home crying, and I told my mother to never let him pick me up again. My mother asked why.

"아빠 미국사람이자나" (Appa Migook saram ijana; Dad is an American [derogatory]), I said in between sobs.

My mother and father laugh about this to this day. They laugh because I said "American" like it was a slur. To my father, this undeserved recognition was a surprise benefit of moving to Korea. He had lived his adult life in places so remote for whites that his mere presence as a white man was worthy of attention, but the respect paid to him by the Koreans, many who had bought into the propaganda that Americans had saved them during the war, was next level. Koreans looked up at him like he was the actual lead singer of the Bee Gees. Or what they were told Jesus looked like. The white savior.

One of the biggest privileges of being white in Korea is that you're allowed to exist without needing to have 눈치 (nunchi; understanding what to do without having to be told). Korean culture is extremely rigid, and there are rules on how to behave in every situation. The rules are so complicated and abundant that it is common for strangers on the street to correct others in social situations when they're doing something wrong. To do something "incorrectly" is shameful in itself, but on top of that it is shameful to cause someone to have to correct you because you inconvenience them with the confrontation. All Koreans develop razor-sharp nunchi to avoid the shame of being wrong, but mostly to avoid burdening the person responsible for correcting you. But Koreans understand that Americans do not know the rules and allow them to play without following them. Americans are very much the younger sibling sitting next to their older brother, playing *Super Mario Bros* with a controller that isn't plugged in.

Having free, positive attention as a white guy, combined with the added benefit of being allowed to not learn any of the complicated social rules, meant my dad's life in Korea was absolute paradise. He could do whatever he wanted. I would cringe with humiliation watching him do something "wrong" in public, and I could overhear Koreans around us say, "역시 미국사람들은다 눈치 없어." (Classic American. No nunchi.) Then they would smile at him and he would smile back, oblivious. Sometimes the Koreans would say it loudly on purpose so that my mother and I could hear it. When someone does something wrong in Korea, Koreans have a burning desire to shame the person. But when the person is a foreigner, they need to pass it on to the closest Korean, the closest person who has shame, something whites do not seem to have. So my father's life in Korea was free of shame because everything he did wrong, my mother and I were made to carry the shame for.

But I was Korean (or at least that's what I thought), and I was obsessed with being Korean correctly and learning the never-ending rules. Korean children are taught to conform at a young age and to never stand out for fear of becoming the wangtta, but there is also a deeper primal fear, the fear of extermination. This might sound hyperbolic, but the eradication of "the other" in Korean society is well documented. The severely high rates of international adoption are the obvious example. But what if they stayed in Korea? What happens then? They become a wangtta. Wangttas regularly meet their end by suicide. Koreans are saddened by the high suicide rate of the relentlessly bullied runts of their society, but they also believe in its necessity and are relieved by their deaths to an extent. Suicide is seen as an individual's weakness. One's inability to cope. But for wangttas, their deaths are nothing short of societally condoned murder. A million hands hold on to theirs as the knife slices through their throat. A reject from the collective society. Then after their death, the society says, "How sad that a child killed themselves. You can see it was their own hand that held the knife."

To be different is to not be Korean. I didn't yet know about the relentless killings of biracial children in postwar Korea, but I could smell their blood on the street. I could sense the danger in the air. To my father, this attention made him feel like a celebrity, but to me it felt like I was being hunted. My only way to survive was to hide. But walking in a crowd, I could feel a pair of eyes catch me and keep staring. I would turn slowly to see the person the eyes belonged to tapping someone else on the shoulder and pointing at me. Then more and more eyes staring. They would keep staring even as I stared back. I stopped looking at people altogether. Whenever I went out, I stared at the ground to avoid any eye contact whatsoever. But I watched all their movements peripherally because I sensed the danger. I watched them without looking. With nunchi.

My parents laughed that I was ashamed of being American since to them, it was a blessing. They could not see that for me it was a curse.

* * *

또라이 아저씨 (TTORAYI AHJUSSHI; PSYCHO MAN)

AFTER MY DAD'S AUTOGRAPH INCIDENT, I would walk home from school by myself. This was actually the standard for all children my age in Jeju—I just had been afraid to before then. But after that embarrassing-ass shit with my dad, I was more than happy to walk alone. Every day I would leave the school building, wearing white stockings under my dumbass velvet lad outfit with gold buttons and lace, clutching the straps of my large, hard rectangular backpack, a leftover from imperial Japan. One day I noticed a man sitting between two parked cars across the street from the school gate, staring at me. He was dark, thin, and sinewy. Koreans lived hard back then, so I'm guessing he was like twenty-eight even though he looked like he was fifty. I saw his eyes and I did what I always did: I watched him peripherally, pretending not to see. I felt the need to keep watching, to make sure he didn't move toward me. As I passed him, I heard him slur between drags of a cigarette, "야! 야! 이리와!!" (Hey! Hey! Come here!!) I didn't know what being drunk was back then, but I distinctly remember he slurred his words, and how he said this sentence is burned into my brain.

Without thinking, I said, "내" (ne; yes) and walked toward him. To be Korean was to listen to adults and do what they told you to do. I walked over to him, and he grabbed my arm and pulled me close to his body. I remember the backpack hitting my back from the jerk; I remember the soju on his breath. "니 어디서왔니?" (Where are you from?)

"내?" (Yes?)

"어디서왔어?" (Where [are you] from?)

I didn't understand the question because I didn't understand that I was supposed to be from somewhere else. I gave him my home address in full. I asked him if he wanted me to show him where it was. I wanted him to let go of my arm because it hurt, but more than that, I wanted to make sure I was answering him correctly. I wanted to make sure my behavior was correct. That I was just like the other normal Korean children. I didn't understand what he was asking me because it had not yet dawned on me that my dad was from somewhere else. I thought 미국사람 (Migook saram) was the name of some sort of deformity my dad and I had. Some weird thing that made people stare at us. But where was I from? I was from Korea, just up the street and around the corner. The drunk man was confused that I was confused. After that he said, "오 알았어 아저씨가 집애대려다줄깨." (Oh, OK, I'll take you home right now.) He pulled my arm and started leading me, and I was happy that he was going to take me home. I was happy that I answered correctly.

At that moment two middle school girls walked up. I remember thinking they were so tall and big, and I knew they were in middle school because they were wearing uniforms and had mandatory blunt bobs. They said loudly, "또라이 아저씨다!" (Ttorayi ahjusshi da!; It's the psycho man!) The word 또라이 (ttorayi; psycho) was a word we used as a joke to one another, and until that day I had not heard it used seriously. The alarmed tone of how they screamed it brought me to reality, and it was only then that I realized this was...sus. The man held my arm tighter. In that moment, I did not feel fear but overwhelming humiliation to be near an outcast of society. These cool girls thought this man was a ttorayi, and they saw me with him. I wanted so badly for them to know I didn't know him and we weren't together. I started pulling my arm away, but this fucker had soju power grip going for him. For some reason soju goes straight to the fingers of Korean men, as any one of us who got pinched too hard by our drunk uncles knows. As I squirmed and wriggled, trying to break free, my humiliation grew. I knew I looked like a fucking loser, trying to wriggle away from this crispy-ass-looking creep. The girls kept screaming, "Ttorayi ahjusshi! Ttorayi ahjusshi!" and that's when I noticed that behind him was a busy street full of adults. All these adults had been there the entire time, but they had not seen me until they heard the screams of the girls. They all stopped one by one and stared at Ttorayi Ahjusshi. They started murmuring and pointing. Realizing he had been perceived by adults, he finally released his grip on me while murmuring, "아니야 아니야 그냥가!" (Aniya, Aniya geunyangga!; It's nothing, it's nothing, just go!)

* * *

눈치 (NUNCHI; TO KNOW HOW TO ACT WITHOUT BEING TOLD)

I DIDN'T RUN WHEN HE LET GO. I just walked off like nothing had happened, because to run would be admitting I was harmed, that I was weak. I walked slowly away to show that I wasn't scared and I was cool. I was a normal Korean. Everything I did, I did so the middle school girls could see. I remember walking closely behind them, finding comfort in the fact that they didn't seem to think this was a big deal either. One of them said, "Did you hear that psycho telling that kid to 'come here'? Complete psycho." They kept talking, recounting the entire incident. They went over, step by step, what they saw that man do, and then they went over the other times they had seen him doing other things to other children. They did this to assure me that they had been watching the entire time and they had always been there to protect me. They did this because they knew I was walking behind them and that I was listening and, although I didn't know it then, that I was scared. They did it peripherally, without looking or talking directly at me. Because they already knew that all the other Koreans stared at me, and they knew that I hated being stared at. They had the decency not to look or talk directly at me, because they could see I was a honhyul, and they knew I hated it. They knew I lived in fear of being the wangtta, because they lived this life too, of constant hiding and worrying if they were doing things wrong, of surviving by not being noticed. In an instant they knew all of this without having to be told, because they had something that my father and other white people did not have: nunchi.

These girls represent everything I love about Koreans. The quiet and steady love and support, given peripherally. Doing good deeds at exactly the right time, without having to be told and without calling attention to it.

I went home and didn't tell my parents what had happened because I knew I would get my ass beat or have to stand in the goddamn corner again for an eternity (ten minutes). I knew by now that being a victim was something I would be punished for. On later occasions, I remember seeing Ttorayi Ahjusshi from time to time, and without hesitation I would scream, "TTORAYI DA!!" and all the children around me would start screaming along as we scurried away. He would drunkenly swat at us with a burning cigarette in his mouth. But I was never afraid of him again, because I knew there were always other children there to protect me.

I remember this incident as comical. The fact that whatever this man had planned to do was foiled by two young girls. I remember it like how my mother remembers the stories of her coming terrifyingly close to death as a child. Many bad things happen in Korea, and many bad people live there. There are "bad things" that happened to me that I will not speak of. But there is a comical element to the ease with which horror is kept at bay. All you have to do is keep staring. Like Hoho Ajumma and the fucking ghosts in *Super Mario Bros.* If you stop looking, they'll kill you. But it's so easy to stop them. Just don't look away.

* * *

정 (JUNG; FAMILIAR ENERGY)

LOOKING BACK AT MY EARLY YEARS in Korea, I remember the children as my protectors and the adults as my abusers. The adults were either not there for me or beating me, making me stand in a corner, staring at me, or attempting to kidnap me. I remember it all with 정 (jung). *Jung* is a word that doesn't exist in English, so it is appropriate that I left it in Korea. If I were to try to translate it, I would say it is as if familiarity were an emotion. However, the definition is way more complicated since it's thought of as an energy force with free will that occurs outside of our control. In Korea, a compliment is to tell someone they have lots of jung, meaning they have the essence of someone who is known to you. Someone who feels immediately comfortable because they feel familiar. Koreans say that the reason divorce is difficult isn't because of love, but because of jung—the bond that is stronger than love, the bond of being used to something. It isn't a positive word like love; it encompasses all the emotions of the familiar, like the bond between siblings. Koreans also use this word for homesickness. You will often hear Koreans traveling abroad blame their indigestion or general discomfort on jung. I have jung for my homeland. It makes me sick to be away from it, but it makes me equally sick to be there. Because for every positive emotion tied to jung, there is an equal negative one.

In 2008, the most well-known rape case in modern Korean history happened. The circumstances of the case were somewhat similar to my incident with Ttorayi Ahjusshi. A drunk man abducted an eight-year-old girl in broad daylight, took her to a Christian church bathroom (somehow the Christian god let this happen), assaulted her, and attempted to murder her. She survived but was disabled for life because of the extent of her injuries. She is no longer able to have children and uses a colostomy bag. I cried for days when I first heard this story. All Koreans did. We were all collectively devastated. I feel like we all felt responsible. I feel like we all felt like we were all supposed to have been there to stop this man. I kept thinking, *Why wasn't anyone there?* Then I remembered the busy street full of adults who had not seen Ttorayi Ahjusshi when he was attempting to do whatever he wanted to do with me. I had the horrifying thought that maybe there had been a street full of adults that had seen this drunk man take this girl too. But where were the two middle school girls? Where were the children who protected me?

Then I realized that all of the children from my past were now adults.

CHAPTER 5

Fat

ISLAS DE LOS LADRONES (THE ISLANDS OF THIEVES)

W~HEN I WAS SIX~, my parents moved our family from Jeju-do to Saipan, in the Commonwealth of the Northern Mariana Islands. It is a small island approximately 135 miles north of Guam, a bigger island and the point of reference for most Americans since it houses a US military base. This is the way I have been made to describe Saipan all my life: it's a place next to a place that Americans might know. If you live in the US and are from a place Americans do not know about, you have to describe it in relation to the closest American reference point. Unfortunately, the most common references for Americans are places they did a movie or a war.

I've heard people describe the nation they're from by referencing a scene in *Mission Impossible.* Imagine if you're from a country and the only way people heard about it was because it was in a *Fast and Furious* movie? And you had to specify which one, like "No, it's not *2 Fast 2 Furious,* it's *The Fate of the Furious.*" As humiliating as that is, it's probably a less weird feeling than being from a place like Afghanistan. Imagine having to tell an ignorant white American you're from Afghanistan and having to withstand the combined look of suspicion and pity. Suspicion and pity for a country that was destroyed by our wars. Saipan is a place Americans did a war. But fortunately, the average American does not know a lot about most of the wars they do, so instead of looking at me with suspicion and pity when I say I am from Saipan, they say, "Taipei? I love Taiwan!"

I know Saipan viscerally. By scent, like how an animal knows its mother. But what I'm supposed to tell you here is the information that they put on the Wikipedia page: geographical information, the population, the weather, and the history. This is the shit that matters to people when they ask you about a place. Saipan is located around 1,500 miles southeast of Japan and it's near the equator so it's always hot. On the Wikipedia page, there is one sentence about evidence of human habitation on Saipan dating back four thousand years before large sections describing each era of colonization. The Spanish were in the Mariana Islands from roughly 1500 to 1800, then the Germans, Japanese, and Americans, who all had "ownership" of the islands since then. That's the focus of the Wikipedia article. There is little mention of the Indigenous population of the Marianas known as Chamorros. There is no mention of how the Chamorros were so advanced in marine navigation that they found these specks of land 3,500 years before the whites did. The white man who "discovered" Saipan was named Ferdinand Magellan. I know his name because the continental breakfast buffet restaurant at the resort my mom worked at was named after him.

There is a reason there's no mention of anything before the colonizers arrived. When they first discovered the Marianas, the Spanish referred to them as "Islas de los Ladrones" (the Islands of Thieves) because upon their arrival, the Chamorros casually jumped aboard their ships and took what they needed without "permission." The Spanish didn't realize that in Chamorro culture, they considered the concept of individual ownership of possessions stupid. Everything was meant for everyone. And because there was no ownership, there was no thievery.

It's not that they didn't understand owning property, it's that they decided that it made more sense to share everything in their culture thousands of years before the Europeans got there. I like to think this was the reason the Chamorros, as with a lot of other Indigenous cultures, didn't really record anything and put their names on places. It makes sense that cultures that evolved away from individual ownership also didn't feel the need to own history or geography. I dislike the romanticization of Indigenous peoples and their belief systems because I find it infantilizing and offensive. Chamorros are not innocent savages like Europeans like to think all people they colonized were. They're human beings and are driven by the same negative and positive feelings that we all have. All people feel greed and self-preservation. Everyone wants to put their name on something. But some of us come from cultures that understand that it's futile. Yes, Europeans recorded their story and therefore took command of Saipan's Wikipedia page. I think a lot of Europeans think that having the foresight and technology to record their point of view and therefore own the narrative was proof that they were smarter than everyone else. But what if it's the opposite? What if other people were just smart enough to recognize how ridiculous that was?

Europeans thought Chamorros were not intelligent enough to see hundreds of years into the future, but what if it's that they were smart enough to see millions of years into the future? What if they saw the entire universe and understood how utterly devastating it was to try to name something after themselves for a blink of an eye on a small floating rock in the endless sky? They saw that we are all part of a whole that will exist forever, and therefore we all are already immortal. Therefore, there was no need to put your name on anything. Ferdinand Magellan was so adamant about pissing his name all over an island that he "discovered" 3,500 years after other people already discovered it. Like a feral cat pissing all over your oak tree, trying to mark its territory. The cat doesn't own shit. The oak tree is going to be there after he's dead. The funny thing is you don't own the oak tree either, because it will be there after you're dead and it's weird you think it's yours just because it's in "your" yard. Childish explorers like Magellan sprayed their urine names all over this earth, over things that belong to no man. He thought the

Chamorros were not smart enough to do the same. He did not realize the Chamorros knew that having a continental breakfast buffet restaurant named after you was a fate worse than being forgotten after death.

The Chamorros were living in an economic system that white people would later pretend they invented and call "socialism" or whatever. They lived on islands for 3,500 years before white people pretended to discover them and call them Islas de los Ladrones. Now the islands are called the Marianas, and I absolutely refuse to look up who they're named after. I don't know who the fuck "Mariana" is, but one thing I know for certain is that she was a thief. Because putting your name on something that belongs to all of us is thievery. They aren't the islands of thieves but islands that are "owned" by one.

This is a story we all know. Because it happened to the Chamorros, the Hawaiians, the Papuans, the Samoans, the Navajo, the Inuits, and the people who the Vikings raped and pillaged who I don't even know the name of. I feel most sorry for the victims of the Vikings because to this day, no one seems to feel bad for them. There is no justice for them because it happened so long ago and also because of the weird white supremacist ideology surrounding Viking pride. Someone once told me that the people who lived in Scandinavia before the white Vikings looked like Björk. Imagine the cool and weird culture the Björk people would have had. We could've had an entire culture of Björks. Now we just have Sven from Sweden who can't shut the fuck up about how his country "invented" socialism four thousand years after the Chamorros did.

But the Björk people did survive. All victims of conflict, war, and colonization survived throughout history through their mixed-race children. That's why randomly you'll see someone from Sweden and they'll look wasian. I bet the blond, blue-eyed Swedes ask them where they're really from all the time. Can you imagine? Those poor Björks. This happened on Saipan too.

The Spaniards showed up on Saipan and pretended they owned

everything, including the Chamorros themselves. They enslaved them. Because ownership takes away bodily autonomy and consent, by definition, they raped them. Today, much like other former Spanish colonies, the wealthy Chamorros are lighter and have Spanish surnames. Some of the wealthy Chamorros have German, Japanese, or American surnames because those people also took turns owning and thus raping the Chamorros.

Mixed-race people from places like Saipan have a profoundly different experience than I did in Korea. In cultures that were mostly replaced by the colonizing culture, the closer the person is to appearing like the colonizer, the more they are rewarded. This is the experience of most mixed-race people in the US. This is the experience most Asian Americans are familiar with, and my identity as a wasian rubs a lot of them the wrong way. They've seen people like me living easier lives growing up in America and resent that I have the nerve to discuss the racism they think they've experienced way more. They are correct in a lot of ways. Although physically I don't appear white, my mannerisms and behaviors are definitely white. I say, "For Christ's sake!" when I want to emphasize something, for Christ's sake. And although I have discussed how shitty my life was in Korea as a biracial, on Saipan I enjoyed a level of privilege that Korean Koreans didn't because everyone on the island could tell I was mixed. A lot of people on Saipan even thought I might be mixed Chamorro, which was a very good thing to be there. So in this period of my life, I did enjoy, dare I say, white privilege. But not from the fucking Koreans.

* * *

MERCY

WHEN I FIRST GOT TO Saipan, my parents sent me to a school called Grace Christian Academy. It was the strictest, most religious of all the schools on Saipan. The children were made to wear stiff gray wool uniforms. For boys, the uniforms were three-piece suits, complete with a necktie and wool vests over crisp white shirts. For girls, the uniforms were exactly the same except instead of pants, we wore gray wool skirts with goddamn Victorian-haunted-child thick white leggings. This shit did not make any sense because the temperature on Saipan was, and is, always eighty-five fucking degrees. My parents thought this school was best because it most resembled the school I had attended on Jeju-do. I think my mom was sold on the uniforms, which to her resembled the little lad velvet outfit she forced me to wear in Korea. Grace Christian Academy was infamous among children on the island because they allegedly implemented corporal punishment. Every week the principal would visit all the classrooms with a giant wooden cricket paddle. He would walk in wearing a gray suit, say good morning, and then ask us if we all knew what he was holding in his hands. We all said yes and then he left. Kind of kinky?

At this point, I still didn't speak English, so I could only really hang out with the other Korean kids. In my class, there was a group of Evil Christian Korean girls who were crueler and more toxically nationalistic than even the Koreans in Korea who I had just left behind. For me to gain acceptance into their crew, I had to prove that I was Korean, which was hard because they didn't think I was by my appearance. Absolute fucking shocker, I know. Also, I was new, and half the time I was in ESL. This was my first experience with the Korean diaspora outside of Korea, whose insecurity about not knowing their own culture made them gatekeep-y and suspicious. They bullied me relentlessly not only for not being Korean enough, but also for secretly being a boy. They said they could tell that I was a boy pretending to be a girl because of the size of my hands. They were not impressed by my "German bones" like my mom was. Every time we had an assignment, before turning it in, the girls would scan my paper to make sure my answers matched all of theirs. If my answer didn't match, they would make me change it, even if I knew I was correct. These girls were not just evil and Christian but sort of dumb (traits that all sort of go hand in hand to be honest). So a lot of times I would be made to erase my correct answer and change it to theirs and then get it wrong. The point wasn't that I got the work right; the point was that we were all the same. That's what being Korean meant.

Once we were made to cut out a profile of George Washington in art class. The teacher handed all of us a piece of white paper with his profile outlined in black. I had a hard time using scissors in school because I'm left-handed. The Evil Christian Korean girls thought one of the most important things in the world was to cut perfectly on the outside of lines in art class. I tried to cut perfectly along the line and immediately messed up. I thought, *Who gives a fuck* and just cut the entire line out so that the profile looked like I had cut it freehand. The "leader" of the Evil Christian Korean girls had a name I can't remember, but it was one of those Korean names that sounds like a brick made of mud, like Dok-Gun. She saw my profile and raised her hand and told the teacher I had done the assignment wrong. The teacher didn't seem to care, but Dok-Gun and the other Korean girls wouldn't let this shit go. They kept asking me why I had cut out the black line, why had I done it "wrong." They laughed and said my hands were too big for the scissors. I looked around the room and saw that some of the other children had done it the way I had too, but none of them were Korean. The Koreans all cut outside the line perfectly. When my mom came to pick me up, she saw the profile and said, "How did you cut it so perfectly? I can't believe you did this by just looking at a quarter!" In that moment, I thought Dok-Gun was a fucking idiot for including the line. By cutting the outline out, I had scammed my mom into thinking that I had talent. She thought I had done this without needing direction. But Dok-Gun wasn't an idiot. Her mom probably saw her George Washington with the line perfectly intact, so precise that it looked like it was done by machine. She probably praised her for following the line perfectly. Who am I kidding? Her mom was Korean, after all. She probably told Dok-Gun that it was good, but it still wasn't good enough.

Dok-Gun's appearance, much like her name, was giving mud brick. Her hair, skin, and eyes were all the same color brown, and she had a big, square-ass head. Her vibe was medium. She was a medium-sized, medium-colored, medium-length-haired medium girl. In this way, she was the Korean dream of what a girl should be. Medium. The middle of the pack. The conformist. Never questioned anything. Rule follower. Probably a Capricorn or, even worse, a Virgo. She was the leader of the children because in every situation, she knew the right Korean thing to do. The medium thing. She came from a long line of brown mud bricks, the Koreans who make up the walls of the prison that is Korean society.

One day Dok-Gun said we were going to play a game called Mercy. The rules were that she would take our wrists and twist them in her hands, causing the thin skin to burn, and whoever could hold out the longest before saying "mercy" would win. Obviously, I would be the first contestant. She grabbed my wrists and said, "Big boy wrists!" I remember her fingers barely being able to wrap all the way around. She started twisting, and immediately the pain was unbearable. I held out for as long as I could, but it was only a few seconds. "Mercy!" I squeaked, trying to make my voice sound less low and boyish. Dok-Gun kept going. "Mercy!" I thought she didn't hear me. "Mercy! Mercy! Mercy!" I realized she definitely had heard me by then but was ignoring me on purpose. I tried to wriggle away from her, but she had my wrists in an evil Korean death grip, somehow without being fueled by soju. I remember how she stared at me, expressionless. I finally wrestled my wrists out of her tiny Korean hands. "왜 이렇게 못참어?" (Why are you so bad at enduring?) She laughed.

Enduring for as long as possible was Korean, and this proved I wasn't. She didn't play the game with the rest of the girls because they didn't need to prove anything to her. I feel like this was the last straw of rejection from Koreans. I had lived my life up to this point doing everything they asked of me. By the time I was six, I was done with their bullshit. This wasn't a game I could win. This was a game set up so I would get hurt. They would not give me mercy, even if I begged them.

After I fled the Koreans, Dok-Gun made a few feeble attempts to assert power over me to try to pull me back in (Al Pacino voice). She hated that I had figured out that belonging to her group was utter bullshit. One time at lunch, she opened up her lunch box and told everyone we could take one of her gimbaps. We all took one, and as I placed mine inside my mouth, she screamed at me, "Not you!!" She immediately started fake-crying, and her minions called the teacher over.

When the teacher walked up, Dok-Gun told her between fake-ass sobs that I stole her lunch. The teacher grabbed me by the cheeks—which, if you're keeping track, was the second fucking time this traumatic maneuver was done to me in childhood—forcing my mouth open so that the gimbap plopped out onto the ground. I felt tears forming in my eyes out of humiliation and terror. The teacher wagged her finger at me and screamed, "NO! NO!" By the time she finally walked away, I was fully crying. I was humiliated and sad.

Then I felt something else, something I don't really remember having felt before. I felt angry. Dok-Gun was mean to me for what? What the fuck had I ever done to this bitch? It wasn't my fault my hands were big and I sucked at using scissors. Why did all this shit matter so much to her? I felt this fucking rage bubbling up through my tears. I started screaming all the Korean cuss words I knew at the time and angrily stomped on the gimbap under the cafeteria table. I stomped over and over again until it was completely mushed into the concrete. I vaguely remember the girls staring at me, but they weren't laughing or making fun of me anymore. They sort of looked like they respected me. Exploding in uncontrollable rage while screaming, "씨발 개년 너

죽일꺼야 쌍년아!" (Fucking bitch, I'll kill you! You fucking slut!) was the most Korean thing in the world, and by doing so I finally won the game. But it was too late. I was no longer playing.

Sitting behind me was a girl who I'll call Jung-Ha. Jung-Ha's mom had been Dok-Gun's mom's best friend before they were born, and the two girls had been essentially raised together since birth. Jung-Ha had the privilege of knowing that Dok-Gun was evil since they were in diapers, and by the time they were in school, she knew to avoid her. So Jung-Ha hung out by herself. When she saw me scream at Dok-Gun, she knew we would get along. I was rage-crying so hard at this point, I could barely catch my breath. She sat next to me and, when I finally calmed down, offered me some of her lunch. Not surprisingly, it was also gimbap.

Jung-Ha was my first real friend. She had jung. I felt as if I, not Dok-Gun, was the one who knew her before birth. Every day after lunch, the teacher would turn the lights off, and the children were made to nap on foam mats that we had to drag under our desks. At nap time I would always crawl across the floor, passing the sleeping bodies of my other classmates to Jung-Ha's desk, where we would hug each other in the dark and tell jokes. The "jokes" were mostly just us saying the word 방구 (bangu; fart) over and over again. Every day, we would end up laughing so hard and making so much noise that the teacher would come over and whisper-scream at us, "Stop! Talking! Stop! Name...chalkboard!" At this point I still didn't understand English very well, so in my memories of this time, people talk in a choppy string of familiar words.

I had figured out that the rule for receiving paddling was that if you did something wrong, the teacher would write your name on the board, then make a check mark for every time after that. Three checks meant you would be sent to the principal's office and get paddled. Because of our nap-time-joke-telling ritual, Jung-Ha and I always had our names on the board along with ten to fifteen checks. After nap time, our names and our checks took up half the chalkboard, and the teacher had to squish the lesson onto the little remaining space. Every day, she would tell us, "Last chance...today...tomorrow...chalkboard...name...three checks...principal...paddle!!" Eventually we stopped believing her. Until one day, after nap time, we got up, wiping tears from our eyes from laughing so hard. The teacher turned on the lights, sighed heavily, and said "Jung-Ha! Youngmi! Principal's...office...now!"

All the children gasped, and Jung-Ha and I looked at each other in shock. We got out of our seats and walked out into the hall. I felt terrified but comforted by the fact that we were going to go together. Even in the face of my worst fear, having her there made everything OK. Part of me even thought it was sort of fun because we got to take a little break together. It was like a free recess or something. Jung-Ha was laughing nervously, which sent both of us into a fit of genuine laughter. We laughed so hard at the ridiculousness of it all. I knew she felt exactly how I felt. This shit was so stupid and funny. We got to the lobby of the principal's office, and as soon as the secretary saw us, she put on a performative disappointed face and went to notify the principal. He came out of his office and said, "Jung-Ha!" Jung-Ha silently got up and followed him inside. I sat listening intently, anticipating the *whap* of the paddle followed by her crying out in pain. But I heard nothing. After a few moments the principal opened the door, and she shuffled out, mouthing the word *ouch* and rubbing her butt. I thought, *Wow, what a badass. She's not even crying.* Then the principal said, "Youngmi!"

I followed him into his office. He was already holding the paddle. I could see a nail behind his head where I assumed he usually hung it. He started talking, and I knew from his tone that he was scolding me. Then he asked, "Do you...why...here?" I nodded and looked around his office. It was tiny. There was barely any room for us to stand far enough apart for me to get paddled. I wondered where Jung-Ha had gotten paddled.

He continued talking, but his tone had shifted, and I kept nodding while trying to comprehend. "So...today...not...next time...paddle." I realized I wasn't going to get paddled. As he continued to talk, I realized Jung-Ha also had not been paddled. Then the thought exploded in my brain that maybe no one ever got paddled. That the whole thing was a fucking scam. An empty, nonexistent threat in order to keep children in line. All the children in the school had lived their lives in fear of something that didn't exist. He opened the door. As I started walking out, he put his finger to his mouth and went, "Shhhh!" I knew from my career as a child gang member in Jeju-do that this was the international sign for "don't rat out the mob." Omertà. But instead of keeping a secret from the authorities, we were the authorities keeping a secret from the public. I was now in on this scam, and the entire thing would come crumbling down if I told gen pop. Paddling wasn't real. That's why Jung-Ha and I hadn't been sent to the office after three checks all those days. That's why only one or two children a year were ever sent to the principal's office, because they couldn't afford to let too many children in on the lie.

As Jung-Ha and I walked back to the classroom, she whispered, "I didn't get paddled, but he told me to tell you that I did because he was really going to paddle you."

I whispered back, "He told me the same thing! I wasn't supposed to tell you!"

When we got back to the classroom, the other children scanned our faces to see if we had been crying. We walked in, rubbing our butts and mouthing, *Ouch.* The teacher smiled. She smiled because we were now part of the gang and had passed our initiation. She smiled because she knew we knew. We knew we would have to uphold this scam. All the children sent to the principal's office always did. All the children inherently knew to uphold the lie of authority. None of them ever revealed the secret. Jung-Ha and I tried to act like we were devastated by being physically assaulted, but before the end of the day we were back at being disobedient little shits and continued to accrue checks behind our names.

Even when we thought getting paddled would actually happen, the threat never worked on me or Jung-Ha. For us, getting punished was worth it to spend those endless nap times in the dark telling weird fart jokes and squeezing each other's cheeks. So what if we got our asses beat? The worst possible thing we could imagine was worth our friendship. Worth love. The threat of the paddle worked on all the other children, especially Dok-Gun. She built her entire life around it. She saw how effective it was in creating order and control, and she emulated it, using fear to manipulate her own following.

The other Korean girls stayed loyal to Dok-Gun. They did everything Dok-Gun told them to do even though she hurt them all the time, and they could never "win." They also behaved in school because the threat of paddling worked on them. They thought the way to gain love was to endure pain and to be afraid of more pain. Love feels so precious that some people believe it must cost something, that we must have to pay for it with pain. But love isn't gained by enduring pain or fearing a paddle. Love isn't gained by not ratting out the mob. Love is found at nap time, when the lights are off, under the desk of your best friend, when everyone else is asleep.

I became fluent in English over the course of a few months. My English became way better than the Evil Christian Korean girls because I made non-Korean friends who were way nicer to me. I learned English well because I needed to get the fuck away from the Koreans. So at this point I spoke English AND Korean better than those idiots. I still do to this day. I am more fluent in both languages than a lot of them. I had to be better at Korean to prove myself to them, and I had to be better at English to get the fuck away from them. I had to be better because I had no other choice.

My parents pulled me out of school in the middle of the year for some reason, but I assume it's because they learned that the principal would do weekly kinky paddle tours. They did not know about the paddle when enrolling my sister and me at Grace Christian Academy. They were OK with hitting me, but they drew the line at another adult hitting me. I assume that when they called, the principal told them the secret, that none of the children actually got paddled. They probably thought it didn't matter if no one got paddled because even the threat of that was harmful, and there is something so weird about an adult walking around rooms full of children brandishing something a lot of them use during sex. It's fucking weird. What my parents didn't realize was that I didn't learn to fear authority in my short time at that school; I learned the exact opposite. I learned to never respect authority out of fear. Because their threats, much like their power, are not real.

*　　*　　*

MUD WALL

I MET UP WITH DOK-GUN and her big-ass square head one time as an adult. It was 2012 and I had just moved to New York City. Shockingly (maybe not so shockingly), she still hung out with the same girls from first grade. We all met up for dinner because she was visiting New York for work, and her two minions agreed to fly out to meet her. I arrived at the restaurant to find all of them dressed like Pam from *The Office,* in pencil skirts, modest heels, and cardigans. We met in a fake-trendy Italian restaurant in Tribeca no one had ever heard of, where Dok-Gun ordered everything before I got to look at the menu. I tried to order myself a martini, but she didn't let me. She said she had purchased a Groupon for seventy-five dollars, which included a course for two and a bottle of red wine. She said if I ordered a thirteen-dollar cocktail, it would ruin the entire point of coming to this restaurant. So I sat there eating food meant for two split among four and drinking red wine, which I don't ever drink since it makes me sick.

The conversation during dinner was the most depressing shit I've ever had to sit through in my life. They all discussed their shitty jobs as mud bricks in some mud-wall corporation. Dok-Gun was in some field so horrifyingly boring that for the life of me I can't remember what it was. Maybe PR? Advertising? Something horrible like that. They were all married or engaged to shitty Christian Korean men and all lived in shitty, horrible cities like Boston. They stopped to congratulate one another after discussing some horrifically depressing raise or vaguely unsatisfying-seeming vacation in Aruba. At one point, Dok-Gun was talking about how beautiful Kate Beckinscott or whoever looked at the Oscars. I remember not knowing who the actress was and Dok-Gun stopped talking, her face in disbelief, and she said, "진짜??" (Really??) Her minions laughed. Like a real point-at-the-loser-and-laugh laugh. Like they truly thought I was pathetic for not knowing who Kate Beck-install or whoever was.

Dok-Gun brought up Grace Christian Academy. All the girls had continued to go there until middle school, long after I left in the first grade. Dok-Gun said, "Remember the paddle? I remember Youngmi and Jung-Ha got paddled! You were both so bad!" It dawned on me that none of the girls knew what Jung-Ha and I knew. None of them had ever done anything to be sent to the principal's office, and therefore none of them had the opportunity to see the truth. None of them had eaten from the tree of knowledge because God said if they did, they would be kicked out of paradise. But their lives were not paradise. They continued to live under the threat of the paddle. In high school, the paddle was replaced with another empty, fake threat that was bigger. In college, it was replaced with an even bigger, even emptier threat, and so on and so on. Today the girls lived working mud-brick jobs, being in mud-brick relationships with mud-brick partners, wearing gray pencil skirts and beige cardigans, afraid of a paddling that didn't exist. That had never existed.

"We didn't get paddled," I said, nursing my allotted two ounces of red wine that was already giving me a headache.

"What?" Dok-Gun said.

"We didn't get paddled. The principal told me and Jung-Ha to pretend that we got paddled. But we didn't. Honestly, I don't think anyone ever got paddled."

"He didn't paddle you because you were girls," she said without missing a beat. "But I remember Greg [not real name] in our class got paddled. I remember he threw up on his desk after coming back from the principal's office because he was paddled so hard."

I remembered Greg throwing up on his desk. This was by far the biggest event of first grade. He threw up because his mommy dropped him off and he couldn't stop crying because he missed her. He threw up because he loved his mom so much that being away from her made him sad. I remember the teacher being gentle and kind to him at that moment, which was rare for her. She cleaned his desk and gave him a hug. She knew she couldn't threaten him with the paddle for loving his mom. The threat of the paddle doesn't work when someone already knows what love is. I felt abysmally sad when I realized that Dok-Gun remembered the incident this way. I felt so sad that she couldn't accept that the paddling wasn't real even as an adult. It was so sad that she needed the threat to be real because she had based her entire life on it. She needed to think she lived in paradise, and the place where Jung-Ha, barfy Greg, and I lived was hell. But the opposite was true.

After dinner all the women thanked her for paying. I had not intended to let her pay for dinner because that would be power, and she abused any speck of power. But I had no option to object because it was prepaid using a Groupon. I thanked her for dinner as well and gritted my teeth at that shit-eating, smug look on her face. The server brought over the check with the tax amount, which wasn't covered by Groupon. It was an amount that was less than ten dollars, and she tipped five dollars on top of that. Five dollars for a bill that was approximately eighty-five dollars after tax. At this point in my life, I worked in restaurants and was familiar with restaurant people, so I knew as soon as we had walked in, the handsome Italian server saw us and said some racist shit about Asians to his coworkers. Then I knew he told them that we split a meal for two among the four of us using a Groupon and made some racist comment about that too. Then I knew when we left, he would show his coworkers the five-dollar bill and they would all laugh at us. Because I knew all this, as the women got up to leave, I furtively pulled a ten out of my wallet and slyly slid it on the table.

Although Koreans have always rejected me, and always will, I still want to protect them. I want so badly to be a part of the mud wall, but I know I can't. But I will still do everything in my power to uphold its dignity and to defend it. I won't let the handsome Italian servers of the world make fun of my people.

*　*　*

THE PADDLE

I ALSO ENDED UP MEETING up with Jung-Ha exactly once while living in New York around the same time. She had moved to the city to attend film school at NYU and then stayed after finding success in her field, which was impressive. When I met up with her, she had already been living here for quite some time. She possibly lives here still. I am not exactly sure why, but I never contacted her after that one time we hung out. We met up at her one-bedroom apartment in the Upper East Side. It was a small, windowless basement space, but impressive for living alone in New York City. We sat in the living room, which looked like the room where suburban people keep their washing machine. The walls had been painted a dark hot pink. She explained that she had once had a roommate who slept out here and had painted the walls before moving out. This was when I had just moved to New York, and the concept of not replacing a roommate seemed luxurious to me, but also lonely. Sitting in the small dark pink room had the effect of sitting in a cold, wet womb.

I asked her if she was dating someone, and she told me that she had secretly married an American GI she had met while still living on Saipan. She showed me a picture of him. By "secretly" married, she meant she had not told her Korean parents about him. He was extremely buff and handsome. He was also Black. She didn't say it was because he was Black, but she didn't have to. I asked her how long she was going to keep the fact that she was married a secret from her parents. She said she wasn't sure but she would figure out when to tell them. This was over ten years ago now, and I am not sure if she ever told them. Jung-Ha and I both learned when we were six years old that the threat of being paddled wasn't real. But I think she forgot this.

I felt as if I'd left all of these people in exactly the same place I had met them. Jung-Ha, with her name on the board followed by an endless string of checks. And Dok-Gun, in a never-ending game of Mercy, forever twisting the wrists of anyone who would let her hold them, taunting them with Kate Beckinscott trivia.

*   *   *

THE LITTLE MERMAID

AFTER MY PARENTS PULLED ME out of Grace Christian Academy in the first grade, I attended a school on the beach called Saipan Community School. Like other schools on the island, it was set up by American Christian missionaries, but this one was set up by the "fun hippie" ones. It was considered the most liberal school on Saipan. My life there was wonderful. The school was so ethnically diverse that there was no real way for the children to form cliques according to race. I wasn't *barely* different from the rest of class; I was *extremely* different from the rest of the class. We all were. Paradoxically, it made us all the same. Every race was represented in this small school. Even the Koreans in the school sort of gave up on their weird racist gatekeeping because they sensed they were outnumbered. No one gave a fuck about being Korean there. Since I was already fluent in English by the time I started, I easily made friends with everyone. I also learned that I was "smart" and that I had just struggled academically before this because all schooling prior was done through negative reinforcement, which absolutely did not work on me. At Saipan Community School, where children were taught through positive reinforcement, I excelled in my studies and quickly moved to the top of my class. To this day, my mom still brings up that I was the smartest kid in the second grade.

This school was paradise compared to the previous one, but one of my most vivid memories of being there is strange and sad. Since the playground was directly on the beach, there was a string of orange cones about twenty or so feet from the water. The children were forbidden to cross the orange cones, and the penalty for doing so was detention, which was a mega harsh punishment for this very chill school. We all knew never to cross the orange cones. But every day after lunch, I would walk out to the cones and longingly stare out into the water and wish I would become a mermaid. *The Little Mermaid* had come out around this time, and I was obsessed. I was convinced I could hear God telling me to just jump the orange cones and go in the water and hold my breath. He said if I was brave enough to break the rules, run into the water, and hold my breath past the point of drowning, I would wake up as a mermaid. This was a test to see how much I actually wanted it. I stood at the cones every day, trying to push myself to jump over them.

The recess chaperone never watched the orange cones because they knew the kids were all too terrified of detention. I still think about how if I had gone ahead with my mermaid plan, it is likely no one would've seen me drown myself. I still think about what would've happened if they had just found my lifeless body, drowned in two feet of water. What would they have thought? As a teenager or younger adult, whenever I remembered this daily ritual, I thought I was a whimsical, fun kid. But now I realize that during those days I stood at the edge of the playground, I wasn't being whimsical—I was contemplating killing myself.

* * *

THE BRADY BUNCH

THIS WAS THE BEST TIME of my life at Saipan Community School. But it was the worst time of my life at home. I was left completely alone with my sister, who was only four years older than me. She ignored me completely. She never made me food or helped me with anything. The only interaction I had with her was when she would beat me. We would sit in the living room and watch TV. I wasn't allowed access to the remote, so we would watch only what she wanted to, which was usually MTV or *Brady Bunch* reruns on Nickelodeon. I found this show to be corny and passé, but for some reason also extremely disturbing. Whenever the intro theme song ended, it would pause on a shot of the exterior of their home in Southern California. Something about what the color correction of the seventies did to the bright sunlight hitting the dark wood home was eerie and nauseating. I would ask her to change the channel, but she would tell me to shut up and punch me. Sometimes the punching didn't stop, and I would run away into my room to hide. But she would find me and continue punching, slapping, and kicking me.

My father was away during this time, flying cargo airplanes in Angola. Pilots are legally required to fly for a certain number of hours before having to take time off. His company merged all of his hours into three-month stretches, followed by one month of "off time." He would spend some of his off time in Thailand with his pilot friends before coming home. Every time they came back, one of his friends would have a new nineteen-year-old Thai wife.

My mom worked at a resort, which was a knockoff of the Club Med in Bali. They literally even copied the signage. My mother was rarely home. I am not sure exactly how long we were left alone, but I remember the dread I felt watching the sun go down. I remember watching the door peripherally for endless hours while watching *The Brady Bunch*. I remember being left alone for so long, my sister and I once filled the entire living room and kitchen with water from the bathtub. We did this to turn the apartment into an indoor Slip 'N Slide. We were able to do this and clean up the mess in time without being caught. We cleaned long into the night. For meals, we would eat cases of instant food and snacks my mother would buy in bulk that she knew my sister and I could cook for ourselves. Because of this, from the ages of six through ten, I gained an enormous amount of weight.

I didn't know when I was supposed to eat or how much. I would drink an entire case of juice boxes and eat boxes and boxes of cereal and Pop-Tarts. I would eat all the rice inside the rice cooker along with five or six scrambled eggs, which was the one thing I knew how to cook. I would eat all this because no one told me I was supposed to eat a certain amount, but also because I found the comfort in food that I was missing from a parent. I was terrified all the time. I was alone with my sister, who was also just a child. My sister seemed to have what I thought was the opposite reaction to negligent abuse; she starved herself. I sought out comfort but my sister sought out control. But even when she controlled everything perfectly, my parents weren't home enough. I think her fear turned into anger, which she took out on me.

When I first started gaining weight, my father had returned home from yet another excursion in Thailand. I think he was repulsed by my weight gain. I believe that my father might have had a severe eating disorder. In my memories of childhood, he rarely ate any food during the day. I remember him never sitting down to eat meals with us. I believe that in his youth, his thinness, the thing that made him look so much like the Bee Gees and ultimately attracted my mother, was his most cherished physical trait. At this point of my childhood, he was in his late forties or early fifties, and although he adhered to his rigid dieting, his body was no longer responding in the way he wanted it to. I think the loss of control over his own body—coupled with the realization that he couldn't control mine, which he possibly saw as an extension of himself—made him extremely afraid, and angry. My body became the outlet on which he would unleash this anger.

*　*　*

SPAGHETTI

ONCE, WHEN I WAS AROUND EIGHT, my dad took me to visit one of his pilot friends. When we walked in, his friend was boiling hot dogs in his kitchen. He looked at my dad and said, "I'm making hot dogs for your kid." He was a very large, marshmallowy-looking white man with hair so blond that it was the same color as his skin. I couldn't tell where his hair started and his face stopped. He wore so much aftershave that his entire apartment smelled like Old Spice. Aside from the fact that he was boiling hot dogs for me, allegedly, he didn't acknowledge my existence and kept talking to my dad using the word *fuck* a lot. I was used to this from my dad's friends; none of them ever talked to me or even looked at me. Next to him on the wall of the kitchen was a large poster of a woman wearing a tiny nineties-style high-cut string bikini. Her nipples were very hard and visible. His harsh language and the overtly sexual poster made me scared of him, because he looked so

95

nonthreatening but obviously had put the poster up there, so he was a 변태 (byuntae; pervert).

Just then, his new Thai wife walked in from the bedroom. She smelled strongly of floral perfume and was wearing a lot of makeup and a pretty dress. She was very thin, probably because she was barely not a child. She came up to me and was immediately familiar. She put her arms around me and squeezed my cheeks while asking me what my name was. Everything about her was beautiful and sweet. Having the attention of an adult, especially a beautiful, nice adult, felt surprising and pleasant. She put me at ease. I thought her husband was a byuntae, but if this nice lady was married to him, he must be safe enough.

Shortly, she left for work. My father and his friend continued their conversation while continuing to not acknowledge my presence, and I felt scared again. This man felt dangerous. I overheard him refer to his wife as a "fucking stripper." I vaguely understood what that word meant, and I knew it was a scary thing. I was confused because I was taught that strippers were unsafe, but she had felt safe. Meanwhile, this man, who looked like the pastor at the Seventh-day Adventist Church, felt unsafe.

My dad's friend brought me one hot dog on a paper plate before sitting down with his own precarious paper plate of five hot dogs. I remember thinking how ridiculous it was to put five hot dogs on one flimsy paper plate and wondered why he didn't just eat them one by one. He took a huge bite and snickered. "As soon as you said you were bringing your fat kid, I started boiling hot dogs." My dad laughed and then turned to look at me, quietly enraged.

We drove home in silence. When we got there, my mother was making spaghetti in the kitchen. I loved spaghetti and became really excited and started dancing behind her, singing, "Spaghetti! Spaghetti!" My dad was making himself a Jim and Coke and pulled ice out of the freezer. He saw me dancing and shouted, "What the fuck are you so excited about?" My mom looked startled and turned to look at him. I stopped dancing. "I said, what the fuck are you so excited about?"

"Spaghetti," I said.

When the spaghetti was ready, my mom put it on the table in a serving bowl along with a plate of garlic bread. I got to the table first so I could scoop a huge portion onto my plate before anyone else sat down. I was already eating when my mom and sister sat down. My mom said, "Youngmi, why did you take so much? What about your dad?" It was a strange thing for her to say because my father never ate. He never joined us for meals. He starved himself all day and then would binge eat at night secretly as we all slept. But I felt embarrassed that I was being greedy, so I started scooping some spaghetti back into the serving bowl.

My father walked up to the table, holding a fresh Jim and Coke. He said, "Did you put all that spaghetti on your plate?" The anger in his voice made me stop what I was doing. He grabbed my plate from my hands and threw all the spaghetti back into the serving bowl. Then he grabbed my mom's and sister's plates and threw their spaghetti back in the bowl too, throwing the empty plates back down.

He pushed the serving bowl in front of me and said, "You wanted to eat all the fucking spaghetti? Well, then, eat all of the spaghetti." I looked at his angry face, and then at my mom and sister. They were smiling. Both of them were probably hungry, but watching me get what I "deserved" was worth more to them than spaghetti.

Aside from the fact that I was fat, I was still my dad's favorite child by far. I excelled at school and had a lot of friends. My sister didn't do well in school and was not very popular. My report cards were straight A-pluses. Everything I did, I did well. I won art contests, music awards, spelling bees, writing contests, math tournaments, everything. The only thing I sucked at was PE, but I don't think my dad gave a shit about sports, so it didn't matter. I think he saw these achievements as his own. My sister

97

had a different dad, so I obviously was great at everything because of my dad's genes. I think my mother and sister were tired of me receiving this praise and failed to see it as what I believe was my father's narcissistic reflex. I don't think they realized that when my dad constantly bragged about me, he was the one talking. I was scared to talk about my own accomplishments because I could see it angered my mother and made my sister sad. When my father was mean to me, I think in their minds it was him taking down a pompous, arrogant asshole (me). In that way, I was deserving of his cruelty.

After hours of trying to finish all the spaghetti and failing, I was finally allowed to get up from the table and was sent to my room for the rest of the night. I cried in my bed for a long time, holding on to a floppy stuffed dog toy. I had named it Ryan. For some reason, all of my stuffed toys were named common white names. I had a stuffed Care Bear named Peter, a set of rabbits named Sandy and Candy, and Ryan. Ryan was actually a car window plush that I had brought into my room because I felt sorry that he had to live in the car, alone. Because he was made to withstand the extreme temperatures of the inside of a car, he was made from neon-green camping tent material, had thick plastic suction cups on his paws, and was way understuffed. I made up a story that he was my invalid child that was born with a deformity, atrophied muscles, and suction cups on his paws. The lack of stuffing caused his limbs to lethargically hang from the heavy pull of the industrial-strength suction cups. Because of his deformity, he couldn't walk or use his paws, and so I had to carry him around everywhere. I held on tightly to Ryan and cried for hours that night, his suction cups flopping helplessly as the tent material stuck to my face. My father barged in after a while, still full of anger. I looked up, Ryan's wet tent skin peeling off my face. My dad stood staring at me, breathing heavily for a moment before ripping him from my arms. He threw Ryan against the wall, screaming, "You don't need to hold this. You can just hold your fat belly!" He left, slamming the door shut behind him.

When I was sure he wasn't coming back, I quietly got out of bed and picked Ryan off the floor where he had landed. I asked Ryan through tears if he was hurt. He was crying but he said he was fine. My father had thrown him against the wall to break him. But what he didn't understand was that Ryan was made to withstand extreme abuse. His tent-material skin, his suction cups, his lack of stuffing that made him too soft—all of the things I saw as deformities were actually the traits that rendered him unbreakable.

* * *

THE LITTLE MERMAID II

OUTSIDE OF BULLYING ME FOR my weight and turning all my accomplishments into his own, my father ignored me. He was very quiet and spent most of his time in his room unless he was drunk, and either inappropriately jovial or angry. Once during his three-month stretches in Angola, he got in a plane crash. I don't know all the details, but I know that his plane crashed into an apartment building, causing the death of many Angolans. I believe all the white pilots survived. I remember looking through photos of the accident he kept in a photo album, pictures of a mangled airplane and then some pictures of the night after when all the pilots went out to drink at a hotel. They got so drunk they all decided to jump into the pool naked, and there were photos of them all bent over with their balls and dicks pressed between their legs. As an adult I learned the term for this is "fruit bowl" because the balls and soft penis in this position look like a decorative bowl of fruit. They did this the same day a few Angolans buried their families, some of them children.

After the accident, I remember that his fits of rage became explosive, followed by extremely long periods of depression. For years, we would have to sit in the dark in our home, with all the curtains pulled

99

closed. We would have to watch TV with the volume turned down very low. My mother came home even less during these times, and when she would come home late after partying or whatever she did, my parents would argue long hours into the night. My father was terrifying and did things to my mother that were extremely difficult to witness as a child.

My mom bullied me about my weight too, but for some reason, all these incidents register as humorous to me. When I remember the words she used to call me, like 뚱땡이 (ttongttengi; fatty) or 돼지새끼 (doeji sekki; pig's baby), I can't help but laugh. I remember laughing even when she called me them as a child. One day she hit me so hard, the spoon she was using snapped in two. She said, "You're so fat you broke my spoon!" And we both burst out laughing. We laughed so hard we started to cry. She forgot why she was beating me in the first place. I still laugh when I remember this memory.

My parents were always either angry or sad, and I never heard them talk about why. So I decided that it was because I was fat. If I just lost the weight, they would be happy and they would come home more because I would no longer be embarrassing to be seen around. However, I had no idea how to lose weight. I thought I would become a mermaid.

During the fall of that same year, my mother took me shopping for my Halloween costume. As soon as I walked into the store, a shiny green fabric caught my eye from the rack. I ran over to it and pulled out the clear plastic package it was in. It was an Ariel costume from *The Little Mermaid*. Inside the bag was a long, iridescent, glittery green skirt with a sequined fin at the bottom, a glittery purple bra sewn into a beige-colored mesh shirt, and a red wig. It also came with a little plastic sheet of bejeweled stickers I could put on my face, to emulate the sparkling reflection of water. I had never in my life seen anything so beautiful. Inside this one package was everything I needed to make all my dreams come true. I pulled the costume off the rack and ran it over to my mother. I was so excited, I was shaking as I held it out in front of me. She looked it over as I patiently waited, hoping she wouldn't say it was too expensive like she usually did when I wanted something. She looked at me while pointing at the mesh shirt through the plastic. "You can't wear this because it shows your stomach. You're fat, remember?"

I was so stupid to think that I could be a mermaid. Mermaids were never fat. All the mermaids in *The Little Mermaid* had the same skinny body. My mom knew that I wasn't good enough to be a mermaid because I was just a fat girl who was so annoying that even my parents hated coming home to me. I was embarrassing. My mom was right to tell me how pathetic it was that I had such a stupid dream.

I stood on the beach, staring out at the water all those days during recess because I was begging God to please turn me into a mermaid. I needed to become a mermaid because the magic that was strong enough to turn my legs into a shimmering tail would be powerful enough to make me skinny. I would be a skinny mermaid and I could just swim away from there forever. I wouldn't have to think about why my parents never came home or why my sister always hit me. I wouldn't have to eat boxes of Pop-Tarts for dinner with my invalid dog-plushie son who had suction cups for paws. I wouldn't have to wake up to my mom's bloody lip. I wouldn't have to go with my dad to the homes of cruel men who ate five hot dogs at a time. I wouldn't have to wonder where my parents were while watching the nauseating *Brady Bunch*, where the worst thing Marcia did to Jan was have pretty hair. God heard me begging to be taken away. He told me that all I had to do to become a mermaid was jump over the orange cones, walk out into the ocean, and hold my head under the water until I stopped breathing.

All I had to do was kill myself.

CHAPTER 6

Skinny

MTV

THE OTHER THING MY SISTER loved to watch besides *The Brady Bunch* was MTV. Whenever my sister would turn on MTV, I would run into my room, close the door, and hide. The reason I didn't want to watch MTV wasn't because it was considered adult and I knew I wasn't supposed to watch it; it was because it terrified me.

The most provocative programming were these try-hard artsy animation shorts that would randomly play in between music videos. There was an animation short called *Æon Flux,* drawn in a grotesquely oversexualized fashion that made the characters appear insect-like. The main character and namesake of the show would slide around a darkened, futuristic landscape in a leather cutout catsuit. As she moved, the focus would zoom in and out of the curves of her sex organs, the animation shifting from soft and round to jagged and scratchy. Probably the most beloved animated show of this era was *Beavis and Butt-Head* and featured some stoned guys breathing heavily into microphones over crude drawings of two teenage boys, Beavis and Butt-Head. Either because of poor quality or by choice, each frame was mismatched, causing the characters to constantly pulse. The backgrounds were hastily drawn as large, vapid rooms, which gave the show the eerie effect of watching a squirming insect stuck under glass.

102

What disturbed me about these animated shorts wasn't the overt sexuality and obscenity, but the pulsing and squirming of the low-budget animation, the terrifying liminal spaces, and the absolute void of ambient sound. As a child, I saw all worlds, animated or otherwise, as real. I imagined that after their shows stopped, the brittle Æon Flux would stand on a hastily drawn gray cliff, her breasts contorting unnaturally with every breath, waiting for us to come back. The deformed children named Beavis and Butt-Head would stare blankly ahead while their bodies nauseatingly pulsed out of their control in a yellow room with no ambient sound, waiting. They didn't know why their bodies were crude and ugly and moved outside of their control. To watch them was to force them to exist in this nightmare, and I didn't want that for them.

Early-nineties MTV is a source of pride for every person my age that wants to pretend that they were cool kids. I think it was because to watch MTV, it meant they would've had to be cool enough to sneakily do it while their parents weren't paying attention. Although MTV was basic cable and played in every household in the US, to have the bravery to watch the channel meant to be part of an exclusive club. But I didn't have parents telling me not to watch these programs. The interesting thing about rebellion in children is that for them to want it, they need an adult to provide not only an oppressive force but also a sense of security. They need to have something to fight against, but also to know that whatever happens, it'll be OK. Watching scary adult TV is a safe way children learn to push against their parents because the worst thing that can happen is to get grounded or lose their access to Nintendo for a week. But without parents present, I had no oppressive force, and no sense of security. If I watched something scary, I would have to sit alone in an empty, soundless yellow room, my distorted features pulsing as the result of my lazy and careless creators.

Although I was scared of the animated shorts, I was never bothered by the live-action music videos, and actually enjoyed them.

The interesting thing is, the live-action music videos were way more obscene. Whatever perversion was displayed in the animated shorts was ten times worse in the videos. But they didn't scare me because unlike the unnerving world of the animations, they took place in a fully fleshed-out reality.

*   *   *

THE DISCOVERY CHANNEL

I LIKED WATCHING REAL-LIFE-SEEMING THINGS on TV. My absolute favorite things to watch were nature documentaries on the Discovery Channel. Nature documentaries were technically even more obscene in content, but like music videos, they didn't disturb me because they were real. I watched animals fucking, animals giving birth, animals killing other animals and dying, sometimes all in one episode. Some of the most fascinating parts of these documentaries to me, though, were when animals killed their own babies.

The narrators in nature documentaries would always take great pains to say how it is OK that parents kill their own children. We should all be OK with it. Because it's natural. Birds push runts out of nests, rodents eat their newborns when they're nervous, alligators will eat any of their hatchlings if they're unlucky enough to accidentally walk in front of their mother shortly after birth. Animals kill the babies of other animals too, and we all have to be OK with that as well. Dolphins rape seal babies to death. A lion will kill a lioness's cubs so she can go back into heat and he can fuck her. All this shit happens all the time, and it is OK. There was a good reason for all of that. Ever since the beginning of reproduction, the first amoeba probably split into two and then one immediately tried to eat the other one. It couldn't see the long game; it was an amoeba. Humans kill their own kids too. All the time. That's totally OK too. Remember there is always a good reason. For example,

104

there was that one guy who choked his baby to death because the baby was interrupting his *Fortnite* game.

We see this shit on the news all the time: accounts of fathers killing their kids who were too loud during their video games, mothers who drowned their kids because their new boyfriend didn't like them, fathers who left their babies to suffocate in a hot car because they wanted to get a divorce and start a new life. These are all good reasons to kill children in the minds of people who feel worthless. People who believe they have no worth believe their children also have no worth by extension. So they can kill them. All the children kicked and screamed when their parents were killing them because they didn't believe they were worthless like their parents did. They were born with the instinct to survive no matter what; before they could understand words or ideas, nature gave them the gift of feeling worthy. But their parents had been sold a lie. They had been infected with a disease that had yet to infect their children. And even if the kids survived, they would've inevitably contracted the illness because it was highly contagious. And ultimately they would've died from it, because the disease of feeling worthless is fatal.

I was infected with this disease by my parents. The disease of self-hatred. They couldn't help it because they were both infected, and to pass it on to me was out of their control. But what I cannot forgive is that as they passed along this disease to me, they smiled. In their eyes, they were handing me a gift. They were giving me the gift of being a 미녀 (minyeo; beautiful girl).

* * *

미녀 (MINYEO; BEAUTIFUL GIRL)

IN KOREAN, THE WORD FOR beautiful girl is 미녀 (美女; minyeo). There is a gravity that is lost in translation, though, because this word has

105

the weight of a title. In English the person is still a girl, and *beauty* is merely an adjective. But in Korean, *minyeo* is one word. She is a completely different thing than 소녀 (sonyeo; girl) or 여성 (yeosung; woman). When someone is called a minyeo, it has the same effect of someone being called "Doctor." And just like the title "Doctor," *minyeo* carries the heavy weight of the collective respect of the entire society.

The first female doctors in Korea came about during the Joseon dynasty, which was established in the 1300s. Their title was 의녀 (Uinyeo; medical woman). I want to pretend this was some sort of girlboss feminist move, but the origins are sort of sad. The Confucian idea of strict gender segregation meant that many women in these times died of illnesses because they were too ashamed to be examined by doctors who were exclusively men. So the royal court decided to train female royal maids, essentially enslaved women, to treat other women. This is a complicated and confusing historical fact when viewed through the lens of Western feminism because it is astonishing that Koreans had female doctors dating back to the 1300s (way before women were allowed this title in Europe), but these doctors, because they were women, were also enslaved.

Probably the most famous uinyeo in Korean history was 대장금 (Dae Jang-Geum; the Great Jang-Geum), because she was the first woman to become the royal physician. The royal physician was the final-boss doctor in Korea, the most skilled doctor who treated the royal family, including the king himself. She was so skilled, she overrode the laws of Confucianism, which ironically was the reason women had to become doctors in Korea in the first place. She was so skilled in medicine that they let her touch not only a man, but the final-boss man. Jang-Geum was awarded the title "Dae" (the Great), which changed the entire feeling of her name. "Jang-Geum" sounds like a lowly slave girl, while "Dae Jang-Geum" sounds like a warrior. But to read about her life perfectly captures the confusing place uinyeo had in society. She was the highest-ranking doctor in all of Korea, but she was also a woman and a slave. Therefore, she toggled between being punished for her errors and being rewarded for her accomplishments. Her punishments were severe and ranged from forced exile and imprisonment to the constant threat of being executed. These punishments came about when she was unable to cure a disease or save the life of a royal family member. Her rewards were comically small in comparison. She would cure the king from a mysterious illness one winter and receive like . . . a bag of beans.

This is what women who are Great in Korea receive. A woman so talented that she breaks the rules of God and Man to become great, and she receives the constant threat of being killed and . . . beans.

While visiting family in Korea when I was twelve, my teenage cousin showed me a college textbook she was studying. It was in English, but the words were so specialized, I couldn't understand a single sentence. I asked her how she read this book because she didn't even speak English, and she said, "나한텐 시워." (For me, it's easy.)

She had just received a scholarship to the most prestigious program in her major in a top-rated university in Korea. In celebration, her father, my uncle, had purchased a small cake from Paris Baguette and we sat around it as he passed out slices. At the table with my cousin and uncle was also my aunt (his elder sister). Although getting into a great school is the top achievement for any Korean student, my cousin looked emotionless. She never expressed any emotion after her mother died when she was ten. When my uncle put a slice of cake in front of my aunt, she ignored it. She then angrily screamed, "쓸데없어! [Worthless!] A girl going to school is worthless! Don't let her go. She needs to get married and have children now."

The next time I saw my cousin was over a decade later. We sat in the same living room where she showed me the textbook as a teenager. My cousin had gone on to graduate at the top of her class and was immediately employed by [insert important Korean company here] after university. She shortly married someone else who worked there and stopped working because she had a son. She had come back home because her marriage was troubled. She sat there talking to my mom about her impending divorce. She talked without showing any emotion. It had been over twenty years since her mother had passed away by this point, but she seemed to have never recovered emotionally.

My mother kept asking why she was getting divorced, since her husband made a lot of money doing the same job she was forced to give up when she had their child. My cousin said that he drank and beat her every day. I don't know why he did this, but he probably thought she was not holding up her end of the bargain, since he worked and she didn't. It didn't occur to him that she was better at doing the same job he did, and the only reason she stopped was to raise their child. My mother looked at my cousin while she told the extent of his brutal abuse, completely void of emotion. Without a single tear. My mom paused, staring at my cousin's blank face with her eyes somewhere very far away, and said, "When men beat you, it's because you deserve it."

For being Great, my cousin got a cake from Paris Baguette and the constant threat of being killed.

I saw this happen over and over again in my life. Women who had the audacity to be Great were punished for not succumbing to the disease of believing they were worthless. They fought against that belief all their lives and walked away brutalized by it. Ripped to shreds. Every moment of their lives was a fight against this relentless disease. There was only one Great woman who was safe. The minyeo. The minyeo didn't challenge men. She just was good at being pretty. Since she didn't scare men, she was rewarded by having champagne poured on her titties in the MTV music videos. The only way to be Great without being punished was to be a minyeo.

* * *

DISEASED LIVER

I LOST A TON OF WEIGHT during the summer I was twelve because I had a growth spurt and grew multiple inches in the span of a few months. By the time I was thirteen, I was the height I am now, 5′6″, and towered over the rest of my classmates for a brief moment before they all caught up. Looking at children now, I realize this is a pretty common growth pattern: children's bodies will put on weight in anticipation of a growth spurt. I can see why many healthcare professionals are against diets for children. I can see that although my weight was considered unhealthy and abnormal, it was just my body preparing for the taxing process of growth during puberty. For me, being overweight was a temporary phase of my growth. My parents were cruel to me during this period because they said they were concerned for my health. I believe that to have been an outright lie. I think if they gave a fuck about my health, they wouldn't have done what they did next, which ended up giving me an actual life-threatening disease.

Even though I became a "normal" weight after my growth spurt, I still wasn't "skinny." This was the late nineties, and something called "heroin chic" was extremely popular. Although as a middle school child, I was shielded from the professional-internalized-misogynist-white-supremacy-upholding face of Kate Moss saying, "Nothing tastes as good as skinny feels," the adult Skeletor zeitgeist had infiltrated all media created for children my age as well. From the girls who graced the Delia's catalogs to the sexualized child pop stars with rail-thin arms sticking out of baby doll shirts, every form of media I consumed was overrun by underweight girls. I didn't look like them and I knew it. I was skinnier but I wasn't skinny enough.

I also knew this was true because my parents told me this. Whenever I would go outside, everyone would compliment me on my weight loss. Every time we would run into a friend of my mother's, they would comment on my amazing weight loss, and my mother would respond by saying, "She lost weight, but not enough. She thinks she looks so good, though. She's becoming a show-off!"

This was comical because I could barely make eye contact, and anyone who saw me would see I was suffering from severe lack of self-esteem. I was terrified of Korean adults because culturally, they are expected to say something cruel and rude to children when they see them. I was relieved that they now said nice things about me. But then my mother would remind them that saying these things would inflame my ego, and they would overcorrect by saying something twice as cruel. When my mother would call me a show-off, they would respond, "Oh, you think you can be a model now because you lost a little weight? 잘났어. [Jalnaseo; you're full of yourself.] You're still way too fat to be a model. You can't be a model unless you lose maybe twenty more pounds."

Korean women all want to be models. To be a model means you are a minyeo, and a minyeo is the "winner" of all women. Korean women hate admitting that they all want to be a minyeo because to do so would be to admit they have an ego. They were taught that the ego was something that could be smothered out. Ever since they were children, they were forced to suffocate it, because Koreans think you can kill the ego this way. But the ego is a natural part of all of us. Like an organ. Like the liver. Forcing someone to pretend it doesn't exist won't make it go away. It has to exist for that person to remain alive. Their relentless pretense that their egos didn't exist made their egos diseased and swollen, like a neglected liver. Because they're denied validation and praise instead of having a healthy yearning for acknowledgment, they feel a burning desire for ultimate superiority above everyone else, the tyrannical rage of wanting to be the winner of all. This mutated desire is humiliating and shameful for them. They can't hold on to it, so they give it to little girls to hold. They gave it to me.

At that point, it had not even occurred to me I could be a minyeo. I was still under the belief that I was a fat kid. I had barely noticed I had lost weight because my growth spurt had happened so quickly. Not only had it not occurred to me that I could be a minyeo, but I had not dreamt of being one. I had never wanted to be a model. What I wanted in life was that feeling when I made a funny joke. What I wanted was the feeling when I got the best score on the reading comprehension test. What I wanted was not to be someone I was not, but to be recognized for who I already was: a funny, smart, and kind person. Who was fat but still cool. But all these rotting-ego Korean women told me that I was wrong. What I really wanted was to be a minyeo, because the minyeo was the best thing a woman could be. I guess I did dream of being a model? They said I did, so it must have been true. This must have been my dream. Then they told me I had already failed at it. So I tried harder. It was my dream after all, so I needed to lose weight in order to achieve it.

I stopped eating for days on end. One time I stopped for an entire week. Before dropping me off at school, my mother turned and said to me, "I'm proud of you." She took me shopping after school, and while I was in the fitting room trying on the smallest jeans I have ever fit into in my entire life, I overheard her bragging to the person working at the clothing store. I walked out to show my mother that the jeans fit. She looked at me, beaming with pride as the shopgirl looked at me with a strange, mixed expression of pity and jealousy.

But after I stopped starving myself, the weight would come back. My mother would run her hands along my back to feel my training bra strap squeezing out excess fat, or wrap her hands around my upper arm to see how far her fingers could go around. She told me she used to think my body was all muscle, but after I lost some weight, she knew it was all fat. My parents would look at everything I ate, every snack

I picked out. If my father ever saw me eating something, he would make a comment in passing about how I was getting pudgy again.

I think they did this because they were afraid that I would become fat again. So, I started binging and purging.

*　*　*

KAREN CARPENTER

ONE DAY MY FATHER TOLD me he had something important to talk to me about.

He said, "I'm really proud of you because you got in shape and lost so much weight. I can tell that you understand, right? You understand how important it is to be thin. It's probably one of the most important things in the world, and I am so glad you get that."

He winked at me and paused. The silence was deeply unsettling. I felt violated and I couldn't tell why. He finally continued, "But I want to tell you about a famous singer I used to listen to named Karen Carpenter. I know you don't know who that is..."

Of course I fucking knew who Karen Carpenter was.

"But, well, she was really skinny. REALLY beautiful. But she couldn't control herself so she ate a lot of food and then made herself sick after. You know what I'm saying? She made herself throw up."

I believe as a child and teen, I saw signs that my father had both anorexia and bulimia. The reason I believe this is because I saw similar patterns of behavior after I developed both diseases. I combed back through my childhood and took note of the things he did that I ended up doing: taking extremely long showers right after lunch, eating only after everyone went to bed, breaking down into fits of anxiety and rage about his weight whenever something bad happened.

By the time we were having this conversation, I was convinced he was sick in the same way I was sick. I listened to him talking about how important it was to be thin and then feigning ignorance of the specifics of the diseases. He talked about the act of throwing up after binge eating as some weird, fucked-up shit that this weird Hollywood white woman did in the seventies. He talked about it like it was alien to him, possibly because perhaps it was alien to him, or perhaps to hide his own behavior. I think he was trying to convey that he thought eating disorders were for silly women. Silly women who couldn't *control* themselves. Not like him. He was a man. Men were always in control. He had the privilege of hiding behind the fact that he was a serious and important man and not some self-absorbed, image-obsessed woman who couldn't control herself around snack cakes.

"Anyway, I just want to say I'm proud of you. You've figured out how important it is to be thin. But I don't want you to get too carried away. Because you know what happened to Karen Carpenter? Her heart stopped."

I've played this conversation over and over again in my head for years since it happened. It always struck me as one of the most disturbing conversations I've ever had with my father, and for the longest time I couldn't figure out why that was. I'm still not sure what he was trying to say, but I think maybe he was telling me to go on. I felt like in my mind, he was giving me the green light to keep doing whatever it took to stay thin. I don't think he was trying to deter me with the story of Karen Carpenter; I think he was trying to tell me that that's just the life we all signed up for. Then it struck me. I saw this conversation as an initiation into a gang. A death cult. I saw it as the final step of him transferring this fatal disease to me. The disease of being worthless.

And what I heard was, for that, he was proud of me.

There have been many moments in my decades-long, still-persistent struggle with eating disorders where I knew they would kill me. At times, when I was walking around at a lethargic pace and feeling the loss of consciousness creeping up like a warm hug, or bent over a toilet bowl after throwing up for the fifth or sixth time in a day, I would feel my heart beating irregularly and think, *This is it. This is where my parents kill me.*

If I had died from eating disorders, all the adults around me would pin their dreams and failures on me. My mom's Korean friends would say, "What a stupid girl who wanted to be a model so bad she killed herself! Showing off was more important to her than living? She would've never been pretty enough to be a minyeo anyway." My mom would agree, saying my ego was so out of control, I barfed myself to death. My dad would see my dead body and feel sad, but also feel validated in his belief that he and I were worthless. A worthless death for a worthless life. All the things they felt for themselves would be projected onto my dead body. But my dream wasn't to be skinny enough to be a model or Karen Carpenter—it was to be skinny enough so that my parents would love me.

My parents did love me, I think, though I felt it being reeled in back and forth depending on the number on the scale. But I believed I was deserving of *unconditional* love. Love that wouldn't go away even if I was fat, stupid, ugly, short, hairy, big boned, not funny, unathletic, dark skinned, poor, or a girl. I thought, like every child who is born, that this was a right given to me by nature: parents who love me no matter what. How pathetic and heartbreaking. Nature never promised me anything. Nature never said that all parents of children love them unconditionally. Nature said the lions, the hamsters in clear cages at the pet store, the woman who drove her car into the lake with her children in the back, they were all parents too. And they all killed their children. Karen Carpenter's parents probably told her she looked amazing the year she turned thirteen and dropped a bunch of weight. And if they did, they killed her. And we all have to be OK with that. Because that's natural.

There is no cure for the disease that my parents passed down to me. There is a huge chance that this disease will ultimately take my life.

But at least I am skinny.

Chapter 7
親 (Chin; Close Person)

FATHER

After I became skinny as a teenager, I started becoming attractive to adult men. I'm being very generous to men here because the truth is that it started happening closer to when I was twelve. I liked the power of it. The power was nauseating but also fucking fun. It's like the ride at the amusement park that swirls you around too hard. But you're in there with your friend's dad, Robert, for some reason and he's looking at your boobs. I enjoyed it even though it made me want to barf. So I started dressing like a slut. This male attention and the nauseating power that it came with coincided with me acting out in school. As a teen, I never realized that those two occurrences were related, but the truth is that they worked hand in hand to destroy my perception of adult reality in a way that was too painful for me to acknowledge then.

When I was a fat kid, the positive attention I received all came from my academic success. Although I never tried, I was really good at school. Later, as an adult, I learned I had ADHD, and my childhood behavioral problems all align with the symptoms of undiagnosed neurodivergence. But even though I spent the majority of the time zoning out and getting in trouble, I was always at the top of the class. I would do all my homework minutes before the bell rang in the morning and still get the highest marks. I excelled at all subjects, but what I was really good at was writing. It became the thing I was known for. Then I became a pretty teen. I didn't know it then, but I was no longer allowed to be smart.

In high school, I switched schools twice on Saipan and once in Korea. The first time I changed schools was because in the ninth grade, I colored my hair blue. The school said I would have to dye it back or get expelled. The strange thing was, a few months prior I had bleached it platinum blonde, which they didn't have a problem with. Since it was almost the end of the year, I opted to wear a Halloween wig every day for the rest of the year instead of washing out the blue dye. I cannot tell you the secondhand embarrassment (firsthand?) I'm getting from remembering my fourteen-year-old self wearing a fucking Party City wig to school for three months. I hid the front of the wig beneath a red bandana à la Bret Michaels, and just like Bret Michaels's "natural" hair, it was very obviously a wig.

The weird thing about the bleached blonde hair was, I think the school sort of liked that I bleached my hair because there were no white kids that went to that school, and me having bleached hair made it look like they had one white kid there. I swear to god this was their reasoning. Even when I switched to the blonde Cinderella wig, they preferred it over the blue hair. By the end of the three months, the humidity and my sweat caused the wig to bunch up so much that it looked like an anxious yellow cat sitting on my head, trying to squeeze itself under the red bandana. I didn't know if I should comb it or try to *pspspsps* it out of there. The most embarrassing memory of the wig was that I used to rip it off my head all dramatically and punk rock as soon as I got in the parking lot after school. I imagined that everyone was looking at me, thinking I was so cool. I thought I had beat them at their own game and this gesture was a big middle finger to the man. I imagined the principal watching me through the window, thinking, *That stupid fucking dumb bitch* and taking a swig out of a flask. I would rip the wig off and jump in my friend's car. We would light up cigarettes and drive around while my wet blue head dried off in the wind.

The next year my parents let me switch schools because they agreed that the no-dyed-hair rule was ridiculous. At my new school, the "writing class" was taught by this old white guy who looked like those Santa Claus figurines you get at the Florida airport, like Santa but in a Hawaiian shirt and flip-flops. His tropical Santa look was complete with advanced skin cancer. His face was peeling off in big red patches and his facial features were distorted and puffy. He also had a greasy seventies-style comb-over, which was weird since it was the early 2000s. Anyway, if you're unfamiliar with the seventies-style comb-over, it's basically when someone balds until they have that Friar Tuck ring of hair around the bottom of the head, and they grow one side out like a foot long, and then they drape that shit over the top of the dome. The problem was that it needed a ton of product to keep it in place, so the end result looked like a deflated cinnamon roll, or Paris Barbie's plastic beret. It looked one billion times worse than just a bald head, which was probably why it went into extinction in the mideighties or so. But people were fucking with this comb-over heavy during the seventies and eighties. Like you can watch pop music videos from that time, and the lead singer will be snapping his fingers, boppin' around with one of those bad boys on his head.

Anyway, Florida Santa was extremely cruel. If he were a woman, he would be described as "a crazy fucking bitch," but because he was a man, people described him as "[his name]." He would fail people for arbitrary things, burst into fits of rage, and just say unnecessarily cruel comments about students. I have a theory about cruelty, and it's that no one really cares about cruelty when it's fair. Like Gordon Ramsay. That asshole is a mean-ass motherfucker, but people let it go because his assessments are always fair. When he calls someone a "stew-ped doughnut," it's because they were being a stew-ped doughnut. No one cares that he is an adult man who acts like a schoolboy during a

Manchester United match, because he's right and he should say it. But Florida Santa was unfair. So, everyone hated him. Until we all found out he was actually dying of skin cancer. Then every unfair failing and angry outburst was tolerated. In life you can be as cruel as you want if you're fair or actively dying.

One day Florida Santa called me into his office. He threw a paper I had written on his desk. He said (not asked), "You plagiarized this." And I said, "No, I didn't," and he said, "Yes, you did. I'm going to fail you."

Just like that, writing, which had been *my thing*, was taken away from me. I didn't put up a fight. I barely reacted. I took the paper and walked out of his office and I never wrote again.

It would be stew-ped of me to blame all of this on one man. My home life was in tatters, I was barely able to be present in school, I never said anything, and I dressed like a slut. It makes sense that this man thought I would just plagiarize something. He didn't realize that writing was extremely easy for me and I had just popped out that paper thirty minutes before class in the school library. In the paper, I referenced Mae West, but I can't really remember why. Imagine being a sixty-year-old white man and reading about Mae West in a paper written by a fifteen-year-old Asian slut with blue hair. Imagine the rage he felt. He was probably like, *How dare this stupid bitch own information that belongs to me.* All women know the rage that comes from a man when he realizes that you also know something he does; he feels like you're taking his one thing away from him.

Another interesting thing I think about all the time is that this man had a teenage Filipina wife. He met her at an illegal strip club. She said she was twenty-two but she looked fifteen. She wore a lot of makeup and ho-y outfits. I think about how he must've treated her. I think about how big he must've felt as a failed writer turned high school English teacher, explaining to her the importance of *Lolita*. My god. Imagine that power. I understand this kind of pathetic little man. Imagine my teacher explaining Mae West to his child bride one day and she said, "Actually, I know who she is." Imagine the betrayal he would feel at the break in their contract: the unspoken contract between racist, misogynistic men and the child lovers and wives they find in Asia to dominate with their "superior" knowledge. Her one job was to not know the things he knew.

"How dare you look like my child wife but also know things!"

I know this type of man very well. The *90 Day Fiancé* white man. The man suffering from the powerful union of the most intoxicating social illnesses known to humankind: white supremacy and misogyny. A white man who suffers from this combination is beyond hope. The diseases are powerful on their own but absolutely lethal together. The reason I didn't put up a fight when he *told* me I plagiarized is because to convince him that I actually wrote it would be to convince him that I was a human being. And that realization would mean that his child wife was also a human being. He would not be able to process that.

I know this type of man. Because I have this type of man as a father.

*   *   *

SISTER

SHORTLY AFTER I STOPPED WRITING because of Florida Santa, I tried to run away. My plan was foiled by my sister, and I never spoke to her again in any meaningful way after this event. I bought a plane ticket to California after saving money all summer from working at a steakhouse. I don't know why I chose to go to California, just like my parents had no idea why they moved anywhere in their entire lives. I just had to get out. I chose to fly out on a certain day knowing my dad would be abroad working and my mom would be on vacation in Korea visiting family. Before leaving to hang with friends prior to my flight that night, I had a heated argument with my sister. She went into my room and found that I had taken a lot of things. She called each and every one of my friends until one of them finally told her I was planning to run away. She planted weed in my room and called the cops on me, saying that I was planning on flying out to transport drugs. By the time I got to the airport, the cops were already there. Because I didn't have drugs on me, and the story she told barely made sense, they decided to take me to a CPS facility until my parents could be contacted and interrogated.

My sister is actually my half sister. Her father was the man my mother married to escape Korea. She divorced him shortly after the birth of my sister because she said he was barely able to hold a conversation and would spend all his time alone in his room, constructing intricate model trains. While pregnant with my sister, my mom had a 태몽 (taemong; pregnancy dream). In Korea, a taemong is thought of as the spirit of the child introducing themselves to their mother. In times before pregnancy tests, Korean women would be able to tell they were pregnant by having this vivid and often nauseating type of dream early on. My mother said in the dream, she picked the most beautiful fruit from a magical-looking tree sitting atop a magical mountain. As she turned it in her hand to examine it, she saw that it was actually rotten. My mother said my sister was born crying and sick and never stopped. My mother had to leave my sister to rot in the care of cheap daycare workers to go work at KFC. She said she would regularly pick my sister up and notice she had been left in a soiled diaper all day long. Eventually she developed a diaper rash so severe, she needed hospitalization. My sister cried for days while recovering. But she always cried.

My sister was not breastfed because my mother, who was new to the States and barely spoke English, was told by her white male doctor that formula was better. He said this because he was receiving a cut from a formula company for every patient he convinced not to breastfeed. My mother gave birth, and he injected her arm with a chemical that dried up her milk.

120

My sister happened to be severely allergic to the formula and developed lifelong complications due to her intense food allergies. I don't know if this is true. This is all what my mother told me. I am not a doctor. I don't receive money for convincing poor immigrant women to use a product that costs thousands of dollars a year instead of using their breasts for what they were intended to do. You would believe me if I were a doctor, because doctors are smart and trustworthy. Doctors back then were mostly white men—white men who became doctors because they had read all the books written by other white men. The knowledge from these books was pure and good and always right. Like the Bible. An Asian woman yearning to put her child to her breast, the pulsation of the universe telling her that it was what she was born to do as a human, as a beast of this earth, that was no match for the white man and his white man books. White men are human. Asian women are beasts. But I am not a doctor. You cannot trust what I tell you to be the truth.

Although she's in her forties now, in my mind's eye my sister is still the age that I last saw her, nineteen. At that age, she had long sun-bleached hair, was extremely thin, and had giant breasts. She was beautiful. Her face was covered in freckles, the kind that explode like a universe all over someone's face and never seem to end. Even her lips were freckled. She looked identical to Sissy Spacek in the film *Badlands*. I haven't seen my sister in so long that the character Sissy played in that movie has fully merged with my memories of my sister. I can only imagine her as a poetically beautiful, listless teenager waiting for Martin Sheen to come and kill her father.

Freckles are considered deeply, deeply unattractive in Korea. Koreans don't just hate freckles as a mark of ugliness but because they're tied to superstition. A freckled person is someone who is bearing a curse and has bad luck. Because of this, my sister was horribly bullied and ridiculed by the Korean adults in our community. As a child I had already been indoctrinated by Western fashion magazines and recognized her freckles as quirky and cool and something at least one of the models in the Benetton ads always seemed to have. However, the Koreans didn't give a shit if Americans thought freckles were cool; that was one beauty standard they would never adopt. Her face, which was the same exact face of a movie star in the US, caused her to be bullied so severely by the Korean community that I assume she still struggles with leaving the house to this day.

My sister was constantly congested throughout her entire life because of food allergies. She also suffered from acute asthma, which led her to being hospitalized throughout her entire childhood. When she was in her midtwenties, her eardrums needed to be replaced after being ravaged due to a lifetime of constant pressure from built-up mucus. She had surgery where they opened up her head to remove all the damaged parts, the tiny, intricate parts of the inner ear that need to be absolutely perfect for each one of us to hear. The parts of the human body that are so perfect that they have me, the most atheist person in the world, sometimes wondering if there is a god. God created this perfect, tiny symphony of bones and organs inside the head of my sister behind a billion freckles scattered across her face like the endless universe. Korean women told her the universe on her face made her worthless. And a white man destroyed the inside of her head for like a $300 check from some drug company.

The one thing my sister had over me was that she was never a threat to my mother and therefore retained her love. She was beautiful but was covered in freckles, which disqualified her in the eyes of Koreans. And so my mother could remain loving her as a child, and not a woman.

*   *   *

MOTHER

I TRIED TO RUN AWAY from home because my mom became distant when I became "attractive." I think she had been told all her life that

122

her only value in this world was that she was pretty, and she couldn't emotionally deal with losing her looks while her daughter was gaining hers. I think in her mind, I had become her competition. I tried to run away because I was so deeply in need of my mother and I couldn't bear her rejection.

After I was taken by CPS to a safe care facility, I slept for a number of days that is unknown to me. I was in shock.

One night I woke up at 11 p.m. and went to the living room, and the CPS man who was in charge of watching me asked me if I was hungry. I said yes because I was starving, but also I was excited that I had gone days without eating and I was SKINNNYYYY, so a big part of me wanted to say no. I sat on the couch and he put pancakes in front of me. They were on a paper plate and the syrup had already soaked through. I ate them all so fast and immediately felt like shit because I was no longer SKINNNYYYY. I thanked him, but he suspiciously avoided eye contact. I was used to this treatment by then. Adult men were either sickeningly interested in me or angry at me. They hated my existence. They hated that they were attracted to me, or the world thought they were attracted to me and they resented that assumption. They made up fake scenarios where I humiliated and rejected them in their heads, and I could see those painful scenarios swirling around in their eyeballs. I thought I was imagining all this, but this was also around the time the Internet blew up and I could just . . . see them say this shit in chat rooms. *Cruel Intentions* was playing on TV. The actors in the movie were supposed to be my age, but I thought their behavior was terrifying. I didn't understand their confidence and cruelty. I had never seen a girl my age behave in this way. I have yet to see a teenage girl behave in this way.

Cruel Intentions was written and directed by an adult man named Roger Kumble, who wrote a movie where the girls act out on each other. The film was a huge hit. Turns out that society as a whole agreed with Roger that these female children were evil deviants. They loved his movie because they saw these girls in real life, and they had unbearable thoughts about them too. Roger put his words into the mouths of female children. Then he convinced himself and us that they are the ones who say those words in real life. Cleansed of his sins, he spread this message to millions around the world, the diseased message being that *cruel intentions* do not belong to adult men but to female children.

I watched this movie while sitting across the living room from a man who was paid to take care of me yet hated me so much he couldn't even make eye contact. He, like Roger, was convinced the dirty thoughts in his mind weren't his but that I had implanted them in there. He couldn't look past his dirty thoughts and hatred of me to see that I was a child crying uncontrollably because she missed her mommy.

This idea that female children are evil and not the men who harm them wasn't invented by Roger Kumble. It is as ancient as rape. As ancient as sex. Did my mom believe this idea? Did she believe the lie that, in fact, it was her daughter who had *cruel intentions* and not the adult men? Is that why she emotionally abandoned me? Maybe it was easier to accept that her child was evil than to accept that every single man in the world was. It was my fault that whenever we went outside together, adult men looked at me, a child, and had stopped looking at her, an adult. It was my fault.

If this is what she believed, and if this was the reason she emotionally abandoned me, it is so very sad. Because I was the one who saw her for who she really was and loved her for that. I didn't care that my mother was aging and becoming less attractive. I saw her. My love for her was what she had been searching for her entire life: unconditional love from someone who really knew her. But since it came from her female child and not a man, it had no value. She became afraid when she sensed her beauty slipping away because that was the only thing the men valued. It's sad that at that moment she couldn't recognize that my love was eternal. She traded in gold for a handful of shit. But who can blame her? All movies are written by men like Roger Kumble. All of them. Even the movies we watched together when I was a child. They convinced her that she was an evil old witch and I was a child princess. She went to her castle on the mountain and asked her mirror, "Who is the prettiest of them all?" The mirror told her the ancient lie. The mirror was a man.

My father's name is also Roger.

*   *   *

ME

When I was returned to my home from the CPS place, Roger wanted to talk to me about something.

"I found your journal," Roger said.

"OK."

"It's really good. You should become a writer. You have a skill. You get it from me. I've always been a great writer."

I had been told this all my life. That I was a good writer because my father was a good writer and it was merely genetics. But I never saw him write anything, so I honestly do not know if it's true. We never talked about my writing after that. But one day, he gave me a book called *On Writing* by the idiot Stephen King. I'm sorry I called him an idiot, but I never read his books because I saw them at the airport, and to me that meant he was corny and stupid. I was a teen in the era where we were all recovering from the Gen X dogma that anything mainstream was not cool, and everyone was pretending to be punk rock. I remember looking at Stephen King on the back cover of the book. He looked like my dad. I never read the book.

What if Florida Santa never failed me all those years ago? What if I had no obstacles in front of me? What if I had been born a man? And my teenage Asian body didn't intimidate and turn on old white men? And I just became a writer using the natural knack I had supposedly inherited from my dad? I would've been a horrible writer, maybe. Maybe I would've written some shitty murder mystery series that you could buy at the airport. Maybe I would've become some insufferable alt-left blue check on Twitter with the amazing skill to turn every national tragedy into something that I'm the personal victim of. Who knows?

As a kid, I had a natural ability with words and could read and decipher basically any book. I had a vast vocabulary. I understood words better than any of my classmates. I knew how to read and interpret a story. But that shit is boring. The thing I inherited from my father is worthless. Who the fuck cares about inherent skill? Who wants to see an eight-year-old play a really hard Beethoven symphony on the piano perfectly? That shit is boring. I know it's pathetic to talk about something I was good at when I was ten. I know I'm being that guy who always talks about how if he didn't have an ankle injury in high school, he would've become an NFL star. But I did suffer an ankle injury of sorts early on, which led me to stop writing completely. A lot of people build their identity around their inherent talent and maybe I feel resentful that I wasn't allowed that luxury. I had to abandon it. But now I realize that what I gained in return was far more valuable.

For people throughout history who weren't allowed to openly shine, we found ways to display our intelligence and talent covertly in the dark. There is a development of a second skill that I don't know what to call. My dad could always say my skill as a writer belonged to him, but he couldn't claim the other thing. My talent now isn't as a writer. My talent is what a crab has, an adaptation to go in a direction that I wasn't meant to go. I was stopped from going one way, so I did something fucking weird and humiliating to survive. There's no name for this skill. There's no way to quantify it. There's no way to record it in a white man's book. Because of that, it is invisible to them. They cannot

126

see it, and they cannot take it away. It is the skill that my mother has. I might not have inherited it from her but she taught it to me, in the way her mother taught it to her for her survival. It was taught to her by my grandmother, who had to teach it to her after they killed her first child for being good at something.

My mother knew I would need this skill because my life would be shitty. For people like us, life is always going to be shitty. She knew that everything I had would be taken away from me by a jealous, stupid man. Just like it had for her. So she gave me this gift. And this is what I'm here to share. Our mothers and daughters will forever be crying. For an endless eternity. My skill is the ability to make anyone laugh while they're crying. My skill is to make your butthole hairy. Most importantly, my skill is to make sure you're not ashamed of your hairy butthole. Because I have one too. And I got it by trying to survive.

Maybe I was born a writer. Maybe I fucking suck at it. But who fucking cares? That's not what I was put in this universe to do. The gift I have can't be taken away. Not even by Florida Santa. Mostly because he's dead (sad emoji).

* * *

TADPOLE

AFTER I ATTEMPTED TO RUN AWAY, my parents decided to move our family back to Korea. In this move, they left my sister on Saipan. Legally she was an adult, and technically she chose to be left behind because she was dating a man who was our neighbor. But I still feel like she was the child left behind, permanently neglected. I still feel like she is waiting there for us.

My sister beat the shit out of me every single day of my life. Because unlike my sister, who had been a sickly child maybe due to the capitalistic greed of a white man or angry Korean spirits who put her soul in a cursed, freckled body, I was born healthy and strong. And within a handful of years after my birth, I became larger and stronger than she was. For a while after I outgrew her, she continued to beat me. And I took it, silently. To receive these beatings was the price I had to pay for being healthy when my sister was failing to thrive. It was unfair. I had nothing to do with it. But it had to be this way. I wondered why my mother allowed my sister to beat me so much. She would never stop it.

My mother's taemong while pregnant with me was her sitting on the floor in the middle of her parents' bedroom. A large, shiny dragon entered the room through the window and swirled around her. Its scales were made of the stars of the heavens and glittered like diamonds. As it swirled, my mother said it seemed like she was flying through the universe among the stars. My mother was filled with wonder at its breathtaking beauty. She grabbed the two sides of her skirt, determined to catch it. The dragon swirled around her faster and faster, in desperation to escape, or perhaps to be caught. The dragon crashed into her, and she quickly closed her skirt around it. When she carefully opened her skirt back up, she was disappointed to see that the magical, glittery star dragon had transformed into a squirming brown tadpole. She was repulsed by it and hated it in that moment. But she knew it was her actions that caused its devastating transformation. It was her fault. She felt forever bound to take care of it. She woke up nauseous and knew she was pregnant.

My mother told me her two dreams signified who my sister and I were as people: my sister the rotten fruit, sick since birth. And me the shiny dragon, powerful and strong. But I always thought the two dreams meant the exact same thing. The most beautiful fruit of the most beautiful tree on a magical mountain top, and the glittering dragon made of the stars of the heavens, both turned rotten by my mother's interference.

CHAPTER 8
Strangers

놀부 (NOLBU; RICH BROTHER)

I FINISHED MY LAST YEAR of high school in Korea. My parents enrolled me in a really expensive English-speaking private school in Seoul. They had no money, so my mom had to borrow a bunch from my uncle, which I don't think she has paid back to this day. Some of the students there were foreign—the children of foreign diplomats or the children of foreign business owners—but most of them were the Korean children of extremely wealthy Korean people. Some of these people had lived abroad and therefore needed to continue sending their children to English-speaking schools, but a lot of them had never left Korea and had just enrolled their children in these schools in order for them to be fluent in English. These extremely wealthy Korean kids were surprisingly not mean or shitty like the regular or poor Koreans I had encountered my entire life. They reminded me of the quote in the movie *Parasite* where Chung-Sook, the wife of the poor man, Ki-Taek, says rich people are nice because they are rich, to which Ki-Taek replies, "Rich people are naive. No resentments."

Some of the students at this school were 재벌 (Jaebol; rich family). In Korea, much like in America, there is a small group of extremely wealthy families who gained an economic upper hand by being shady during times of political conflict and now influence the government and control everything. The wealthiest handful of these families own the vast majority of the wealth and are known as *Jaebol*. The families are known by the household name brands that each of them own. As a South Korean, I am as afraid to piss these people off as a North Korean would be to poke fun at Kim Jong Un, so I'm not going to tell you what the names of the brands are, but I don't have to because chances are you are sitting in a room with one of these products in it right now. You might even be reading this book off one of their smartphones or listening to it inside one of their cars. But for the sake of this anecdote, I'm going to refer to all of the brands and the families that own them as ShamShung.

The conspicuous power of Jaebol in South Korea is comical because Koreans don't seem to mind that everything they eat, drink, drive, watch, and wear is owned by two or three companies. In the US, corporations sense that we would be terrified if everything was honestly labeled by the conglomerate that owns it. So, although two or three companies might own everything in your home—including the news station you're watching—all of those things will have different brand names so that when you wake up in the morning, it doesn't feel so *1984*. But in Korea, Koreans will wake up in an apartment building with ShamShung painted on the side of it, in a ShamShung bed, then brush their teeth with ShamShung toothpaste, turn on the ShamShung News channel, and pour ShamShung-brand cereal and ShamShung milk into a ShamShung bowl. Then they'll get in their ShamShung car and drive to work ... at ShamShung.

The reason why American companies try to hide the fact that they own everything is because Americans have a very different relationship with power and control. Americans are told they are individuals and are free and no one is controlling them. They know this because they have seven hundred options when it comes to breakfast cereal. It would depress them if they found out two companies own all the cereal AND also financed the war in Iraq, but that's another story. But not Koreans. Koreans are not scared of having everything owned by Jaebol because in Korean culture, they don't think the biggest company became the biggest company by shady backroom wartime deals; they think the biggest company became the biggest because they made the best products. All the products that the ShamShung companies make are the best; that's why all of them are rich. Because they are smart people and they made a good thing (not because they lightweight sided with the Japanese and Americans during the wars or whatever).

By definition, a ShamShung product is the best you could get, and why would it be upsetting that everything has the mark of high quality? It is a privilege to live a life that is all ShamShung. Remember that Koreans were poor as shit one generation ago. They were made fun of because they didn't have shoes. Now their country makes the best affordable sedan on the global market. They wear the mark of ShamShung like someone who just won the lottery and is now dressed from head to toe in Louis Vuitton Monogram. If you try to tell a Korean that's an embarrassing fashion choice, they will say, "Louis Vuitton is expensive and good, so why would Louis Vuitton Monogram be embarrassing?" The funny thing now is that Gen Z Koreans are hyper aware of not wanting to look nouveau riche, so they dress in head-to-toe Margiela or Eckhaus Latta instead without understanding that the embarrassing part is to be a walking label.

Anyway, I went to school with some actual ShamShungs or ShamShung-adjacent kids. And they dressed for that role, like CEOs on a leadership retreat. Some of the students wore American high school clothes popular at that time, like lace tank tops, low-rise jeans, and Vans, but it was not unusual to see a student wearing an actual suit. During this time, I was "punk." I had brightly colored hair that was regularly shaved into a mohawk or something equally stupid. I wore eyeliner down to my goddamn nipples, which were pierced, as were my nose and lips. I also had a few tattoos already because I had gotten some while still living on Saipan, where no one ever checked my ID. I wore spiky chokers, studded belts, and PVC jackets with patches safety-pinned onto them. I wore ripped shirts with bands on them like Operation Ivy. Kind of embarrassing, yes, but honestly, not half as bad as wearing a fucking suit to school, bro, WTF.

I did not fit in, but it wasn't because of the way I was dressed; it was because I was poor. I was so extremely poor. My mom had borrowed $10,000 for me to go to this school for one year but had neglected to realize I would need money for food and other shit to maintain the illusion of being in the same class. I never had any food and had to walk everywhere. It sucked.

We lived in a tiny apartment in Ilsan, which is a northern suburb of Seoul. The fancy private school was located behind Yonsei University in the center of Seoul, and because the school was so far away, I had to take an express intercity bus to get there. On the very first day of school, the express bus dropped me off and I saw a large, sprawling campus and assumed this was the fancy, rich high school I was being sent to. I walked around the campus for what seemed like hours until I realized I was at Yonsei University. After I asked a bunch of people who had never heard of an English-language high school near Yonsei, one old security guard told me it was at the back of the campus. I walked to the back of the campus, and there I found a brick wall overgrown with vines. By then I was in a panic since I was so late and it was the first day of school. I realized this stupid wall separated the two campuses and I would have to walk all the way to the entrance and circle around, but then I found a small, rusty metal door. I walked through the door to find the cutest, most idyllic school I'd ever seen in my entire life. This school, which included grades K–12, sat atop an adorable cherry-blossom-tree-filled hill surrounded by vine-covered brick walls. Compared to the rest of Seoul, full of the harsh gray lines of joyless office buildings and the haphazardly placed, messy storefronts and food stalls, it looked like the hobbit village where the hobbits took off from in *The Lord of the Rings*. I walked into the lobby and was led to my first class. I was two hours late for school on the first day. It was because I was poor.

The other students were rich. They were driven to school in black cars, with private drivers who would drop them off in the front of the campus, accessed through a private driveway on a road on the other side of the hill from where Yonsei University was. After dropping them off, the drivers would park the fancy black cars in a multistory private lot in front of the school and sit there and wait until the students were finished. The drivers all wore suits. The thing about Korea is that the working class is the same race as the wealthy class, so the students in their suits looked exactly like their drivers, who looked exactly like the students' fathers. If I knew about men's suits, watches, and shoes, I would be able to differentiate the classes by texture of fabric or brand of watch, but I didn't. So, whenever I walked past the garage after school, I couldn't tell who was father, son, or holy Ki-Taek from *Parasite*.

Anyway, since I was the only *poor* who had to walk to school from the bus, I was one of the only people who knew about the door in the back wall that led to Yonsei University. During lunch, I would go smoke cigarettes on the university campus using the door. One day, a few of my ShamShung classmates saw me walking back there and asked me where I was going. I told them that I was going to the university and they were confused. I showed them the door, and they were excited AF because they had not known of its existence.

We were on the Yonsei University campus smoking, me in punk attire and them in suits—the two most humiliating outfits known to humans. I wasn't used to being around people this wealthy before, and I felt nervous because I thought they were judging me for being poor. But what I didn't realize was that my punk outfit transcended wealth and class. Punk was a movement started by kids from poor and working-class communities in the UK and the US in the seventies but very quickly evolved into a costume adapted by the wealthier white children living in wealthy suburbs of the West. By the early 2000s when I was doing it, the vast majority of people who adhered to the aesthetics of the punk movement were rich white kids appropriating the look and ideas of the poor. So by dressing in torn-up fishnet stockings and shirts pieced together by safety pins, I had unknowingly camouflaged myself as a *rich* cosplaying as a *poor.* The ShamShungs treated me as such. I could sense they almost respected me, because not only did they think I was a *rich,* but they thought I was the type of rich that didn't care what my parents said. That was some gangster-ass shit to them.

I knew one of them was a Jaebol whose family owned a popular beverage company, ShamShung Cola, let's call it. He was wearing a gray ahjusshi business suit. He turned to me and said, out of the fucking blue, in what I can only refer to as an LA Koreatown I-love-my-hyungs accent, "Ya! Did you know I'm a gigolo?"

This was right after that shitty movie *Deuce Bigalow: Male Gigolo* had come out, so he overpronounced the word *gigolo* in a way that revealed he had just learned what it meant. I was confused when he said this because he was fucking rich and also he was not that attractive (sorry if you're reading this).

"What do you mean you're a gigolo? Like a prostitute?" I said.

"I swear," he said.

"Yeah, right."

"No, jinjja! I swear, bro, I swear."

"What? Why are you gigolo? Cuz you're getting laid?"

He continued in an LA Koreatown accent, "Yeah, I was, like, fucking so many hookers and spending, like, jonna lots of money, like *baekman* [one million won, approximately $750] in one week. I swear. So I thought I would do it to save money. But honestly, now it's like my kink."

"It's your kink to get paid for sex?"

He told me that he very quickly realized that the job didn't only consist of getting laid. It mostly consisted of another, more violent, and therefore more Korean, act: getting beat up.

In Korea, there is a regimen to going out. Yes, for Koreans, even when cutting loose there are rules. The rules follow the order and system of families, school, and the government. The oldest person or oldest male person must pay for everything, but they also are awarded the privilege of choosing what everyone eats and drinks, where everyone goes, and what everyone does for entertainment. The younger people then must pour the drinks of the older people in order of age. I know this sounds like an exaggeration, but everyone follows these rules. For most Koreans, it comes naturally without thought. Also, there is a schedule for a night out. There are steps referred to as 차 (cha). Usually, a night out will consist of:

1. 일차 (ilcha; first step): eating at a restaurant and drinking
2. 이차 (icha; second step): drinking at a bar
3. 삼차 (samcha; third step): drinking at noraebang

However, it is slightly different for groups of men going out with their coworkers and their boss. For them, there is usually (but not always) a fourth step: hostess bar, massage parlor, or other vague expression for an establishment that is basically a brothel. When it is a work group, the person holding the highest position, regardless of age, becomes the superior. The superior pays for everything and gets to decide where they go, what they eat and drink, how much they drink, what activities they do, and also when any of the inferiors can leave. The inferiors can never say no. Inferiors are not allowed to reject alcohol and are not allowed to leave until the superior decides that they can. This culture is so rigid in Korea that some inferiors adopt religion as a way to opt out of it. However, they know rejecting the drinking culture will greatly reduce their chances of getting ahead at work, therefore greatly reducing the chance they will become a superior themselves. A lot of them are indoctrinated into this culture during the two years of mandatory military service that all Korean men are obligated to do. Their superiors in the military force them to drink to the extreme, beat them up for no reason, and commit other horrific acts of abuse in the ritual of hazing to see how far their loyalty to the hierarchy goes. If the inferiors act out or complain in any way, they are severely punished. I truly believe one of the reasons South Korea still implements mandatory military conscription for men is for them to learn this system of abuse so they can perpetuate it as civilians, so that by the time they reach full adulthood and get jobs in the "real world," Korean men have been broken in.

In a school or university setting, the word for superior/senior in Korean is 선배 (Sunbae). They don't usually call workplace superiors "Sunbae"; they call them by whatever title they hold at the company: 화장님 (Hwajangnim; president) or 과장님 (Gwajangnim; manager). But as a whole, they are understood as Sunbae. The word for the inferior/junior is 후배 (Hoobae).

The rigidity of Korean culture means that no one can do what they want until they're the Sunbae. But by the time a Hoobae becomes a Sunbae, they are so fucking damaged by the years of being forced to do things they didn't want to do, all they know how to do is inflict that pathological control onto others. They force Hoobaes to binge on soju and throw up in the streets. They force these men to fuck prostitutes, even if they're happily married. Whether the Hoobaes like fucking the prostitutes or not, there is an anger and resentment that brews in them from not being able to do what they want to do.

In my time living in Korea, I've met many sex workers, most of whom are (trans or cis) women or gay men. They have told me over and over that a lot of their work involves being beaten up. The men who visit them need to beat them up because that's the regaining of control. They couldn't even choose what they ate for dinner that night, or the songs they sang at noraebang, because their Sunbae did.

All of that gets bottled up and pounded into a prostitute's pussy and face. (Sorry, I know, but it's true!) They also told me that Sunbaes beat them up too, but there's a way higher chance that they will just be extremely gentle and nice. One of my friends had a Sunbae sugar daddy who would just fly her out to places to have dinner with him and she wouldn't even have to fuck him after. It made sense to me that Sunbaes had less repressed anger, because they could expel it all day on other men.

I always found the behavior of Hoobaes so funny because all they have to do is say no. But for some reason, they just can't say it to their Sunbae. A lot of this is because they got their asses beat so hard in the military. Since Hoobaes are literally incapable of saying no, they go along and eat what the Sunbae wants to eat, drink soju even if they don't want to, and sit in a noraebang and watch him sing "Yesterday" by the Beatles fifteen times in a row and clap like he did a good job. Then he tells them it's time to go fuck prostitutes, and whether they want to or not, they go. I'm sorry, that's so fucking funny and pathetic to me.

I remember that during this time, a drunk, old, rich man screamed at me on the street for smoking. Smoking outdoors for women was illegal in Korea until 1997, and this was probably around 2002. I shouted at him, "닥쳐 개놈아!" (Shut up, you son of a bitch!), and he just walked away. Hoobaes are unable to do that.

My classmate, the Jaebol Gigolo, continued his story: His entire clientele base was female prostitutes who would hire him after a night of working. They spent their shifts getting beat up by rage-and-soju-filled Hoobaes, but then the women ended up filled with rage and soju so they had to take it out on someone else. Enter my classmate, Sham-Shung Bigalow: Jaebol Gigolo.

So, the son of a Jaebol, a ShamShung in his own right, the top of Korean society, received the beatings that went down the entire chain of command. From Jaebol, to Sunbae, to Hoobae, to sex worker, to him. It's entirely possible that the top of that line of abuse was his own father.

He said at first he was confused that most of the time he was just being beat up. But he kept being a gigolo because a lot of the women ended up fucking him after the ass-whooping. He then said he discovered he actually enjoyed being beat up, and realized it was his kink. I think he liked getting beat up because he was literally 재벌집 막내 아들 (youngest kid of a Jaebol, also the title of a popular Korean drama). His whole life, he was probably never punished for anything. I think he felt that not only did he deserve this punishment, but he longed for it. He felt that it was rightfully his and had sought it out and found it.

At the time, I remember listening to this story and thinking it was bullshit. I thought he was telling me this so I would think he was cool. He was trying to impress the cool punk girl who he thought was so rich she was cosplaying as a *poor*. But now, I know for a fact that this story was true.

Because in Korea, we all know this story to be true. We all know the hierarchy is not a line.

It's a circle.

* * *

흥부 (HEUNGBU; POOR BROTHER)

THE KIDS WHO WENT TO this school were filthy rich and very proper. But they went out binge drinking every weekend in the surrounding neighborhoods of Sinchon, Hongdae, and Itaewon, as well as the wealthier neighborhoods south of the river: Apgujeong and Gangnam. Because they all spoke English, the Koreans who worked at bars and nightclubs assumed they were college-aged and no one ever got carded. However, I only partied with them a handful of times because there was something fucking off about these fuckers.

The ShamShungs had this extremely volatile mixture of "inno-cent, sheltered rich kid" meets "demented secret sadomasochist perv." When I first met them, they seemed soft and nice, but I realized they had just compartmentalized the "dark" sides of their personalities they needed to hide from their families. I didn't think there was anything wrong about sex, drugs, and rock 'n' roll since by then I was doing all three. I thought that shit was cool. I thought it was cool as hell that that guy was a gigolo. He probably sensed that from me, which is why he told me that right off the bat, but he sure as hell wasn't telling his Jaebol mom and dad and friends about it.

I don't think there's anything inherently wrong with any behavior, but in the act of trying to hide it and come off as a Goody Two-shoes, the ShamShungs appeared unsavory and dishonest to me. If you see someone with a neck tattoo on the street shooting up heroin, that's fine, but if you see someone in luxury golf leisure doing that, that's fucking disturbing. There's nothing wrong with being a freak, but there's something so very wrong about pretending to be a normie when you're a freak. This is why the ShamShungs rubbed me the wrong way. So I didn't really hang out with them that much. Also, to be completely honest, I couldn't really afford to go to all those fancy nightclubs and restaurants. Instead, I hung out with the *poors*. By the *poors* I mean the kids and young adults who made up the Seoul punk rock scene.

As soon as I moved to Seoul, I used the thing that we referred to as the Internet back then to connect with a handful of punk kids who lived in the city. Since the scene was so small and close-knit, I quickly met most of them by just going to a few shows. The most influential people in this scene lived in a basement club. The club is known as the first "punk" club in Seoul, and considered akin to CBGB in New York, but shortly closed down after my move there. I honestly can't remem-ber what it was called. But before it shut down, I remember walking down the mildew-smelling steps after school to find the entire floor covered in a mass of sleeping bodies. It didn't matter if it was 8 a.m. or 4 p.m., they were always dead asleep from the night before. Sticking out of leather vests, spiky leather straps, and patches of brightly colored hair were the limbs and drooling faces of... Koreans. I had never met Koreans like this before: high school dropouts, drug addicts, children of single parents, sex workers, etc. For some reason, none of their marginalizations scandalized me as much as the high school dropouts. Before this time in my life, I didn't even realize high school dropouts existed in Korea. But here on the floor of this soon-to-be-doomed club, they slept.

These were Koreans born in the seventies and eighties. Back then, any sort of dysfunction in the family was considered grounds for becoming a wangtta. All the punks I met in Seoul came from broken homes and almost all of them had grown up poor. That meant they were discarded from society at a young age. A group of Koreans that was and is so well hidden from the rest of the world, even some Koreans don't know they exist.

The way that punk had infiltrated Korean culture before the Internet was mostly through Japan. Japan is humiliatingly obsessed with Europe, so they like to copy and paste a lot of things from them. But Koreans embarrassingly copy and paste things from Japan. Literally as soon as punk mutated out of rock bands in poor communities all over the UK, there were "punks" in Japan donning leather jackets and ripped jeans. And very soon after, "punks" started popping up in Korea. This is the strain of the punk disease that infiltrated Korea, the Japanese one via the British one.

The Korean punks saw kids who lived just like them from factory-working blue-collar towns in the UK. Kids who were bred to work and die in factories, creating wealth for a wormy-faced queen. They related to the desperation in the voices of the children who knew they were born to not matter. They understood better than anyone else, even possibly better than the poor British kids themselves, what it felt like to not be able to escape the hierarchy. But these British kids weren't just going along and being depressed about it; they were opting out. They realized that being at the bottom of the hierarchy with no way out gives you freedom. The idea that nothing matters, born out of being told that they didn't matter. Nihilism and anarchy. In a lot of ways Korean society is more rigid and unforgiving, meaning to be punk in Korea is actually way more punk than being punk in the UK.

In my first week of meeting them, one of the punk girls who went by some really bland English name like Sherry ordered a tattoo gun off the Internet. Within three days she had tattooed full sleeves on the entire scene. I remember one of my friends, who was the bassist in one of the more popular bands, showing me all of his tattoos.

"This one is a map of Alaska."

"Why did you get the map of Alaska tattooed on your arm?" I asked.

"I don't know," he said.

I had sex with him.

I had sex with a lot of people during this time. All of them were in their mid to late twenties. Starting when I was sixteen and until I moved away from Seoul at the age of twenty, I had sex with Koreans who dropped out of high school. Koreans who robbed people. Koreans who played in bands. Koreans who got into fistfights in that now legendary Hongdae park.

When I was seventeen, I got into a relationship with a drummer in one of these bands. He was abusive. When we met, he was twenty-six. I moved in with him after I (barely) graduated from high school at eighteen years old. We lived in an apartment near Sangsu subway station until I moved to the US at the age of twenty. I moved to the States in order to escape this relationship and, shortly after, heard that my ex had entered into a psychiatric hospital in order to escape the mandatory two-year military conscription.

The first time I visited Korea after moving to America, we met up. He had gained a massive amount of weight from all the antipsychotic drugs he was forced to take in the psychiatric hospital. We smoked cigarettes in a pajun/makgeolli restaurant designed to look like a traditional Korean Hanok. We got there by taking an elevator to the fourth floor in a high-rise in Hongdae. The sleek glass elevator doors opened up to a bar with walls covered in brown earth, ceilings covered in hay and twigs, and signs written in calligraphy on handmade paper. The signs were written in Chinese characters like they would have been in the old days. Makgeolli was served in yellow aluminum dented 주전자 (jujeonja; kettles) and poured out into yellow aluminum bowls. We drank and ate as I chain-smoked Marlboro Lights. He asked me what the US was like. I took a long drag of my cigarette and said, "미국애서는 식당않아서 담배못펴." (Migookaeseoneun sikdanganaeseo dambae motpyeo; In America you can't smoke indoors.)

"좃같은나라" (jot gateun nara; shit country), he said in a thick Busan accent.

My ex had grown up poor in Busan with a single mom. His dad died when he was a baby, but it didn't matter to his classmates and community why he didn't have a father. All that mattered was that he had no father, and thus his family was unable to rank in the Hoobae/Sunbae rat race. He was born a wangtta, a reject from society, even though he had no hand in the circumstances. He grew up hating the game that had disqualified him before he even knew he was playing. In high school, he and a few of his wangtta friends started a punk band and became popular enough for them to move to Seoul. This is where we had met and started a relationship. His ultimate dream was to leave Korea. I think in a lot of ways, he knew I was an American citizen and could be his ticket out. But then he started beating my ass and I just left by myself.

After I left, he decided to fake mental illness (he thought he was faking it, but maybe without even realizing, he hadn't been faking it). He entered the psychiatric hospital and realized quickly that it was a huge mistake. In Korea, the worst thing someone can be is crazy. The worst slur to be called there is a 미친놈 (michin nom; crazy guy). In his desperation to break free from the system, he bolted himself into it. We both knew it was impossible for him to leave now. Korean men who do not fulfill their obligatory military sentence suffer extreme restrictions in their day-to-day lives. Every official record is marked. It becomes difficult to find work and almost impossible to travel abroad. The restrictions resemble those placed on former incarcerated Americans. And just like in the US, the government claims that these restrictions are for the safety of society as a whole, but in reality, they're just to control a population of people they hate.

He asked me why I had left him. I said I just wanted to move away from Korea because it was so strict and rigid. He nodded his head because he understood that. That was partially true, but what I didn't realize at the time was that there was a much bigger reason: I left to get away from him. I had become the sex worker getting beat up by a Hoobae. I had entered into a hierarchy. However, it was with someone who didn't think he was participating. But neither of us realized at the time that we were both participating. Everyone is always participating. There is no escape from the circle.

It's been so many years since I've been "punk." As a teenager, it was my entire identity. I was obsessed with knowing and listening to all the bands and reading all the zines. At the birth of the Internet, the vast majority of what I looked up was punk stuff. Today I don't know where my inherent beliefs end and the beliefs I collected during this punk phase of my teens begin. It shows up in countless ways. I consider myself a socialist to this day because I read so much Aaron Cometbus and his writings about being a socialist that I ended up reading a bunch of books about it. At any point, I'll be sitting in a bar and a Black Flag song will come on and I will know all the words for some reason. Every time a weird punk thing bubbles up in me, it feels as though I'm being visited by a ghost. A ghost with a patch that says "Fuck Off!" safety-pinned to her jacket (embarrassing).

143

The reason I stopped being punk was because I could no longer lie to myself that it meant not being part of the system. I think a lot of people who hold on to this movement to this day don't understand that there is actually no way to escape the hierarchy. For me, being punk still meant getting my ass beat by a man who's mad at another man. And I wasn't about to hire a gigolo to take it out on. I left Korea and this man because I refused to take it out on anyone else.

I broke the circle.

* * *

흥부와 놀부 (HEUNGBU AND NOLBU; POOR BROTHER AND RICH BROTHER)

ONE OF THE MOST POPULAR folktales in Korea is the fable of Heungbu (Kind, Poor Brother) and Nolbu (Greedy, Rich Brother).

There are endless variations of the story of Heungbu and Nolbu because it was a 판소리 (pansori; traditional story told orally). But here's the general storyline: During an exceptionally frigid winter and time of famine, Heungbu gives all of his food and belongings away. His family dies of starvation, and he loses all his possessions. He becomes a homeless, wandering beggar. When he realizes he is on the brink of starving to death, he goes to the home of his rich, greedy brother, Nolbu, despite knowing he will not help him. Nolbu hears him knocking, and knowing Heungbu is there to beg for food and even though he has more than enough, he tells his wife to go and turn him away. She goes outside and screams at Heungbu to go away. When he refuses to leave without rice, she hits him across the face with her rice paddle. Heungbu realizes that a lot of rice has stuck to his face. While laughing, he begs her to hit him again. She thinks he's mocking her and hits him across the other cheek, enraged. Heungbu is able to use the rice stuck to both of his cheeks to survive the winter.

Heungbu struggles like this through the winter. One day in spring, he finds a wounded baby bird and nurses it back to health. The bird turns out to be a magical spirit who repays him with a magical gourd seed, which he plants. When it ripens, he splits it open to find it full of gold. He becomes one hundred times wealthier than his brother and buys land, a massive home, and acquires a new wife and has more children. When Nolbu hears the story, he purposefully breaks a baby bird's leg and nurses it back to health. This bird also turns out to be magic and gives Nolbu a gourd seed as well. When his gourd ripens, he splits it open to find it full of snakes, 도깨비 (dokkaebi; demons), and curses. They destroy his home and kill his family. Now Nolbu has become the homeless, wandering beggar. Nolbu goes to ask Heungbu for money, but instead of turning him away, Heungbu gives his brother half of his wealth, which Nolbu uses to buy land and a home, find a new wife, and have more children. Nolbu also finds out that Heungbu has already shared most of his wealth with all his neighbors and is still way wealthier than Nolbu had ever been. They live out the rest of their lives, both brothers having learned a lesson: Heungbu gives away any excess but is careful to keep enough to sustain him and his family. Nolbu also gives away his excess, shedding his greed, and only keeps enough for him and his.

In these pansoris, the brothers don't represent actual people. They represent two extremes of existence, which, according to 도교 (Dogyo; Taoism), can be both destructive or positive. Unlike Western religions, there isn't an emphasis on one being "better" than the other, just the idea that both need to exist in balance.

Heungbu represents passivity, gentleness, generosity, and lack of self-preservation. These are seen as good traits to many, but in the story, it leads to the death of his children and wife, and to the absolute destruction of his entire life. Too much of one thing destroys. But there is no man alive who is actually so passive, generous, and gentle that he would kill his own family. Or is there?

145

After I was born, my parents struggled financially for a few months. They had spent all their money on moving the family to Korea, and my dad was unemployed for a few months before starting his new job. My mom said they were down to their last few dollars one day when my father decided to go out and drink at a bar. She found him hours later at a bar in Songtan, wasted. She was pissed because he was drunk and also they had so little money left for the week. She yelled at him to come home, and as he got up, she saw him hand the sexy bartender two 10,000-won bills (about twenty US dollars) as a tip. Although tipping isn't customary in Korea, in Songtan, where the patrons were mostly American GIs, the bartenders expected them. The Americans usually left a smaller tip than they would back home because they knew Koreans weren't "used to" receiving them. A 20,000-won tip in the eighties was absolutely unheard of. My mom said the bartender made a huge deal of it and my dad acted like it wasn't a big deal.

This entire time, my mother was carrying me 어부바 (ububa; piggyback, also the word for wearing a baby in a specialized ububa blanket). As they walked home, I started to cry. At this point, I was old enough to know some words and kept repeating "주스" (ju seu; juice). My mom asked my drunk dad to go into a little store and grab an apple juice. My father pulled out his wallet and my mother saw that he only had enough money left for one juice.

"Roger, why you give that lady twenty thousand won?" she screamed.

"What?" My dad was drunk.

"Go get juice!" my mom yelled.

My father bought the apple juice and walked back out toward my mother, swinging the small glass jar in a plastic bag. He drunkenly swung the bag against a brick wall, and the glass shattered everywhere, spilling the juice. They walked home in silence, while I was wrapped up against my mother's back, screaming for juice.

This is my mother's favorite story about my father. This is the story she used to describe what kind of father he was. She said for my father, it was so important for him to be a show-off in front of the sexy woman at the bar that he didn't even care that his crying baby wanted juice.

Heungbu was so generous, he gave away all of his food. His wife watched him give all their food away to the sexy bartender. He came home drunk and his children were crying. They were starving. His wife asked him if he had any food left for them. He slapped her across the face and beat his children. His wife and children fell asleep huddled together, crying. The next morning when he woke up, they had all died of starvation. Heungbu, the good brother.

My mother was a born-again Christian. But her entire life, she was raised with the principles of Dogyo and Buddhism. The thing about religion (and punk rock) is that it is a viral disease. It moves like a virus and has no brain. A virus has no true objective beyond survival. Mutant strains of Christianity exist throughout this world, covering pagan gods and rituals with a fake white veneer. It has no core; it only has the objective of spreading. My mother wears the skin of Christianity, but her insides know better. Among her organs, pulsing with the blood and breathing in and out with the lungs, are the beliefs handed down to her from her people for millennia. No white man can convince an animal what it knows in between its organs. No white man is good. Because no man is good. But I think sometimes she forgot that no man is evil either.

My father probably gave the sexy bartender a huge tip because he wanted to impress her, yes. That was a selfish act, yes. But nothing is ever truly only a good or a bad act. I believe he did it partially out of some kindness. He probably felt bad for her. Or maybe he was just wasted and didn't realize what he was doing. Who knows? But therein lies the beauty of the story of Heungbu and Nolbu. Heungbu gave all his food away but then his brother's wife slapped him with the rice paddle, and he survived. His good act killed his children, but her bad act let him live. Although my father's actions were selfish and done to soothe his own ego, once the money left his hands, none of us know what happened to it. None of us know which direction it went, good or bad.

I wonder what happened to that 20,000 won. Most likely the sexy bartender was also a sex worker, and whatever money she made went directly to her pimp. What did the pimp do with the money? Maybe he went home and bought juice for his children. What about the bartender? Did she go to a brothel after her shift? Did she spend all night getting beat up by Hoobaes? Then what? Did she go hire a gigolo? Was the gigolo the son of a Jaebol?

There is no good person or bad person. There are no good acts and bad acts. There are people who give away too much and sacrifice themselves for others. But in the real world, there are no magical spirits to bring them gourd seeds. A few years ago, a migrant ship carrying Syrian refugees capsized in the Mediterranean. Among the migrants was a family: a man, his wife, and their two toddler sons. Two brothers. The man only thought to save himself and swam to shore while his wife tried to hold up their two babies. She drowned with them while her husband lived. I am assuming the man has a new wife and new children now, just like Heungbu and Nolbu. I am assuming the original story of the two brothers was written by men, and therefore there is an unfairness they forgot to address: the women and children in the folktale don't matter. Their lives don't register into the cosmic balance. But in real life, of course they do. Women represent the dark side of the yin-yang. The side so passive, it fails to register to most men. The side that receives so much of the brutal unfairness of the world, they leave it out when they write stories of humanity.

None of us are going to encounter a magical spirit bird, but a lot of us will die because of our stupid husbands. They will live and get a new wife and kids to replace us. This is the way of the universe. There is no reward for good and no punishment for evil. The Jaebol control everything in South Korea. A lot of them gained massive amounts of wealth by fucking over other Koreans. Countless Koreans died so they could acquire wealth. We don't know any of their names, just like we don't know the names of Heungbu's and Nolbu's dead wives. But we know Heungbu and Nolbu. We know ShamShung. They make the best TVs.

My mother is the one who taught me the story of Heungbu and Nolbu. For her this is the moral that lives in her organs and was not removed even after she was born again: We can choose not to enact violence. We can choose to only create kindness. But there is no guarantee that those acts will come back to us in the way they left. That is why we do things with no hope of reward and no fear of punishment. Doing good things just for a reward is not good. But there is nothing wrong with being not good. Being selfish is bad. But there is nothing wrong with being bad. Because all of it needs to exist, and all of it will exist even if we try to make it stop. It is out of our control, and we must be at peace with that.

There is nothing for us to do but laugh and cry.

*　*　*

태극 (TAEGUK; YIN-YANG)

KOREA IS A LAND OF EXTREMES. Two sides. Two parts. In the center of the flag of South Korea is the 태극 (Taeguk; yin-yang) in red and blue. Bad and good. North and south. Jaebol and punk. Anger and love. Sunbae and Hoobae. Winner and loser. People see the Taeguk as a division of two opposing sides that will never touch. But that's not what it is at all. The two sides are not divided; they are bound together. In all of us.

In a circle.

CHAPTER 9

Rich

KOOL-AID

WHEN I WAS IN GRADE SCHOOL, my mom would force us to wake up on Saturdays at the crack of dawn and make a giant vat of Kool-Aid in a yellow ten-gallon Igloo cooler. We would then take this cooler to tourist destinations all throughout Saipan, where we would sell the drinks for two dollars a cup. After spending hours out in the hot sun, we would go back home with a profit of twenty dollars. My mother would tell us, "This is the life we have to live because your father is lazy."

Although my father was a pilot, he had yearslong bouts of what I suspect to be PTSD-induced depression where he couldn't get out of bed. During the times when he was unemployed, we would slowly fall into poverty. The shift happened gradually because we could live comfortably on our savings for a few months. The feeling of slipping into economic hardship reminds me of the boiling frog experiment. A frog thrown into boiling water panics, knowing exactly the amount of pain it's in before death, but a frog placed in water that turns hot slowly barely notices and dies peacefully. One by one, things that weren't "necessities" were taken away until the day I woke up and realized I owned only one pair of shorts and the power had been off for weeks.

It's humorous to me that my mother lacked the understanding of mental illness to the point that someone lying in bed for years at a time read to her as laziness. Looking back, I find it sad that my father didn't have access to the care that he so desperately needed, but during that time, I could only focus on what I saw was the immense unfairness of my mother's life. Not only did she work full time, but then she would come home every day and do all the domestic labor and childcare. My father did absolutely nothing for years besides drink Jim Beam and Cokes and watch TV. Somehow, we always had money for Jim Beam and Coke. Coke was a luxury to us as children, a nonnecessity that we could never justify spending money on. But we always had Coke for my father's cocktails. We were forbidden from drinking it. My father would see me reaching for it and say, "Don't drink that. It makes you fat."

As a child, I couldn't help but see my mother as a savior and my father as a bum. As an adult, I can see that both of their reactions—my father's inability to do anything and my mother's frantic inability to sit still for a second—were caused by mental illness and out of their control. I now understand that people react differently to trauma and hardship and it's not fair to compare the two. Also, I now understand that my mother's behavior was just as destructive as my father's.

It took me years to realize that my mother could've easily made twenty dollars doing literally anything else for an entire day, but she chose to drag us to the equivalent of the town square to sell Kool-Aid. The Kool-Aid selling wasn't about the money; it was about the humiliation. It was about being out in front of people, parading around our shame.

In the old days in Korea, when children wet the bed past the age when it was appropriate, their mothers would force them to walk around with a basket on their backs and collect salt from the neighbors. I'm not exactly sure why, but I think the salt was used in deep cleaning the bedding. The practice was done under the pretense that salt was so expensive that no one could afford the amount it would take to cleanse the bedding of urine and would therefore need to collect it from neighbors. Like a deranged old-timey Korean GoFundMe for pissing the sheets. However, it was obviously just an excuse to publicly humiliate the child in an attempt to shame them into stopping from peeing the bed. In the same way, the Kool-Aid selling wasn't about earning twenty dollars, it was about teaching us that we were poor kids and that we needed to know our place in society.

My sister and I hated selling the Kool-Aid on weekends because that shit was embarrassing. We would see our friends and classmates all the time. One time a white kid from my class came to the Kool-Aid stand with her parents. I was burning with shame, but my classmate thought it was cool. She asked me how much money I had made. Her dad asked for cups of Kool-Aid for all of them and then handed us a twenty-dollar bill and didn't ask for change. He didn't seem to think this was embarrassing at all. He seemed impressed.

I realized he thought that my sister and I had set up this drink stand in the way that rich white kids set up lemonade stands in the suburbs. They sell one-dollar glasses of lemonade and save the money they make to buy themselves the Nintendo they really wanted all year. Their parents knew they had generational wealth and their kids would never have to actually sell things on the street to survive. They had college funds for them. Their kids would never grow up to do menial tasks like this in the real world, so this was all just a game. But the game wasn't just meant to teach their children the value of an honest dollar. It was also meant to teach them that working to survive was easy. Rich people make their children set up lemonade stands to show them that this is childish, simpleton work, meant for inferiors. By the time these rich white kids become adults, they have a built-in sense of superiority over anyone who does menial labor. Lemonade stands teach rich children to look down on street vendors, housekeepers, retail workers, restaurant servers, drug dealers, prostitutes, and anyone who does a job that's actually important. They all believe the work is valueless because any eight-year-old can do it. They believe this because they were able to buy themselves a Nintendo selling lemonade on a weekend when they were eight. They are unaware of the fact that their rich parents secretly put $200 in their money jar when they weren't looking and that to actually afford a Nintendo, they would have had to be outside selling lemonade for years.

Rich white parents who do this to their kids are essentially doing the same thing my mom was doing to us. They are teaching their children where they belong. They are also teaching them that no matter how little work they do, they will always deserve a Nintendo, because the system is set up to give it to them. Whether it's their white families with generational wealth, a school system set up to make sure they come out on top no matter how bad their grades are, or a police system set up to protect their property, especially if their property was inherited and not earned through hard work, there is always an invisible hand behind rich white people that supplements the Nintendo. My mom's role in this was to teach us that we were the poors. She was teaching us that our time—and essentially, our existence—was worth twenty dollars.

After my white classmate's family walked away, I showed my mom the twenty-dollar bill her dad had left. I thought she would be excited since this was an entire day's earnings for us. She snatched it from my hand and said, "What a fucking show-off" with the anger of a donkey tied to a plow.

My white classmate's dad thought it was cute that we were selling lemonade on the street like little moguls, but he didn't realize that standing behind us was my mother, riddled with anxiety, telling us we wouldn't be able to eat dinner that night. The thing is, though, we always had dinner. I never found out what our actual financial situation was. I am unsure if we were really on the brink of starvation, or if it was just my mother's residual trauma from childhood. I have the suspicion that our situation wasn't as dire as my mother made it

153

seem. I think my mom thought having this constant fear of starving to death would make me into a hard worker. This wasn't something my mom did knowingly to humiliate us; this was something she had been made to do as a child by her parents too. Koreans love making their kids feel shame. They think the shame will motivate them to get up and change things. They think shame will stop a child whose bladder grew slower than the rest of their body from peeing while asleep.

However, being in a perpetual state of anxiety throughout my childhood had the opposite effect on me. It manifested as debilitating depression in my early adulthood, causing me to lie catatonically in bed for years. My mother would call me during this time, and finding out I was still in bed at 1 p.m., she would say, "Lazy just like your father."

* * *

TREASURE ISLAND

THE WAY THAT I ENDED up moving to America is a story I rarely share because it embarrasses me for some reason. My story is the classic immigrant poor person scraping together money to flee their homeland, but I don't think it fits the idea of who I am in my mind. But this is how it went:

After I (barely) graduated from high school, I moved in with my punk drummer boyfriend and was excited to be away from my horrible parents. I worked as an English tutor, tutoring young Korean students. I had to dye my hair back to brown and take out all my piercings and hide my tattoos under long-sleeved shirts, even in humid eighty-degree Korean summer weather. I eventually got a job as a textbook editor for a children's English textbook company. I had to ride the bus to Gangnam every day and go to an office and wear a blazer. I was nineteen years old. The textbook editing job paid 2.5 million won (approximately $2,100) a month, which was way more money than I had ever seen in my entire life. Since my boyfriend was a drummer in a band, he didn't make any money.

The month I turned twenty years old, I became pregnant. I got an abortion, which I had to pay for on my own. This was difficult since, like I mentioned, I was supporting my boyfriend. After the abortion, we had to stay in and eat instant ramyun for a few weeks. I remember feeling trapped and depressed while my boyfriend played video games all day and all night long.

The abortion was the breaking point for me. I felt that I had gotten dangerously close to an entire life of whatever the fuck this was. Afterward, I saved every fucking won I made in order to get away. I decided that I needed to move far, far away to get away from my boyfriend and my parents. Although I had never been to America outside of two vacations to Disneyland and New York City when I was a small child, I was a US citizen because both my parents were citizens at the time of my birth. I also spoke fluent English because of my schooling, so I thought I should move to America. I knew my boyfriend wouldn't "allow" me to move, so I purchased a round-trip ticket to San Francisco after my childhood friend from Saipan told me she would be vacationing there. I told my boyfriend I was going on vacation, packed a small suitcase, and fled.

After I arrived in San Francisco in the summer of 2005, I met up with my childhood friend at her cousin's house in Palo Alto. Her cousin was out of town, and she was house-sitting for her during her vacation in California. The day I got there, we sat in the backyard, smoking cigarettes and drinking beer. The backyard was fenced in by ancient trees, blowing wildly in the cold breeze. Although the wind was frigid, the sun was hot. We sat in the sun without shoes. I had no idea that I was sitting in the backyard of a home that cost millions of dollars. I had no way to distinguish what in America was a wealthy neighborhood because I had no point of reference for what wealth looked like here. I thought every neighborhood in America looked like Palo Alto.

The next day I went to the office of the airline and refunded my return-trip ticket, like I had planned to do all along. With the refunded money and the little I had brought for my trip, I had $700. Whenever I tell people I moved to the States with $700, they seem shocked. I'm not sure why. Seven hundred dollars is a lot of money. It's an amount that is life-changing to most people on this planet.

I used my friend's cousin's home PC and found a room for rent in San Francisco on Craigslist for $550 a month. It was the only room available where they weren't requiring a deposit. I called the number in the ad, and my potential new roommate gave me the address over the phone. Her house was located on Treasure Island. I told her I would come over right away to pay the first month's rent.

Treasure Island is an artificial island that sits in the center of the bay that separates San Francisco and the East Bay. The island was created to house some sort of military base or barracks. Since the houses were built for military use, they have the look of all US public architecture: prison. They were identical, covered in gray paneling, and painted with those prison stencil numbers. Treasure Island is accessible via the Bay Bridge by taking the 25 bus from the scary transit center in downtown San Francisco. That day, I went from the millionaire neighborhood of Palo Alto to the prison-vibe public housing hellhole known as Treasure Island. But to me it all looked the same. I thought Treasure Island was just as beautiful as Palo Alto. I stepped off the bus into the frigid ocean wind that made the trees dance on this magical speck of artificial land in the center of a glittering bay surrounded by a shimmering city. I felt like it was some sort of dream to have the privilege to live here. I thought there was no way this could possibly be my home.

I got to the house and knocked. A very skinny blonde woman who looked exactly like Shelley Duvall opened the door. She led me into the house, which was immaculately clean and sparse. All the art on the walls seemed like the art that hangs in the lobby of a Best Western. There were no hints to who she was in any of the home decor: no band posters, no specific style of art, no sign of any sort of personality. The only thing that stood out was a large pet snake in a glass vivarium. She pulled the snake out and carried it on her shoulders as she gave me a tour of the spacious two-floor home. There was a thunderously loud central heating system that tripped on and off as we walked through the house. It sounded like the ominous white noise that plays during the scary parts of horror movies and made me jump each time it came on. Blonde Shelley Duvall said it was always freezing on Treasure Island, and the central heating provided by the US military for free was a huge plus. The north side of the house faced out onto the water, and I watched the tumultuous waves crashing against the large rocks through the window of the room I was about to rent. I gave her my $550 and she made me sign a piece of paper that said "Youngmi Mayer paid rent 8/1/2005" and handed me a set of keys.

I moved in on the first of August, 2005, and met the one other roommate, who looked like Jeffrey Dahmer, complete with tinted gradation glasses. There was also a tiny ginger man who looked like a leprechaun who was not officially a roommate but would just be sleeping in random corners of the house all day. Blonde Shelley Duvall said he was her childhood friend and was "crashing" for a few weeks. I met Blonde Shelley Duvall's boyfriend, who was a sweaty, fast-talking Vegas magician type. He told me I could get a job at the café he worked at. I went with him to the café in Union Square the day after I met him and was hired on the spot. So within two weeks of moving to San Francisco, I had an apartment and a job. It all felt like a movie.

It ended up being a horror movie. Turns out all my roommates were addicted to meth. I was living in a meth house on Treasure Island. It all made sense now: the ridiculously clean apartment, the eerie lack of personality in the home decor, the sleepy leprechaun, the sweaty

157

magician—these were all meth people. Funnily enough, the only one who wasn't a meth person was Jeffrey Dahmer, who became my only friend by default. Until one night I woke up to him on top of me, rubbing his boner on my butt. I pushed him off and told him to get the fuck out. He proceeded to just stand in my doorway, staring at me Jeffrey Dahmer–style, as the ominous heating system roared above us. I knew I had to get out of there, but I couldn't afford it. So I just continued to live there for months, locking my door at night. One day there was a new girl who started working at the café. She also looked like Shelley Duvall but had brown hair. She took me to a party after her first shift.

That's where I tried doing heroin for the first time. After I snorted it, I immediately projectile-vomited everywhere. I started doing heroin with Brown-Hair Shelley Duvall before, during, and after work. For some reason I decided that I would become a junkie. I cannot tell you why I purposefully made the decision to become addicted to heroin, but I did. Every time I would snort it, though, I would projectile-vomit. Brown-Hair Shelley Duvall was living with her boyfriend, who was a skateboarder, in a really shitty apartment in the Tenderloin. Her boyfriend looked exactly like the lead singer of the band Incubus (hot). The other people who lived there were junkies and skateboarders. When I first started partying with them, they were all super hot and cool looking. Within months, they looked like scary zombies.

Even after a few months of attempting to snort heroin all the time, I didn't get addicted. Brown-Hair Shelley Duvall would complain about withdrawal symptoms and shake and moan at work. I had no idea what she was talking about because I never experienced those symptoms. But I also never felt high. I did notice that literally every time I snorted the heroin, I violently vomited everywhere, though. When her parents found out she was doing heroin, they made her move back home and go to rehab. I stopped doing heroin the day she left and didn't really feel the need to ever do it again. Years later, I found out from a dentist that I am allergic to opioids, which is probably the reason I kept throwing up every time I did the heroin. Then even later another doctor told me it was impossible to be "allergic" to opioids. So I don't know if I'm allergic or not, but I sure know it makes me barf. Luckily, I think this saved me from ever becoming addicted to it. Allergic or not, it just didn't stick.

I also was doing a shit ton of cocaine. I started doing cocaine every day when I started dating a cocaine addict who lived with the guy who sold cocaine to everyone in San Francisco. The cocaine dealer also looked exactly like the lead singer of the band Incubus, but he was Mexican. I was doing all this cocaine, but I kept falling asleep every time I did it. I would literally snort rails and fall asleep in my boyfriend's bedroom while everyone partied with Mexican Incubus Guy in the next room over. I did cocaine every day until the day I broke up with Mexican Incubus Guy's roommate. After we broke up, I stopped and never felt the need to do it again. Years later I was diagnosed with ADHD. Apparently, one of the signs of having undiagnosed ADHD is that stimulants relax you. Luckily, I think this is the reason I never really became addicted to it. But again, I have no idea if this is true. I tried so hard to become addicted to drugs and be destitute and homeless because I felt like that life fit what I felt on the inside. But I just for the life of me could not become addicted to anything. This is all sad and funny. But some of the shit that happened during this time was just sad.

During this time, I was raped.

During this time, I started doing sex work.

I don't really want to talk about these things, but it's important to tell you that these things did happen. I need for you to know that they happened.

I started doing sex work and was blown away by the amount of money I made. However, as soon as I started, I could tell I couldn't continue for more than a few weeks because of the enormous strain on my mental health. I had an obligation to fulfill with someone I worked with, and as soon as I did, I stopped working there and never did it again. In the few weeks I did sex work, I made enough money to not only move out of the meth house but also buy a plane ticket to visit my family and ex-boyfriend in Korea. Although I had been dying to get out only a year before, I found myself missing my parents and my ex a lot.

So a little over one year after I moved to the States, I returned to Korea. This was when I met up with my ex at the restaurant and he asked me what America was like. I wanted to tell him that I had done heroin and cocaine, and been raped, and met multiple people who looked like Shelley Duvall. I wanted to tell him about Treasure Island and the Tenderloin and Palo Alto. I wanted to tell him about the life of privilege I was able to live. This life that eluded him. But he was bloated and incoherent from the antipsychotic drugs that had been administered without his consent. I didn't think there was room for me to complain about how bad my life was, because his life seemed way worse. My life was bad because of my free will; his life was bad because of the lack of his.

What I had learned all those weekend days selling Kool-Aid wasn't to "work hard" like my mother had anticipated. What I learned was that I deserved nothing. I was destined to be a Kool-Aid seller on the street. Because I truly believed that I was deserving of nothing, anything I got seemed like a gift. It seemed like a gift to be living in a meth house on Treasure Island. It seemed like a gift to meet all these drug addicts and drug dealers. After all, it could have been much worse: I could've been stuck in Korea with a baby and a husband in a psychiatric hospital. I could've been stuck selling Kool-Aid on the street forever.

* * *

THE TENDERLOIN

I FINISHED MOVING INTO MY new apartment in the Tenderloin when I got back from Korea. The Tenderloin is literally the worst neighborhood in America. It is the skid row of San Francisco, but something about it feels decidedly worse than any other skid row. I once heard someone say that the Indigenous population of San Francisco avoided that area because they believed it was cursed. For anyone who's ever been, that rings extremely true. The neighborhood is only about an eight-block radius between downtown and the super fancy neighborhoods of San Francisco. In this eight-block radius, the only people walking on the street are in terrifying levels of decay from prolonged drug use. To see the houseless people walking around the Tenderloin is to see firsthand the terrorism the American government subjects its forgotten citizens to. They look like the war- and famine-torn citizens you see on BBC World News. It's fascinating that when Americans see people in other countries looking like this on the street, they are able to understand that it is the fault of the foreign country's government that its citizens live that way, but if they see people like that in the US, they see it as a moral failure of that individual.

I was still working at the café that paid no money and had burned through the money I had made doing sex work. The only real friend I had during this time was my coworker at the café, Alicia. We got along because we were both in our early twenties and were the only two people there not addicted to drugs. Alicia wasn't addicted to drugs because she didn't do drugs. I wasn't addicted to drugs because I tried and failed. We also were the only two "hipsters" who worked there. This was around 2005 to 2007 and we dressed like it. We both had long brown bangs that we swept to the side of our faces and wore headbands across our foreheads à la MGMT that obscured our heavily eyeliner-lined eyes. We had uniforms for work, but when we would hang out outside of work, we would wear our hipster uniforms: skinny jeans and ripped band tees. Alicia and I were extremely close, and I wasn't sure why because we had such different upbringings; I grew up in Korea and she grew up in Oakland. But looking back, I realized we had both grown up really poor. When she broke up with her boyfriend and had no place to live, there was no question that she would move in with me. There is an unspoken understanding among people who grew up poor that these things are just things we take care of for each other. We spoke the same language. I didn't realize that most people in the US didn't speak this language. I had roommates who were extremely angry that I'd used some of their butter or drank one of their cans of seltzer. These roommates were usually from middle-class or wealthy families. They had never understood what it felt like to be in need. But Alicia wasn't like this.

It wasn't a coincidence Alicia and I worked at this café that paid so poorly when other people our age wouldn't have even bothered. We were used to receiving nothing, so the meager paycheck seemed not only fair but actually too good. We didn't think we were even worthy of it. Needless to say, we were always broke. The week after Alicia moved in, we decided to go out after work for drinks.

"I want to get a drink, but I have twenty-five dollars until payday," she said.

"I have thirty dollars!" I said. We were four days away from getting paid. We decided to go to a bar.

We had a few rounds of "shot and a beer" specials at a dive bar nearby. Afterward, we counted the money we had left over. We had ten dollars for food. For four days. We were in a drunken and silly mood and skipped to the corner store in front of my apartment to see how far we could stretch the money we had left over. We drunkenly laughed and joked loudly about how poor we were as we took turns grabbing items off the shelves and showing them to each other. She grabbed a giant jar of pickled pepperoncini. "It's only eight dollars! Look how big it is!"

"We can't just eat peppers for four days!" I laughed.

We laughed hard because we were both finally free from the humiliation of poverty. The early twenties for poor people are a liberating time because to be poor in your early twenties is to be disguised from your class background. Everyone in their early twenties is broke. Even rich kids in their twenties have no real disposable income because they're reliant on an allowance while in college. So there is no shame associated with having no money at this age. Also you're hot. In your early twenties, you can wear a sundress from H&M and look better than any old person wearing a $10,000 Chanel suit. Alicia and I laughed because for the first time in our lives, it was no longer humiliating to admit that we couldn't afford food. So we announced it to the entire corner store.

We finally agreed on a box of spaghetti, a jar of spaghetti sauce, and a box of Betty Crocker brownie mix we could make without eggs. While we danced and laughed and screamed loudly about how we were poor, a very cool-looking Asian guy with long hair followed us around. A few times he almost looked like he was about to talk to us, but we kept bouncing away just out of his reach. At the checkout line, where we were held hostage by the obligation to pay, he walked up to us and said, "Spaghetti and brownie mix. Seems like a party!"

"We only have ten dollars and we need to make it last until Friday!" I slurred.

Alicia and I walked out of the store with him, where he leaned against a light blue single-speed bike that was Kryptonite-locked to a pole. Alicia said, "Oh my god, is that your bike? It's so awesome."

He said, "Yeah."

In the early aughts, the single-speed bike was the utmost status symbol for hipsters. It signaled an incredibly high level of taste and culture. Alicia and I started scrutinizing his appearance. He was dressed exactly like us: black bangs obscuring eyeliner-lined eyes, deep V-neck tank top, skinny jeans, etc. However, he was more hipstery. Back in these days, when all hipsters dressed alike, the elite hipsters would gatekeep the perfect brand of deep V or skinny jeans. They would secretly all buy the *correct* eyeliner and headbands. The differences were minimal, but you could tell by how a tank sat on someone's torso or where the rip was located in the skinny jeans that this was a top-tier hipster. This Asian guy was a top-tier hipster. A *Mission* hipster. Alicia and I were "uncool" in the social hierarchy of San Francisco because we worked in Union Square and lived in the Tenderloin and had minimal access to the cool kids who worked and lived in the Mission. This Asian guy was definitely part of the Mission hipster class, a class we were trying to penetrate. Alicia and I psychically communicated that we needed to befriend this cool guy to tap into the cool-people scene. But neither of us knew what to do or say, so we just stood there holding the spaghetti and brownie mix in our arms.

"Well, I better get to work. I'm late," he said, motioning with a nod to a restaurant next to the store. I turned to look at the restaurant, which was super fancy. It was the kind of restaurant meant for the rich old people of San Francisco, a restaurant I would be too scared to even enter as a *poor*.

"Oh, you work here?" I asked.

"Yeah. I'm a chef. My name is Danny. You should come in to eat sometime. The food's really good."

Alicia and I looked at each other and smiled sheepishly.

He quickly added, "Oh! On me, of course. I can do whatever I want here. It's my friend's place. All my friends eat for free."

Alicia said, "Oh good, because I don't think we can afford that place. We're poor!"

We both laughed and walked off into the night holding our ten dollars' worth of food as Danny Bowien went back to work.

We got back to my place and Alicia said, "We need to friend that guy. He's def one of those bike messenger hipsters that live in the Mission. He is soooo, like, in love with you. Next time we see him, you need to flirt with him. You have to!"

I rolled my eyes and started making the spaghetti and brownies.

Alicia pulled a small bottle of Royal Gate Vodka out of my underwear drawer. We always kept a quarter pint of it at home and referred to it as our "emergency vodka." Alicia would take swigs of it whenever she felt sad about her recent breakup. She took a swig and gagged trying to swallow it. She handed it to me. I took a sip and almost threw up.

"Emergency vodka," we said to each other between dry heaves.

*   *   *

CITY HALL

A FEW WEEKS LATER, we saw Danny hanging out outside of work. We said hi as we walked past and Alicia nudged me toward him. I blurted out, "Hey, are you Korean?"

"Yeah? How'd you know?" He seemed genuinely confused.

"Just a guess. Just asking," I said, realizing what I said was fucking weird and mega awkward.

He continued, "I'm adopted, though, so I don't really know anything about Korea. I'm actually trying to learn how to speak Kore—"

"I could teach you! I'm fluent. And also, I was a tutor!" I practically screamed. As I was saying this, Alicia had already started writing my number down on a piece of paper. She handed it to Danny.

"This is her number. You should call her. We are going to the Hemlock tonight. Do you want to meet us there later?" she said, forcing the piece of paper into his hand.

"Sure. I'll swing by after work. I gotta go back inside, though." He rushed back into the restaurant, looking as relieved as I was that the encounter was over.

He never showed up. That night Alicia and I went to the Hemlock, which was a dive bar popular among young hipsters in the Tenderloin. Alicia and I both met guys who were Mission hipsters that we ended

165

up dating for a few months. We had our way into the cool scene, and both of us sort of forgot about Danny.

That same night after work, Danny told his coworker he wanted to go meet up with a hot girl he'd met (me) but didn't have enough money to buy her a drink. His coworker said he should just go anyway. He biked home instead and threw the piece of paper with my phone number on it under his bed.

Eight months later, I broke up with the cocaine hipster I'd met at the Hemlock that night. By then I was working as a waitress at a twenty-four-hour diner, which was almost worse than the sex work and for far less money. I had also moved out of the Tenderloin and now lived in SoMa with a roommate. Alicia had moved to her own place in Oakland. She called me the day she got a new job as a bartender at a fancy Italian restaurant in the Mission. "Oh my god, I just got here for my first shift and guess who's the chef de cuisine here? That guy Danny!"

"Oh my god!! The Korean hipster single-speed guy?" I said.

"Yeah. I walked in and said hi, and he recognized me and asked me about you! That's so funny that I saw him literally the day you became single again," she said.

"Oh my god, seriously, it's wild timing."

"We're all going out after work. Do you want to come?"

That night I went to have a drink at the fancy Italian restaurant Alicia and Danny worked at. I put on a skintight purple bodycon American Apparel minidress that was cut extremely low in the back. I wore a long necklace backward so that the pendant hung down to the middle of my back and placed a bejeweled headband across my forehead, holding my black bangs down over my heavily eyeliner-lined eyes. I sat at the bar and had a glass of wine. The kitchen was visible to the right of the bar, and I could see Danny scrambling around the kitchen, cooking pasta or whatever.

After the restaurant closed, I followed Alicia and Danny and a bunch of their coworkers to a dive bar down the street. After a few drinks I went home with Danny and spent the night. From that day on, we were together for the next twelve years.

Six months later, we got married and didn't tell anybody. We went to the city hall in San Francisco. I wore a plum vintage lace dress that I bought for thirty dollars at a thrift store and the usual bejeweled headband. Danny wore an H&M suit and a headband. The San Francisco city hall has a dome in the center of it, and if you get married there, the ceremony takes place under the dome pierced with skylights. The clerk asked us if we brought witnesses. We had not, so she asked one of her associates to bear witness. She walked us over to stand under the dome and recited the legal vows.

What we hadn't noticed was that while we were listening to her recite the legal vows, a class of small school children was having a field trip and had ascended the stairs to the dome. There they quietly looked down on us while we were getting married. When we both said, "I do," the children all erupted in cheers and applause. Danny and I looked up, surprised, and in the sun-drenched terraces, we saw the innocent and pure faces of these children, cheering and laughing as they looked down on us like angels from the heavens, reveling at our small victory against a relentless and agonizing mortal existence.

I don't know why we didn't tell anyone that we got married. I think we thought people wouldn't approve. Or maybe we thought it was something that was meant to be a secret. A few years later we did end up getting married "officially" in Korea and no one really asked if we had gone to the city clerk to get our legal marriage license yet, so we didn't have to tell anyone we had done it years ago. I think about the fact that there is no photographic or video proof of this secret wedding. The only people who know this happened were me and Danny, the clerk, her associate, and two dozen nameless children. This was the year 2008, before every moment of my life became documented. I was twenty-three years old.

* * *

OKLAHOMA

THE PERSON I MARRIED WAS Danny Bowien. He's a Korean adoptee who grew up in Oklahoma and was raised by two extremely Christian white people. His parents adopted him and another young boy from Korea who was his younger (not biological) brother. Before they adopted them, they adopted a seven-year-old girl from their own community. Danny grew up knowing her as his older sister. When she became a teenager, she started smoking weed and hanging out with boys, as teenage girls do. Danny's mother was a religious extremist who suffered from Munchausen syndrome among many other mental illnesses. She punished his sister by unadopting her and sending her back into the foster care system, which she stayed in until she turned eighteen. Danny's mother also inflicted severe punishments on him and his younger brother.

Danny was made to attend church almost every day, where he suffered sexual, physical, and emotional abuse. He never stood up to his abusers, and he allowed them to take advantage of him because he was the only Asian kid besides his brother and had a severe need to want to fit in. At home, his mother constantly threatened him with unadoption, using his sister as an example. He was constantly in a state of fear of abandonment.

As a teenager, he finally told his mother about the sexual abuse he was enduring at church, and she, a victim of childhood sexual assault herself, promptly brought it up with the board of the church. The problem was that Danny's main abuser was the family member of someone in an extremely high position at the church. This person and their family had an unspeakable amount of wealth and power in their community. The church was the size of a football stadium. The board reacted to Danny's mom bringing to light the abuse by exiling their family from the church, which meant the entire community. Overnight, Danny's family was shunned to live a life disconnected from everyone they knew. No one would talk to them; they would get harsh stares in public. Their lives were essentially destroyed.

Although Danny's mom had initially done the right thing and probably knew deep down she was correct for calling out the abuser, she turned against Danny when she lost her footing in her community. The shunning from her white Christian community caused her immense psychological harm, and she took out her pain on her adopted children. Following the exile, her abuse toward them became extreme. After Danny spent his childhood following his mom around to various hospitals where she would convince doctors to prescribe her a never-ending list of medications, she actually developed breast cancer when he was twelve years old. She took five horrific years to die, during which time Danny and his younger brother were made to become her caretakers and nurses. When she finally died, Danny was seventeen years old. Danny said he didn't understand what he felt at the time, but now he knows that the name of what he felt was relief.

He dropped out of high school, but the principal felt sorry for him because his mother had just died and issued him a high school diploma. He then moved to San Francisco to attend culinary school at Le Cordon Bleu. During this time, the campus of this vocational school was located in the worst part of the Tenderloin. Many young people went to school there only to end up addicted to heroin or crack. The school charged something outrageous like $60,000 a year to learn the skills of and enter into a profession averaging an annual salary of $20,000. After graduating, Danny started working in restaurants around San Francisco. He moved to New York City but was so severely physically abused by the chefs at one fancy restaurant there that he moved back to San Francisco after a few months. That's when we met.

Danny had a shitty life. All of it stemmed from the catastrophic loss of his biological mother. I think about the magnitude of that loss all the time. I think about the fact that this is the same loss that led Siddhartha Gautama to start Buddhism. All adoptees and motherless children understand the experience that started one of the most profound ideologies known to humans. I don't think there is a human alive who doesn't understand the absolute devastation of losing your mom, though. Even white people get sad when their moms die.

Koreans have a primitive and animalistic attachment to their mothers. In Korean culture, so full of rigidity, patriarchal conformity, and coldness, all is forgiven in the event of the death of your mother. Korean people of any class and rank will lose their minds, their civility, and all traces of the rigid performance of conformity in the event of the death of their mother. This is one of the only times you are allowed to make an animal sound. Koreans take this opportunity to unleash everything that was held in them from years of abuse from their Sunbaes and their fathers. The sacred bond between mother and child in Korea transcends the thousands of years of patriarchal philosophy and misogynistic brainwashing.

Danny has in his body the power that started the entire religion of Buddhism. So do all other Korean adoptees. The power of losing your mother at birth. As a Korean, when meeting a Korean adoptee, I feel a negative charge. It feels like rubbing the wrong part of two batteries together. A painful repelling that is supposed to be an attraction. Korean adoptees have told me time and time again that they feel abandoned and neglected. But what they do not know is that Koreans also feel a longing for them. The longing for the lost child, the lost sibling. Like when people look at the Taeguk and see the dividing line and ignore the fact that a circle binds them together. A big reason I married Danny was because I needed to show him that we all missed him. I needed to accept him with the open arms denied me so many times by Koreans.

At the time of our marriage, Danny was the chef de cuisine at a fancy Italian restaurant. The executive chef was a well-known Italian chef who was friends with the multimillionaire restaurateur who seemed to me (ALLEGEDLY) like just a wealthy person looking to launder money in the US. The restaurateur planned to send the Italian chef to the Pesto World Championship (LOL) in Italy in hopes that he would earn a title and they could display the award in the restaurant. The Italian chef insisted Danny come with. Danny had never left the United States since he had entered as a one-month-old and didn't have a passport. He told his boss he couldn't go because the flight was in five days. He came home from work at 1 a.m. and told me this had happened. The next day at 8 a.m., I woke him up and told him we were going to get his passport expedited so he could go to the Pesto World Championship (LOL). We drove around all day going from one place to the other, collecting paperwork and submitting it to the expediter. It cost $500. This was all the money we had collectively. Whenever Danny hit a speed bump, he would say he wanted to give up, and I told him no, we were going to get his passport no matter what. He ended up filing for his passport and receiving it two days later, just in time for this flight to Genoa, Italy.

That year, he ended up winning the award for Pesto Champion of the World (LOL). He appeared in newspapers nationwide in Italy. The thing is, I knew he would win. There was something about Danny that I couldn't explain. It was the thing that the Italian chef saw when he randomly took him under his wing as chef de cuisine. It was something I saw right away. Danny is a genius. This was the first time I had ever been in the presence of a genius. *Genius* is a word that is commonly thrown around without thought, but in the presence of one, it is strikingly obvious. Also, it is not necessarily a positive thing. A genius is a tortured individual. It is torture to be gifted in a singular pursuit. In the "Heungbu and Nolbu" Dogyo narrative, it is the destructive extreme. His singular obsessive focus and inherent talent made Danny one of the most talented chefs in the world, but to be around him was to see the corrosive effects of it firsthand. To me his talent seemed like an energy that lives in the flesh puppet of its host. It ate away at him. Danny would obsessively spend every free moment he had on perfecting a skill. He would read all of the books, he would learn all of the techniques. So many geniuses like Danny go unnoticed in this world because their singular mindset makes them antisocial. But Danny also had the gift of having an entire childhood based on likability. This constant anxiety of wanting to be wanted or not wanting to be discarded. This childhood of emotional and financial poverty created the perfect storm of inherent talent and personability.

A few weeks after winning the title of Pesto Champion of the World (LOL), I came home from work after a brunch shift at 4 p.m. I rode my bike to the apartment building where we lived to find Danny sitting on the sidewalk (a side effect of Danny being a genius was that he always was losing his keys, wallet, and phone on a weekly basis). I jumped off my bike. "What are you doing here? Aren't you supposed to be at work?"

"I got in a fight with the owner and I quit," he said, still sitting on the sidewalk.

Danny disliked the owner of this fancy Italian restaurant, but he put up with him because after the Pesto World Championship (LOL), he gave him a $5,000 bonus every quarter. This was more money than either of us had ever seen in our entire lives. When Danny got back from Italy, they gave him his first-ever $5,000 check and we were excited AF. We went to Barneys and bought clothes and went to a fancy restaurant and drank champagne all day while singing, "We got five thousand dollars" from the *Wayne's World* movie. Danny probably thought that if he walked away from this job, I would probably leave him or something. But I didn't give a shit. The quarterly $5,000 meant nothing to me because money meant nothing to me. I had never had it my entire life, so having it taken away didn't mean anything.

"Good. That guy fucking sucked," I said.

Danny's mood drastically changed. He had been used to living a life with an abusive mother whose love was conditional based on whether his behavior served her or not. He had not been around someone who cared about his best interests.

"Danny, who gives a shit? You're so good at being a chef, you'll get a new job," I said.

Danny smiled and we both went up to the apartment and drank beers while he made duck confit or something probably.

*　*　*

THE MISSION

ONE MORNING WHILE LYING IN bed a few days after he quit, Danny told me about this chef at Foreign Cinema who was sick of being a chef for rich white people and had rented a taco truck to make fancy sandwiches for drunk people late at night. These were the first days of Twitter, and San Francisco was filled with tech losers who were jumping all over the app. The fancy food truck blew up on Twitter solely because it was only traceable by the app. It made the tech losers feel like they had the in on some special food thing. For some reason, tech losers love being in on something that no one else knows, but they rarely have this privilege because they're, well, losers.

The chef turned out to be Anthony Myint and his taco truck "pop-up" shortly got shut down by the health department. Then he moved his operation into a Chinese restaurant called Lung Shan on Mission and Eighteenth. He asked the owners if he could rent out the kitchen every Thursday to make the same sandwiches he had been making in the taco truck. The owners said yes. Part of the reason they said yes is because Anthony spoke Cantonese and they trusted him. So, he started making the sandwiches there but then had the great idea to invite all his chef friends to make whatever they wanted to on Thursdays when he had the kitchen. He had a huge network of important chefs around the Bay Area from working at Foreign Cinema. Every week, patrons would get to taste a special menu made by the chef of a fancy multiple–Michelin Star restaurant for extremely cheap inside a take-out Chinese spot in the heart of the sketchy part of the Mission. Anthony called his pop-up Mission Street Food. It was one of the first viral pop-up restaurants of that era and exploded in popularity, not only in San Francisco but across the nation.

By the time Danny quit his job at the Italian place, a handful of his successful friends had had a night of cooking at Mission Street Food. His chef friends boasted about their menus and how there were two-to-three-hour waits, the freedom to make whatever they wanted to, and the large amount of money they and their staff made for one night of work. The concept was popular not only among patrons but also among chefs, who all also hated making food for rich white people. Anthony had essentially cut out the middleman by renting out the kitchen and dining area of a Chinese restaurant that relied mostly on take-out orders.

Lung Shan was run by a Chinese family who owned the building. The family collected rent from tenants in the building and mostly used the restaurant as a place to hang out with their friends as they casually fulfilled the dozen or so delivery orders a night. Anthony gave them something like $500 every Thursday to use the kitchen and dining area.

The family that owned Lung Shan didn't seem to mind that once a week, their sleepy take-out joint was filled to the brim with white tech people and hipsters waiting in line in the frigid San Francisco wind for hours for food served in paper boats and cocktails served in plastic dentist spit cups. The famous chefs got to have fun for a night and make money, and the patrons got to tell their friends that they ate food made by the chef of Chez Panisse or the French Laundry at a pop-up. Everybody won.

At the height of Mission Street Food's popularity, Anthony invited Danny to cook. He was billed as the Pesto Champion of the World

(LOL). It was one week before our "official" wedding in Korea. Danny made a Korean menu and I went to work as a "line cook." The menu consisted of bibimbap, kongguksu, and some other things I can't remember. It was one of the most popular nights of Mission Street Food to date. Danny and I made some bonkers amount of money in one night (like $800). Then we went off to Korea to get married, feeling on top of the world.

When we got back, Anthony approached Danny. Mission Street Food was a lot of work to produce every week, and the novelty of having a new chef every week had waned. Some nights were extremely popular, but it all depended on the reputation of the chef who was cooking. Anthony was troubled by the lack of sustainability in this kind of pop-up and was looking for stability. He was impressed by Danny's skill because he too could see that Danny was a genius, but he was also impressed by his malleable personality. He asked Danny if he wanted to do a more permanent concept together. He told Danny he could do whatever he wanted.

Danny told me that Anthony wanted to have a serious discussion about it and asked if I wanted to join the meeting. We met at a restaurant called Spices II in the Richmond District. This was the first time in my life that I had ever had "authentic" Sichuan food. Spices II was a Sichuan-style restaurant from Taiwan. This type of trendy, fun mala hot pot restaurant was extremely popular among young, hip people in Taiwan and China at the time, but in 2010 it had yet to have broad appeal in the US. There were already a few people trying to introduce it in America with relative success: Xi'an Famous Foods on the East Coast, featuring foods of the Xi'an province that were somewhat like Sichuan cuisine, and a rogue Sichuan chef who was doing chaotic pop-ups in Atlanta. However, outside of the chef world, nothing had broken into the mainstream.

As we ate a mala hot pot of squid and pig buttholes, a plate of cold and tingly sliced pig ear, and a plate of fried chicken pieces completely covered in fried chilis, Anthony said, "What if you made food like this but for white people? And we brought it to the Mission?" Then Danny said, "I don't want to dumb it down for white people. I'll just make this exactly how it is."

I remember the thought exploding in my brain. In that moment, I knew it was going to be huge. I remember thinking we were going to make one billion dollars. I had never had food that tasted like this, and to me it was new. I know for a lot of people it wasn't. But I wondered why I had never encountered it like I had encountered Thai food or sushi or Vietnamese food. To me, Sichuan food was like the best food I had ever had that no one had ever told me about. Like if someone introduced Garfield to lasagna at the age of twenty-five. If I had not heard of it, I was sure a lot of other people had not either. I remember sitting there knowing that this was going to explode. In the following weeks, Danny developed a menu based on what we had at Spices II. Danny put his own genius spin on it by obsessively making each dish "perfect" according to authentic, old recipes and using the meat-cooking skills he acquired by working in European fine-dining restaurants. Since this was a spin-off of Mission Street Food, Anthony and Danny decided to call it Mission Chinese Food.

This was also the beginning of the end of me and Danny being poor. We had been poor our entire lives. We had nothing and no one. Being poor for me meant I had the freedom to do whatever I wanted. I didn't have to act according to the whims of my parents, who couldn't do anything for me anyway. Maybe I didn't have parents to pay for my college, but that also meant I had no parents to tell me I couldn't do heroin. Being poor meant I didn't owe anyone loyalty. I didn't have to suck anyone's dick. Except for the few weeks when I had to suck some people's dicks. What I mean is I didn't have to pretend to be Republican so that my dad could buy me a penthouse apartment.

Danny also had resilience and fearlessness from being poor, but he wasn't as OK with it as I was. Throughout his childhood, Danny spent weekends at Walmart, where he was paid half of minimum wage to clear out shelves. He went there with his dad. His dad told him they had to do this work to put food on the table. I don't know if this was true or if it was just the way his dad was teaching him, like my mom taught me, the place where we belonged. Because Danny was poor, he was conned into going to a vocational school that had television commercials that played twenty-four seven on basic cable. It cost $60,000, which left him severely in debt in a career where he was unable to make enough to pay it back. But he had something inherent that money couldn't buy: he was a genius.

Not to sound like a fucking cliché, but at this point of our lives, the poorest point, we were wealthy beyond measure. Because we both had something that could not be bought, born of poverty: I had the freedom, resilience, and loyalty that made me a ride-or-die to the nth degree, and Danny had inherent talent. None of these things are obtainable with money. There is no rich person alive who can buy these things because they cannot be bought. They can't pay for loyal friends because the act of paying for them makes it conditional, and they sure as fuck can't pay for talent no matter how hard their nepo babies all try to write a cookbook. At this time of my life, I was rich—not in the sense that I had money but that I had things impossible to obtain with money. But I had also just married someone with $60,000 of Le Cordon Bleu debt. I was actually poorer than I had ever been.

CHAPTER 10

Poor

DIAMONDS

THE NEXT CHAPTER OF MY life has been thoroughly documented because it coincided with the creation of Instagram in 2010. For those of us around at the genesis, we remember a fleeting moment before the app's introduction where another photo editing app reigned supreme. The app was called Hipstamatic and its only function was to provide an endless number of filters to give digital images in your phone the appearance of being film photos. The most popular filters were sepia-toned and had faux ripped-edge borders, making the images look vintage. I think it was popular with millennials, who were the young, cool kids back then, because of the old-timey aesthetic. This was around the time men were sporting suspenders and waxed mustaches, and every restaurant had Edison light bulbs and served cocktails in mason jars. Everyone was using Hipstamatic filters for their Facebook and Myspace posts, and when Instagram started, a lot of us just saw it as Hipstamatic with a built-in sharing option. For this reason, all the first posts during the birth of Instagram have the look of flashback scenes from the old country in *The Godfather*. It's an interesting coincidence that unknowingly, we, the first people of Instagram, made the first photos on the most powerful image-sharing tool in human history look "vintage."

My first posts on Instagram look like anyone else's: heavily filtered high-contrast photos of my cats, a Christmas tree, my nails, a sandwich. But one of the oldest posts is of an olive-colored Celine Luggage Tote sitting on the take-out counter inside Lung Shan. The date of the post is around December 2011. To most people this doesn't mean anything, but to a handbag enthusiast this is extraordinary. The Celine Luggage Tote was the most sought-after luxury handbag of that time. It was the "you can't even buy it because it's sold out everywhere" bag of that era. There were online blogs outlining the journeys of wealthy women flying to different cities around the globe to obtain one in the color they wanted. Even celebrities had a hard time procuring them, and the hierarchy of fame and power could be traced by which celebrity was smart enough to be seen with one first. Yet here I was, less than one year after helping Danny start a food pop-up, posting one with a Mayfair filter on Instagram.

A few months before I posted this photo, I showed Danny an article about how the purse was impossible to purchase. The article introduced me to a whole new world, and before long I was obsessively reading luxury handbag blogs on a daily basis. The level of wealth it took not only to purchase one of the handbags, which were priced around $1,500 to $10,000 back then, but to own a collection of them fascinated me. I read these luxury handbag blogs out of pure fantasy, without ever thinking I would ever be able to afford one. My interest was fueled by dreams of the wildly out of reach but also by the hideous silliness of it all. For some reason, seeing someone spend $5,000 on something made being poor funny. It made me realize how nothing was actually real.

I don't know how to describe the hypnotic allure of luxury goods to anyone lucky enough not to feel that desire. As a kid, I remember watching a film adaptation of *Gulliver's Travels* with my dad. In the scene where the "savages" known as Yahoos are seen digging for colorful stones in the dirt, my dad said disgustedly, "This is like how those idiots act about diamonds." He seemed kind of proud that he made this observation, which is funny because the metaphor is so on the nose. My dad was repulsed by people who coveted diamonds because he spent so much time in Africa and saw the horrific ways they were mined. He was also disturbed by the fact that the big companies that own the diamond mines release only a small fraction of the diamonds into the world market, manufacturing their value by creating a false scarcity. He was right to be repulsed. What a horrific system put in place, all for shiny rocks.

However, I think there is also something endearing about loving something that has no purpose and is made to feel just out of reach. Like, imagine the first person who found a diamond while digging in the dirt for worms or something. I like to imagine she was a cavegirl. I imagine her living a shit life full of scavenging for food and being cold and wet in a cave. Then she finds this shiny thing in the dirt and goes to wash it off in the river. I imagine she looks at it and it's sparkly. She can't eat it, she can't fuck it, and it won't keep her warm. But for some reason it means something to her. It makes her feel strange, like when she's looking at the stars at night. It makes her feel like maybe there's something more out there. She looks at it all day, fantasizing about whatever primitive cavegirls fantasized about. Then the chief caveman sees it and punches her in the face and takes it from her. The next day she sees his girlfriend wearing it in her fur. She no longer has the diamond, but how the diamond made her feel is forever in her. She tells her kids about it. Her kids tell their kids and their kids. Now we all covet this useless shiny thing that we can't afford because of that one silly cavegirl.

Diamonds, like all nonessential goods, are procured in today's world in the worst ways possible. I, like my father, am repulsed by the conspicuous display of them on wealthy people. But I think for people who are poor, like our cavegirl ancestor who found the first diamond, there is beauty in the longing for something that has no purpose. For people who toil and suffer all day just to have food and shelter, an item that exists only for beauty represents something else. It represents hope.

* * *

CELINE LUGGAGE TOTE

THERE IS ANOTHER REASON MY life was well documented starting around this time, because Danny and Anthony's restaurant pop-up, Mission Chinese Food, blew the fuck up. Mission Chinese Food started in June 2010, and by June 2011, it had been written up in the *San Francisco Chronicle*, the *New York Times*, *Bon Appétit*, *Gourmet*, and other newspapers and magazines. The lines were out the door the minute we opened. Every night there was a minimum three-hour wait. Famous chefs from all over the world were flying in to eat at this hole-in-the-wall Chinese restaurant. Martha Stewart came to eat there. The food media, which is run by failed writer-wannabe losers, for once in their cursed careers got something right: they recognized his genius. A year ago, Danny had been sitting on the sidewalk in front of my apartment, depressed that he couldn't even keep a middle-management kitchen job, and now he was eating late-night burgers with Anthony Bourdain.

Danny worked the kitchen, and Anthony (Myint) and I worked front of house. I was the only server for the first few weeks, but when the popularity quickly exploded, I started asking my friends from former restaurant jobs to help me. Since I was the only "manager," there were no rules and we would just show up for shifts and drink beers and be really mean to all the customers.

Danny and I were hired at Lung Shan as "consultants" and were paid a percentage of sales. The amount of money we were making seemed astronomical to us. Every two weeks, we would get one paycheck for both of us. The first few checks were $2,500, meaning we both were making $1,250 per two weeks. That was enough for us to both quit our other jobs. Very quickly the checks became larger and larger and averaged out to around $6,000, meaning in one month, we were making $12,000 collectively. Every time we would receive a paycheck, Danny and I would sing the "We got five thousand dollars" song from *Wayne's World,* substituting "five thousand" with however much the paycheck was for.

On my birthday in 2011, I arrived to work my shift at Lung Shan, and Danny handed me a large shopping tote from Barneys. I cried because I already knew what was inside. Never in my life had I imagined that I would own something as beautiful and useless as a Celine Luggage Tote. Never in my life did I think I would be the one who got to own the shiny rock.

*   *   *

CUSTOMERS

DANNY AND I HAD TWO very distinct views on wealthy people. I hated them and he liked them. This didn't matter when we first got married because we were poor and we didn't really interact with them, but unfortunately, we started making a little money, and the rift became more and more apparent. I want to take a moment and note that our ascending of class was quite extraordinary. The American Dream states that this happens to basically anyone who tries hard, but it's complete fucking bullshit. The American economic system is actually set up to make sure this never happens. The only rich people here are people who were born rich. For people in the restaurant industry, this is nearly impossible despite what Food Network tries to sell us. When I said we were making $6,000 per month each, a lot of people probably read that number as simply adequate. But I know for anyone reading who is in the restaurant biz, that number seems fantastical. It was fantastical. A fantasy. A dream. It was an unheard-of amount of money for us. And I fucking loved having it. But I still saw my "new" socioeconomic peer group as the enemy. Danny saw them as his friends.

Most of the patrons of Mission Chinese Food were rich tech people. They were the people who would think $6,000 a month was nothing. These were the rich white kids who grew up selling lemonade on the street. They had fake jobs like "financial consultant" where they treated the economic system of this country like a poker game at a frat. The millionaires of San Francisco were twenty-three-year-olds who went to Stanford and worked in offices that had free beer on tap and foosball tables, and they looked down on *us*. They were horrible people.

When I moved to San Francisco, my first impression of the wealthy people there was that they were very Christian. Like cult-level-FLDS-sister-wife Christian. San Francisco liberals will not understand this because they pride themselves on being the most atheist, progressive, liberal city in the US. Their food is organic, they recycle, and they only wear jackets from Patagonia because it's an ethical corporation (whatever the fuck that means). But a lot like my mom, who wore the skin of a Christian over her core Asian ideologies, American liberals move in a way that betrays their facades. They wear a liberal sheepskin over their wolf bodies, holding on to the core tenant of white Christianity: supremacy.

In San Francisco, I would go to thirty-five-dollar trendy exercise classes, and the instructors were white women who looked like they were created in a lab to look sexually appealing to guys named Kyle. The exercise classes reminded me of the Seventh-day Adventist Church I went to once as a kid with my white neighbor. The instructors always started with a sermon about having "good vibes only" and then they would end with a hymnal. Except instead of hard pews, which are purposefully made to be uncomfortable to stop you from masturbating, you're sitting on a SoulCycle bike. You're not supposed to be comfortable; you're supposed to push yourself! The "hymnal" at the end is a dance remix of a Maroon 5 song. I remember looking around and seeing these white women cry real-ass tears (for once) on these bikes while the Maroon 5 guy sang about his twenty-three-year-old girlfriend. Maybe they cried because the sermon moved them and they realized that they needed to fight the devil's bad vibes. Or, they cried because they were starving. They weren't allowed to eat processed foods like the other Americans because it was against their religion. The only thing allowed by their god was mason jars full of threateningly organic kale, quinoa, and a squeeze of lemon. The flavorlessness of the kale salad was intentional. Not only did their god demand that the food was flavorless and organic, but it also had to be sourced within five miles of where they lived. If it wasn't, they were judged harshly by their religious peers. Delicious foods (like pancakes) were a sin. Remember! Pleasure is a sin and penitence is a virtue. The women would occasionally indulge in these evil pleasures at a religious ritual known as Sunday brunch. But then they had to pay for their sins the next day by beating themselves on the back with a leather belt. Just kidding. They just had to do extra cardio.

The billionaires of San Francisco are famous for being pious in their choice of clothing. No loud colors. No conspicuously expensive labels. They hide their wealth in the same way they hide the fact that they own everything, and therefore are the exact opposite of the Jaebol of Korea who cover everything they own with the name ShamShung and the monogram of Louis Vuitton. Their lack of flashiness is a mark of their status in the ecology of San Francisco. The only thing missing from Steve Jobs's turtleneck was that stupid white thing. Mark Zuckerberg's wife has a wedding ring that is small and inexpensive; this is the mark of her high status and religious purity. They look down on people who show off their wealth with luxury handbags and sports cars because it shows they are further away from God than they are. Gucci belt buckles are a sin.

This type of rich person is not exclusive to that city. They exist in Brooklyn, Portland, Copenhagen, LA, and at this point any large city that has a substantial white population, liberal or not. These are the alt-rich people. They're like the Christian missionaries who wear tie-dye and Birkenstocks. They think this makes them completely different from the missionaries who wear suits and have military haircuts. The funniest thing about these people is that they want so badly to display their wealth, but their religion insists on their forced modesty. But you can literally see on their faces how badly they want to wear the shiny things. Instead of wearing a Birkin and a Cartier bracelet, they go to parties dressed in $1,300 nondescript linen potato-sack jumpsuits, $900 nondescript Swedish wooden clogs, and *New Yorker* totes. There they are met with twenty other people who are all wearing the same exact getup. Sister wives. Then they have a little orange wine. After a few hours, this civil get-together mutates into a group of drunk millionaire white people screaming over one another about how they just bought a house in Montauk or how their kid goes to school with Chloë Sevigny's kid or how they just bought a horse farm in Bolivia. They start telling everyone their potato-sack jumpsuit costs $1,300 BUT IT'S WORTH IT because it's made by women in Cambodia who are paid a "living wage" ($5 a day). They try so hard to hold in their pride and be good, modest Christians. But that orange wine goes straight to their heads because their stomachs are only full of kale and a squeeze of lemon—the body and blood of Christ.

*   *   *

WORKERS

AT THE VERY BEGINNING OF Mission Chinese Food, this rift between Danny and me came into play. I related with the people whom I thought were my socioeconomic group while Danny sided with the wealthy, whom he aspired to be part of. The people who worked at Mission were my friends from former restaurant jobs. They were chaotic, fun, and authentic, and all came from similar poor backgrounds. After a while, some conflict started between them and the owners of the restaurant. The family who owned Lung Shan ran the restaurant in a different way than the servers were used to. Danny and I were spared a lot of the resentment from the staff because we were technically also employees.

In the US, there is a belief that poor people are the ones who are the most susceptible to religious indoctrination, but I don't think it's the fact that they're poor, I think it's the fact that they have been made to believe *they're* the ones with original sin. Poor people are always believed to be inherently bad while rich people are believed to be good. For that reason, poor people think they're the ones in need of being cleansed. However, wealth or the lack of it has nothing to do with virtue. The people I met in the US from my class were "bad" in the sense that they stole and cheated. However, so did the rich people. The only difference was that the poor people were always punished for it. They were always made to admit to it while the rich were not. In this way, the poor seemed trustworthy to me, because if they did something wrong, they owned up to it. They went to jail for it. They got fired for it. Yet the rich people who caused recessions and went to Epstein Island never ever, ever, ever did. Rich people in San Francisco reaped all the benefits of Christianity while the poor absorbed all the blame.

This is why when the servers started stealing money from Mission, I took their side. In their eyes, they believed it was payback for their unfair treatment by the owners. At Mission, we would write all the checks on pieces of paper and turn the checks in with all the cash at the end of the night. Some servers started throwing away these paper checks and just pocketing the entire amount. The restaurant was so busy that it was barely noticed, but the owners, who were seasoned restaurateurs, could always tell. They had no proof, so it went on for a while, until one server threw away a check that had a king crab on it. King crabs were ordered in advance, and since the owner knew how many were ordered in one night, she could tell that one check was missing. The server responsible was fired, and the resentment grew.

I got into an argument with Danny over this. I defended the servers. I didn't think that our friend should've been fired. I knew that they were wrong, but I also agreed with their complaints against the owner. Danny was the brains of the operation; it was his gift that propelled the project into astronomical success. But I also had a gift: a gift to be a mediator and to listen to people. The servers would come and complain, and I would listen and advocate for them. I think—for a lot of them—my presence was what smoothed over their resentment. I think I also smoothed over Danny's hostility toward the staff who were stealing. Danny had been brought up in the kitchen and, like most kitchen staff, resented who they thought were drunk, careless front-of-house employees who came in for way shorter shifts and collected larger sums via tips. But after this argument, Danny "fired" me. He went up to the calendar on the wall and angrily Sharpied out any time my name was written on the schedule. That was the last time I worked at Mission Chinese Food. It was January 2012. From then on, I stayed home, as a stay-at-home wife and soon a stay-at-home mom.

Mission Chinese went on to become a huge success. We opened a few restaurants in New York. But this rift stayed between me and Danny. In my mind, I was a poor person. In his mind, he was a rich person who had accidentally been born poor. It caused us to behave in two very distinct ways. I believe it also eventually led to the ultimate failure of Mission Chinese.

*   *   *

BIRKIN

THE RISE AND FALL OF Mission Chinese can be detected covertly through my Instagram feed. From 2011 on, Danny started making a bunch of money doing endorsement deals and sponsorships. He had an appearance fee in the tens of thousands. My Instagram feed was speckled with conspicuous yet strategically placed markers of wealth. These photos map the expeditious rise of Danny's success, as well as our move from San Francisco to New York City. The fine-dining meals posted from San Francisco and the Bay Area were shortly followed by meals from three–Michelin Star places in New York City. Then Paris. Then San Sebastián. Then Tokyo. Then a pair of suede Miu Miu pumps. Then a picture of me and Danny in a loft apartment with black hardwood floors in Little Italy in Manhattan. The apartment is empty save for a giant crystal chandelier. Then a picture of me in Copenhagen, wearing a gold-buttoned white Fendi dress. Then a picture of food at Noma. Then a bunch of pictures of food in restaurants in New York City. Then a picture of a Chanel classic flap bag. Then a picture of a line that wraps around the block in front of Mission Chinese Food on Orchard Street in the Lower East Side. Then a picture of us on the red carpet at the James Beard Awards; Danny is wearing Fendi and I'm wearing Alexander Wang. Then a picture of Danny inside a limousine, staring at the gold James Beard medallion around his neck.

Then the birth of our son, Mino. James Mino Bowien was born on February 18, 2014, at NewYork-Presbyterian Lower Manhattan Hospital. The markers of success and wealth continued as a backdrop to his development. On the day he was born, next to a post of him fresh out of the womb, is a post showing me eating $300 worth of sushi from Sushi Yasuda in my hospital bed. The day I brought him home from the hospital, I posted a picture of him next to a Mansur Gavriel tote that was Celine Luggage Tote–levels of hard to get in 2014. Mino's first solid food at five months old was sushi rice at Tsukiji Fish Market. He took his first steps at eleven months old in the Bulgari Hotel in Milan. His first fine-dining meal was at L'Arpège when he was one year old. The pictures of our apartments changed from the open loft in Nolita, to a two-bedroom in a luxury building in the Lower East Side, to a two-floor apartment in NoHo. Danny got me a Birkin for my thirtieth birthday. For some reason, the Birkin was the one thing I didn't post. I think even I knew this was too fucking much.

*   *   *

NO MORE BIRKIN

DESPITE MY INSTAGRAM FEED BEING straight fucking fire during this era, I was miserable. I had suffered from depression all my life. I distinctly have a memory of being in the fourth grade and seeing an ad for antidepressants and realizing I had all the symptoms. The actress in the commercial was a dreary-ass-looking woman wearing a beige cardigan and holding a mug of tea. It seemed impossible that she and I were one and the same. I didn't tell anybody, mostly because no one was home. Even if my parents were home, if I told them I was depressed they would've told me it was because I was too fat to move around so it was my fault.

My understanding of depression is that it's caused by the withholding of negative emotion. Emotions occur naturally, and a lot of time without rationality. To withhold them is to deny your body a biological function. With nowhere to go, the withheld emotions settle to the bottom like the sediments in a bottle of natural wine. After time, the sediments make up most of the bottle that is your mental capacity. The bottle of wine ferments and is under great pressure. This is the anxiety that comes hand in hand with depression.

My entire life, I was made to withhold negative emotions. Displaying them would cause me to get punished and ridiculed. Displaying them would deem me the villain. If I cried because of something my mom did, my mom would cry louder, leading me to apologize. What I learned was that there was never any room for my emotions, and showing them would only lead to me being hurt more. But I was

189

holding in something else: my hopes and dreams. All my life I wanted to be so many things: an artist, a writer, a comedian, an actor. But every time I would hint at my dreams, my mother would mock me and say that I wasn't good enough. I learned to hide my dreams from the world, while also learning that I was not good enough to achieve any of them.

I was in this state of depressed withholding when I got married. Being married made it ten thousand times worse. All the dreams I was too afraid to say out loud were still inside me, and now I was devastatingly far away from that life. I was a waitress who had married a line cook who randomly got famous, and now I was a housewife. No handbag was expensive enough to make the pain of that go away. Not even a Birkin.

I used to wonder why I got married when there was no one telling me to do so. Then I realized that there was someone who made me do it. They made me do it nearly one hundred years before I got married.

My great-grandfather forced me to get married when he forced my fifteen-year-old grandmother to. What she learned was that she didn't deserve her dreams. She wasn't born to live her life; she was born to take care of a man. She passed that down to her daughter, my mother. My mother passed that down to me. Because my grandmother had lost her dream, she beat out any dreams my mother had as well. My mother learned that her dreams must be swallowed. She married any man who would have her. She taught me to do the same. When I met Danny and he seemed to like me, I married him immediately. I was taught that I was nothing, and for anyone to want me was a privilege. I married a poor, hardworking man because that's what I thought I deserved. Just like my grandfather, Danny randomly became rich and successful. Just like my grandmother and my mother, I was deeply depressed because I believed that I wasn't allowed to live my dreams.

Then Mino was born. And I realized that I had value. I had value because Mino was so special, which meant that his mother had to also be special. It is ironic that to see my worth as a human being, I had to see it through my proximity to someone else. Then I realized something else. I didn't learn that I had to be a woman who took care of a man from the words of my mother. In fact, she rarely, if ever, talked about the obligations to get married and have children as a woman. I learned this through her actions. All my life, my mother said things that were the opposite of what she was doing. She told me I could do anything I wanted, while waiting hand and foot on a man she allegedly hated. She never told me I had to do the same, but she didn't realize I wasn't just listening to her—I was watching her.

A lot of women stay in unhappy marriages because they assume it is beneficial to their children. My mother used to say she stayed with our horrible father for our sake. But by staying in unhappy situations, these women teach their children the extremely harmful lesson that their lives are supposed to be like that. They teach them that misery is to be expected and that happiness isn't worth fighting for. If I showed Mino the same behavior, he would grow up thinking marriage was supposed to be torture and women were supposed to sacrifice their lives for his benefit (if his partners turn out to be cishet women). I couldn't let that happen.

I got a divorce. I moved out. I moved into a shitty apartment. I call it that because the first time Mino came over, he said, "This is a shitty apartment."

I had to sell my Birkin a few months after my divorce to pay three months of back rent, but I still have a handful of luxury handbags, jewelry, and shoes. They sit on a shelf made of plywood in my bedroom. Every once in a while, I'll sell one off when I run out of money.

I started doing stand-up comedy after my divorce and making Internet comedy content. All of the Mission Chinese restaurants in New York City eventually closed, and as part owner, I am in a terrifying amount of debt. With the debt, I am even poorer than I was when I met Danny.

I found the shiny rock in the dirt while I was digging for worms. I washed it off in the river, and I saw all the stars of the heavens in it. To me it stood for something. I saw something in it that was beyond value. The shiny rock was taken from me, but truthfully, it never belonged to me. The shiny rock now sits on the finger of a rich man's girlfriend. But I realized that the value it had to me, what it represented, was never inside the shiny rock. It was inside of me. I was the shiny rock. I didn't need it. I never needed it. All I needed was to be able to shine.

And Mino.

*　*　*

[UNNAMED RAP GROUP]

THE YEAR BEFORE I GOT divorced, 2017, was pretty epic. I started microdosing mushrooms and painting at home. I took the mushrooms all day long, and most days I was pretty high by noon. A few months went by like this. In the summer, Danny met a famous rap group (whom I will refer to as "Unnamed Rap Group Which May or May Not Have White Members in It" or URGWMOMNHWMII) and he was going to go on the Mexican leg of their tour with them. He said he was leaving straight from work and wouldn't be back for a few days. I was like, OK????? Danny later called me from Tulum and told me to meet him there. Mino and I flew to Cancun and took a car from the airport to Reserva de la Biósfera Sian Ka'an, which was a nature reserve south of Tulum. The reserve was closed off to the public at night, except for people who owned homes in it. URGWMOMNHWMII had rented a mansion on the beach there, giving us access to this exclusive rich-people place.

When I got there, I immediately saw one of the members, who was known as the actual star of the group (who may or may not be white) and whom I'll call "Rap Group Member 1," getting out of an infinity pool. She had a very specific hairdo (which I will not describe in any detail), body modifications, and tattoos, which gave her the appearance of an alien. She did these body modifications to mask the fact that she was a conventionally attractive (may or may not be white) woman. Without the artsy haircut and tattoos, she would look like the hottest girl in Dallas, Texas.

I was really high on mushrooms as I watched her walk out of the infinity pool in slo-mo like she was the hot mom in an eighties movie, water dripping off her body as she tossed her hair and stared seductively into a camera that wasn't there. I introduced myself to her and two backup dancers. Later I met another member (who also may or may not be white) whom I'll call "Rap Group Member 2." RGM2 and RGM1 may or may not have been a couple. According to some of the other guests staying with them, RGM2 was sleeping with some or all of the backup dancers and everything had come to a head right before I got there. That explained why RGM1 would randomly burst into tears and drearily walk around by herself all day throughout the vacation. The backup dancers were also extremely attractive and were dressed in string bikinis and Insane Clown Posse–esque rubber Halloween masks at all times. They were openly hostile toward me because I think they thought I was just another ho looking to fuck Rap Group Member 2. One of them even flipped me off when I said hi to her. I was terrified of them and spent most of my time hiding in my room, coloring with and reading books to Mino.

At one point they asked us to go zip-lining with them. We took a private Mercedes van to the zip line located in the middle of the jungle, over crystal clear beautiful cenotes. We followed RGM2 onto the four-story-high wooden platform that the zip line took off from. RGM1 and the dancers sat on the beach and watched us. RGM2 was high as shit and started explaining his theory on race. He was spit-screaming and using the N-word a lot (which he possibly could or could not use depending on if he was or was not white). He said white people seemed to be better at most things but he couldn't understand why Asians were better at some things. He said the only explanation for this was that Asians were aliens sent to fuck with white people. He sort of threateningly screamed this to Danny and me, and I started feeling anxious that he was mad at us for being Asian.

He got so wrapped up in his storytelling that he forgot to keep walking up the plank. At some point unbeknownst to RGM2, a large tour bus dropped off a bunch of British tourists who lined up behind us. I was concerned that the Brits would get angry that there was some crazy-looking tattooed dude holding up the line. I tried to step away from RGM2 so it would appear that Danny, Mino, and I were just a nice Chinese tourist family that unfortunately got stuck behind him. However, the tourists were not upset at all because they recognized RGM2 as a celebrity. They started excitedly whispering among themselves and listened patiently to his deranged race theory, sneaking in selfies with him in the background.

RGM2 realized his audience had grown and started spit-screaming even louder so even the people in the back could hear. At this point, he was describing the physical features of Asians that gave away their alien ancestry. For some reason this part also included a lot of him using the N-word (which he possibly was or was not allowed to say). The tourists never lost their patience, even when RGM2 started pointing at them and screaming, "Why are you all so fat? You're disgusting! Ya gonna make this whole thing collapse!! Get back!!" They sort of all nodded like he was right. He was a celebrity, and he was allowed to do whatever he wanted, including body-shaming his fans.

RGM2 suddenly remembered where he was after calling all the tourists fat and walked up to the top. The zip line guy hurriedly hooked me and Mino up, anxious about how long the line had gotten. Mino said, "Mommy, I'm scared!" But I had no choice but to hurriedly jump off because RGM2 started screaming, "Asians are aliens!" again. We whizzed off the platform and flew through the tops of the jungle as his "Asians are aliens!" got softer and softer behind us. Mino started laughing. At the end he said, "Again! Again!"

RGM2 seemed to really enjoy the power he had over the British tourists. I didn't understand any of it. Why would you want to listen to someone so stupid and racist, even if he was a famous rapper? Why did it matter that he was "famous"? He sucked. Why did RGM2 want the power to hold tourists hostage on a zip line platform? What did that do for him? Everyone around him seemed to hate him. Even RGM1 seemed to be dying to get away from him. I was thankful at first that they invited us on vacation with them but quickly realized that none of this shit was worth being around RGM2. Not the mansion. Not the free zip-lining. Not even being really high on mushrooms the entire time made it bearable. By the end of our few days there, I was dying to get away from that weird, racist asshole.

Multiple accusations have been made against URGWMOMN-HWMII on credible media outlets in the following years, and I believe all of them because I witnessed similar behavior firsthand. This was one of the more intimate experiences I had with celebrities of this caliber, and I walked away being really confused why anyone would want to be around them. The strange thing was that during the entire trip, we were surrounded by people who were bending over backward just to treat them well. Everywhere we went, hotel concierges, airport workers, restaurant managers, business owners, drivers, and their own crew—including the dancers being (ALLEGEDLY) sexually exploited by them—treated them like gods. I realized that for RGM2, this was the entire reason he had sought out being famous. I am sure he loved creating art and music, or felt like he had something to say. But I don't think that was his true goal. What he seemed to want was to be elevated on any platform, no matter how pathetic, like a zip line platform. There, however slightly, he was above everyone else. His wanting of this elevation, and the automatic respect it earned from the British tourists, made me view celebrity with disdain.

* * *

ANTHONY BOURDAIN

LATER THAT YEAR, IN OCTOBER, Danny was scheduled to film a promo
with Anthony Bourdain because they had shot a documentary film
together about food waste. To promote the film, they booked a seg-
ment in one of those TV shows that plays inside yellow cabs. Danny
asked me to come to Mission Chinese to help with the filming. By then,
Mission Chinese on Orchard had closed due to a rodent infestation.
Danny and Anthony (Myint) had purchased an outdoor space that had
been converted illegally to an indoor space. When the rodent-control
guy came, we explained that we were spending $2,000 a week on pest
control but couldn't get rid of them. The rodent-control person said of
course not. He said essentially the restaurant was a few pieces of wood
nailed to the dirt and there was no way we could keep animals "out"
because we were . . . outside. The landlord had scammed us into literally paying for a patch of dirt between four buildings. So the restaurant was moved to a real space on East Broadway.

During this era, Danny was always on TV. He did *The Tonight Show*
a few times and even shot an entire series of a travel cooking show. He
was also pretty friendly with Anthony Bourdain to the point that they
texted each other all the time and Bourdain seemed to actually talk to
him like they were buds. Nevertheless, it made him extremely nervous
to be around Bourdain. It made all of us nervous. We couldn't look past
our own feelings to notice that Bourdain also seemed very nervous and
was smoking a lot outside. He kept trying to talk about Harvey Weinstein, but none of us had really been paying attention to the story at that
point. Also, we were shocked to be in his presence and couldn't communicate with him like a regular human being.

This was a day or two after the *New York Times* had released the
article outlining Harvey Weinstein's abuse that led to the Me Too

movement. Although most people remember how huge that story was, I think a lot of people forgot that for a few days, the article was actively being buried by Weinstein's team. It took a solid week for the story to push past the suppression and blow up. Bourdain was in a state of panic because his partner at the time was one of the main victims coming forward and it was looking like the story was going to be swept aside. He was jittery throughout the shoot. Looking back, I realized he was showing so many signs of emotional turmoil, but none of us were picking up on it because we were overwhelmed by his celebrity. It's like he walked up to us after being in a car crash, asking for help, and all of us were just like, "Oh my god!! Are you Anthony Bourdain??!?" None of us noticed he was covered in blood.

After he died, when people were in disbelief that someone so famous and beloved could've taken his own life, I thought of this incident. I thought of how lonely it must've felt. He looked just as sad as RGM1 had in Mexico.

I think what I learned by being around super famous people is that some people become famous because they're just genuinely good at something. They go out in the world, showing everyone who they are, and people genuinely love them. Like Anthony Bourdain. But then there are people who have nothing inside of them. They only want fame because they want the power to hold a busload of British tourists hostage. Like RGM2. Then they spew garbage out of their mouths that barely makes any sense about how Asians are aliens. The two types of famous people are real ones and grifters.

*   *   *

RICH AND SAD

DANNY IS A REAL ONE. He became famous because he had a gift. Although it's hard for people to recognize which celebrities are grifters or not, their own peers can make that distinction. I just look at how their own community treats them. Danny had the respect of all the famous chefs of the world because they recognized he was one of them. An obsessive savant. At this point, Danny wasn't a household name like Bourdain or RGM2, but he was very famous in his circle. It's hard to describe what it's like to be in the proximity of this kind of celebrity because it's a world of extremes. In his industry, he was a superstar and was treated as such at restaurant-related events, but the general public had no idea who he was and treated him like a normal person, a.k.a. like shit. He would get invited to exclusive events and have a black car chauffeur him around and have cocktails and hors d'oeuvres with Mario Batali, then come home to be mistaken for a Grubhub delivery driver by the doorman in our building.

The thing I found so sad about my few experiences with celebrities was that they were at arm's length from everyone else because no one was capable of seeing through the intense glass of fame to see that they were just people too. What to RGM2 seemed to be a desirable elevation, to Bourdain seemed like an unbearable distance. Away from humanity. Away from connection.

All his life, Danny had tried to establish secure connections with people after being abandoned by his biological mother. Unfortunately, all the people who were in charge of caring for him were abusive. I think what he learned from that was that human connection was inherently painful. I think he craved stable, authentic connections, but deep down inside he distrusted all of them. For that reason, he found comfort in the transactional relationships from people who wanted something from him. The transactional relationship of fans of fame. He could figure out exactly what they wanted because they told him what it was. He liked fame for the reasons I thought it was horrible: because it was isolating. He liked the people it drew to him for the same reason I hated them: they were fake. For him, it was comforting to be removed from everyone and everything, and for me it looked like the worst life imaginable.

By the time Danny and I got divorced, we were strangers. We were so distant that when we separated, it barely felt like anything had happened. Danny didn't come home, but he never had before. The divorce was smooth, and I moved out in a few months. I never felt sad. I felt relieved. I think Danny was sad at first, but then he started dating around and felt better. One of his first new flings was with some fashion designer who lived in Paris. I think it was important to him that this was her "title." The people I fucked after the divorce were interns and open mic comedians. We gravitated to the people we thought were in our socioeconomic class. Him, the top. Me, the bottom.

I cried exactly two times about the divorce.

The first time I cried was when I went into Mission Chinese after the divorce, and out of nowhere Danny had made everything black. The large dragon sculptures were spray-painted black, the banquettes were reupholstered in black leather, and all the plates, chopsticks, and tableware were replaced with black ones. It felt like walking into a morgue. All the lights were off because it was preservice. I cried alone in a dark, black dining room. I don't know if Danny did this subconsciously because he was sad about the divorce or if it was just the influence of the Balenciaga/*Matrix*/Y2K/future aesthetic of that era, but it moved me.

The second time was about a year after that. I woke up and suddenly I remembered the day when I came home from working a brunch shift as a twenty-three-year-old poor kid in San Francisco to find Danny sitting outside the apartment. He was wearing neon bicycle shorts and a threateningly low-cut tank top. He had long hair covering his face. He told me he quit his job. He was terrified of my reaction. He was scared because all his life, love was only given to him for good behavior. I remember seeing how upset he was and being confused because I didn't care what he did. I loved him no matter what.

I cried violently and bitterly. I cried because I had forgotten about that Danny. He had been replaced years ago by a cold, arrogant skinny guy who wore giant, ridiculous Balenciaga sunglasses and leather hal-ter tops. I cried because the Danny who sat on the sidewalk that day no longer existed.

And I missed him so much.

*   *   *

POOR AND HAPPY

MISSION CHINESE ENDED QUITE DRAMATICALLY yet gradually. The final years involved a racial-discrimination lawsuit, false accusations, clout-chasing grifters, and other juicy schadenfreude-inducing scan-dals. This is also all documented on my Instagram feed. I also covered it in my podcast *Feeling Asian*.

I feel conflicted discussing the racial-discrimination lawsuit because I want to make sure the victims are heard, but all of this happened during the time I was getting a divorce, and I was not present at all. The only thing I can really touch on is my experience. I was part owner of a business that ended up being a toxic workplace environment for a lot of people. The upper management and chefs turned out to be quite abusive, and the fact that I neglected my responsibilities as an owner is my fault. I think about all those years ago when Danny "fired" me for sticking up for the servers who stole tips. I think I should've stayed at the restaurant and advocated for people who worked there. But I didn't. I hated it there. I hated working at a restaurant. I had the option not to. A lot of the employees didn't. Only rich people have the privi-lege of having an option not to work at a restaurant. I had become the rich asshole. I remember during the Instagram pointing-fingers shit show that went down after the lawsuit, one of the former employees said that all I ever did was show up with my new Celine handbags. I laughed so hard when I read that comment. And then I cried. Because it was true. That's all I ever did. What a stupid idiot I was. What a stupid fucking cave girlfriend of the cave chief with a diamond stuck to her dirty fur. I deserved that.

The rift between how Danny and I thought of rich and poor people made Danny antagonistic toward the staff. He saw them as people who were attacking him and who wished for his downfall. I saw them as people we had to stand up and fight for. Except I wasn't there to stand up and fight for them. I left. Like a coward. Without anyone advocating for them, the staff was abused. They fought back. They were right to do this. I agree with them. I am proud of the people who stood up and sued Mission. I know that is a strange thing to say here because the lawsuit ultimately led to the failure of the business and attributed to a lot of my debilitating personal debt. But I am. I am proud of them. They did something I was not strong enough to do.

Sometimes I think about how much I fucking hate rich people. One of the things I hate most about them is that they seem to never do the right thing. A billionaire could end world hunger by giving up just a fraction of their wealth. But they never do.

I was also given an option. And I did the wrong thing. I ran away.

I am no longer rich. I live in a shitty apartment and have a mountain of debt.

But I feel clean. I feel cleansed of the evil shiny rock I found in the dirt that made me terrified every second it was in my possession. It never belonged to me. It belonged to the people who are cold and sociopathic enough to think they deserve it. It belongs to Rap Group Member 2.

I am poor. I am happy.

CHAPTER 11

Eternity

A MOMENT

ONE DAY IN DECEMBER 2017, I walked into my therapist's office, sat down on the couch, and told her I wanted to get a divorce. She had seen it coming. She had seen that I lived an ill-fitting life out of an obligation I didn't even know I'd made one hundred years before I was born. She asked me a few questions to make sure that divorce was something I truly wanted and that I was in a clear headspace, before telling me she supported my decision. Our session came to an end, and I felt relief, excitement, and fear. As I stood up from the couch, I said, "Oh, and one more thing. I want to be a stand-up comedian."

Mid-standing she said, "What?"

"I want to be a stand-up comedian."

"Oh, OK. How long have you wanted to do that?"

I went to grab my purse off a hook on the wall. "All my life."

I felt her staring at the back of my head.

"I've never heard you say . . ."

I turned around. "It's the first time I've ever said it out loud. But I've always wanted to."

"For all of your life?"

"All of my life. Since I can remember. Since I was a little kid."

She was surprised but smiled very big. She had not seen this coming. "Well, that's great! You should try out an open mic."

She opened the door and I walked out.

* * *

IT'S FASHION

THE DAY AFTER I SAID, "I want to be a stand-up comedian" for the first time in my life, I went to an open mic. I went to two more that week. The week after that I went to four. Then I went to two or three open mics every single night until I started getting booked on shows. I went to open mics and shows every night my son was with his dad for the next two years.

These years were a blur. My days were spent taking care of my kid, and my nights were spent doing stand-up. The comedy shows I did were usually for rooms of three to seven people in the back of dive bars. Sometimes I did shows in comedy clubs for huge rooms of tourists, which was somehow a million times worse than performing for three drunk people in Bushwick. I performed in the worst basement shitholes you could ever imagine, sometimes taking hour-long subway rides to the outskirts of the city. I performed at a Jewish retirement home (they hated it). I performed at a jazz club in the Upper East Side for extremely wealthy people (they hated it). I performed at a seafood restaurant by the train station in Yonkers (they...kind of loved it?). But all of it was horrible. I was so bad at stand-up, but I insisted on doing it every night. I have absolutely zero memory of anyone ever laughing at any of my jokes. To be fair, I think it was because a lot of my jokes were about extremely niche parts of being Korean or biracial. I had a joke about laughing and crying at the same time and my butthole being hairy. The audience was confused because they thought I was going to go the generic Korean route and didn't know how to respond to niche Korean content. For

203

some reason, stand-up audiences are stuck in the nineties. They heard the word *Korean* and anticipated a dog-eating joke or a joke about Kim Jong Un. Occasionally, a rogue Korean person in the audience would shit their pants laughing at something I said, but that was it. I also told jokes about my sex life as a single mom, which made everyone uncomfortable. I discovered that no one wants to hear about someone's mom sucking dick and eating ass. In these beginning years, my career went nowhere. I was the happiest I had ever been in my entire life. Finally, for the first time, I was doing something I wanted to do. And I fucking sucked at it. How glorious.

I think people might think my late start into a creative career was because I was afraid of failure. But it wasn't that at all. I believed I didn't even deserve failure. I had lived my entire life thinking I didn't even deserve the right to say, "I want to do stand-up." I didn't deserve to even try.

I kept my dream of being a comedian a secret from everyone for so long because my mom destroyed all my dreams as a child. When I was small, I would test-run telling my mom small side dreams I had. I knew I could tell her these small dreams because even if she destroyed them, they weren't the main one. In high school, I remember telling her that I wanted to be a fashion designer. This was a side-quest dream I had had since middle school. Every day I made myself draw four different "looks" in a page of a sketchbook. By the time I brought it up to my mom, I had stacks of sketchbooks in my room. She never noticed them or bothered to look through them. When I told her I wanted to be a fashion designer, I was prepared to show her my sketchbooks to prove to her that I was worthy of having this dream. I didn't even get that far. As soon as I said the words, she did a 코방구 (ko bangu; "nose fart," a phrase describing a short sigh through the nose to show mocking disbelief) and said, "You think you're some cool person from Paris? Someone like you could never be a fashion designer. No one would take you seriously."

I believed her. I couldn't be a fashion designer because I was a loser. But I still had this desire to create clothes. So, I decided I would just make the cool things I couldn't afford to buy for myself. One day I saw a really cool skirt in a Delia's magazine. It was super low-rise and hit at the calf, fanning out at the bottom. I could see immediately that this skirt was just a pair of jeans that had been cut on the inseam, then sewn open with a triangular pattern in the front and back. I had an old bag of jeans I had grown out of and I decided to try to make the skirt since my parents would never buy it for me. I undid the inseam of one pair of jeans and sewed in panels of square denim I cut out from another. I kept the button fly intact but cut the back of the waist-band and added an extra panel of denim so the too-small jeans would become low-rise. I finished the skirt. It wasn't amazing and was very clearly sewn by an amateur, but I thought it sort of looked like those high-fashion looks made with raw, frayed denim. I was happy with it. I wore it to school one day, making sure my mom didn't see me leaving the house. I instinctively knew I couldn't show it to her. When I came back home, I could hear her in the living room with a friend. My mother's friends were always the cruelest, skinniest, most heavily perfumed Korean women from church. The fact that my mom met them all at church always confused me because they seemed like the least "Christian" people you could ever meet. For them to make it to heaven would be harder than it would for a camel to pass through the eye of a needle for sure.

These women were way skinnier than my skinny mother and always wealthy. My mother's friends were always rich because she enjoyed being "poor" by comparison. She humored them with her funny stories of working hard and being married to a lazy man. The bulk of their conversations revolved around her making fun of my dad and her own pathetic existence. This was valuable to the wealthy women because they could feel superior and all of their hardships seemed relatively frivolous. They would share stories about how their husbands couldn't stop fucking prostitutes, but then my mom would tell a story about how she didn't have enough money to buy food for her kids. Then she would add a joke about me being fat despite not having enough food, because not only did she openly share these self-deprecating stories with ease, she had the ability to make them funny. She knew exactly when to pull the plug when shit got too depressing. The rich women would laugh, feel better about themselves, and then pay for her dinner or buy her a Louis Vuitton scarf. Both parties benefited. Symbiosis.

That day, I could hear my mom in the living room with one of these skinny, rich church women. I walked in and quickly shuffled through the living room, bowing and saying a polite hello while averting my eyes. I saw peripherally that they were sitting on the couch; my mother was probably in the middle of some story about how my dad sucked and was faced away from me. However, the skinny, rich woman was facing me and quickly picked up on the fact that I appeared to be trying to not be seen. She saw the poorly sewn denim skirt and said, "어모! [Oooh!] Youngmi, did you make that skirt??"

I looked at her peripherally with my back still turned and said with a shy laugh, "네? 어 . . . 네." (Yes? Oh . . . Yes.)

The skinny, rich woman said, "완전 패션이다!" (It's fashion!)

My mother glanced at me, seemingly annoyed that someone else was getting her rich benefactor's attention, and said, "Yeah. It looks really good. Too bad you're too fat to wear something low-rise."

At the time, I took what she said at face value. I thought I looked fat and that fat people didn't deserve to wear nice clothes or become fashion designers. Later, I thought back to that time and realized this was during my peak bulimia days. So why would she have said that? Was it because she knew I was hypersensitive to that particular insult? But even then, why would it matter if I was fat? What did being fat have to do with being creative? Why couldn't I wear something I made proudly just because I was fat? I didn't have the logical adult mind I have now to question my mother's own motives. I just went with what she said. I never made anything ever again. I threw away all the sketchbooks that she had never even bothered to look through.

Later as an adult I realized she was just using me for comedic relief. The skinny, wealthy woman was giving me a compliment, and the three of us were having an intimate and touching moment. A moment where a woman gives a girl validation and guidance for coming into her own. My mother was uncomfortable with this because she saw me as an extension of herself. Her role in their friendship was to be the pathetic loser, and her daughter had to be the pathetic loser's daughter, or else the entire dynamic would be off. My mother had said that to make the rich woman laugh. And she did in fact laugh. She had not expected my mother to say something so cruel in a moment so sweet.

In comedy there is a theory about where laughter originates: the first laughter was a reflexive sound our primitive ancestors made when something extremely unexpected happened. The popular example is the story of a primitive man walking through tall grass. He sees shaking grass up ahead. He immediately raises his spear in fear and anticipation of a lion jumping out and killing him, but the wind blows and he sees that it's a pair of monkeys fucking. He lets out a sound, and this was our species' first-ever laugh. Relief.

My mom and her friend laughed from relief. Relief that they didn't have to think about the fact that maybe I was good at something. Because if I was good enough, that meant they were probably good enough to achieve whatever dreams they gave up on when they were little girls. And that thought was too painful. They didn't want to think about it. They wanted to laugh.

* * *

FAILING AT SUCCESS

IN ORDER TO PROTECT MY real dreams from being destroyed by my mom, I pretended to not have any dreams. She saw my uninterest and criticized it as a lack of passion. My two options were either to be into something and be told I wasn't good enough to do it, or to not be into anything and be told I had no passion. In middle school she told me to join the volleyball team because she had loved playing volleyball as a girl. I did and I was extremely bad at it. This hobby was perfect because it was safe for both of us. It was safe for me because I didn't care about it enough for her criticisms to hurt me. It was safe for her because I would never be that good at it, and therefore never stoke her jealousy.

Unfortunately, since I didn't care about it, I allowed myself to try really hard and eventually got kind of good. I was placed into the varsity team as a sophomore and got to travel to Okinawa as part of the official teen volleyball team for Saipan. Around this time, without my understanding why, I quit volleyball altogether. I quit by just not showing up to practice. My coach tried to contact me multiple times to ask what was going on but eventually stopped calling. One day he drove to my house and told me I had won an island-wide award for Most Improved Player and the award ceremony was happening in a few hours at a fancy resort nearby. He said the local newspaper was going to be there and it would be great if I went because the team would be recognized. I said I would go. I didn't go.

Although I didn't receive that award that night, throughout my life I had received many trophies and awards for being good at things I didn't care about. I threw all of them away just like I threw all my sketchbooks away.

I threw away my awards and hid my dreams from my mother,

because if she saw them, they would hurt her. Just like her awards and dreams had hurt her mother.

I was never afraid of failure. I was afraid of success.

* * *

SUCCEEDING AT FAILURE

I LOVED STAND-UP BECAUSE EVEN when you succeed at stand-up, it is a failure. Because you're still standing in front of four people in a basement. Success in stand-up is making four drunk people laugh. Even when a stand-up comedian becomes so successful they're selling out multiple nights at Madison Square Garden, they're still sort of…pathetic? There's something about the medium that is inherently pathetic. I loved doing something where even being good at it was pathetic. I loved the failure. I thrived in it. Because of the years of stifling my dreams, the pain and humiliation of failure made me feel alive. It felt as if I had been stuck at the starting line for thirty-three years, and now that I was actually running, my body burned with the pain of sprinting. But I never regretted it for a second, because I could still remember the absolute horror of being stuck for an eternity. An eternity of nothing.

Now that I said the fake, humble Korean thing to appease my mother, I must say the truth. The truth is that I didn't suck at stand-up. I had a natural knack for it. I was good at it. Within two years, I was getting booked on shows other comedians of my caliber could only dream of. A lot of them were white guys who would constantly accuse me of getting shows as a "diversity hire." LOL. Those fucking idiots were jealous I was getting booked for a show at some horrible place like the Grisly Pear. It brings me joy to say that they truly sucked at stand-up. Some of them had been doing it for years before I did and couldn't land one joke.

Stand-up was the perfect medium for me because it required a lot of hard work for very little reward, and I hated reward.

* * *

LEFT-HANDED

AFTER MY DIVORCE, I HAD to reacquaint myself with dating. Right away, I got into two relationships back to back. These relationships were not good and I saw a pattern of behavior I was replicating over and over. Then I realized I had not gone longer than maybe three months without being in a relationship since I was seventeen. So I decided to force myself into a year of being single.

What I was trying to do with this year of being single was to heal myself of the idea that I had value because of my proximity to a man. I had to stand in my own worth. To change this perspective in my mind felt a lot like retraining an incorrect movement of muscles. When I was playing volleyball in high school, I served the ball right-handed, even though I was a lefty. I did this because I thought I was only allowed to use my right hand. One day I overheard my coach talking about how amazing left-handed servers are because their serves go in unexpected directions, secretly making them the strongest players.

I told him I was actually left-handed, and he was like, why the fuck are you serving with your right hand, then? I set off to retrain my muscles to be able to serve left-handed. This is what it felt like to recenter my wants and needs in a relationship instead of doing whatever a man wanted. I was retraining myself to act in the way that nature intended, to serve left-handed—a thing that would've come naturally to me if I hadn't been taught to think it was wrong.

My therapist gave me "homework" and said I wasn't allowed to date people who approached me, but instead had to approach people I was attracted to. This is going to sound hilarious, but in my entire life it had never occurred to me to go after someone I was attracted to instead of just waiting for someone who seemed obsessed with me to roll through.

This was the first time in my life I did what I think people call "flirting." This was the first time in my life that I was rejected. I got into situationships with fuckbois (I'm so sorry, but I think I have to write it like that for official reasons) that tore me apart. I had casual sex with people who fell in love with me, but I would ghost them for fear of falling into a relationship. I broke people's hearts. I got my heart broken. I didn't just get my heart broken; I got it destroyed. It was fucking amazing. I felt alive. Not even halfway through the year of being single, I realized I loved this life. I couldn't imagine ever going back to being in relationships. I liked the chaos. I liked the excitement. I loved sleeping with two or three different people a week.

*   *   *

THE WOMAN

ONE NIGHT I WENT OUT to a birthday party. The party was for an acquaintance who was a comedy writer who I will call "Henry." He was successful. He wrote for a show. A good show. It wasn't *Big Mouth* but it was like *Big Mouth*. He told me he was feeling depressed because he was turning forty and he felt like a failure. He said he had some Molly but honestly didn't even feel like doing it. I grabbed him by the hunched shoulders and screamed, "Look!! This is what's going to happen! Let's go do the Molly and we will dance and then we will have sex and it will be great! It's going to be amazing!"

We went to the bathroom and took the Molly and started kissing. It was awkward because I thought my kissing him would put him in a better mood, but he was still mega bummed. I looked at him and kept screaming, "We're going to have sex!!" And finally, he started to seem

211

happier. "All right, all right! You're right. This is going to be fun! Let me go say goodbye to everyone, then we can head to my place!"

He disappeared into a crowd of comedians in their ironic oversized glasses and brown hoodies. Unfortunately, that's when the Molly kicked in for me. His roommate, a wild, tiny comic-book artist, who I will refer to as "Sam," was already hours deep into rolling. She had been aggressively thrashing around the dance floor all night, dry humping anyone who got in her way. We crashed into each other like two fucked-up dandelion stems twirling around the dance floor, squeezing each other's faces, and running our arms through each other's hair. We went to go pee together. This was a different bathroom. Maybe it was the same bathroom but it existed in another dimension. The walls were covered in mirrors. The mirrors created an infinity effect. This tiny Asian comic-book artist with severe cat-eye makeup and blunt bangs that turned into butt-length black hair, and me. I looked at our reflection. I was large. I was sweaty. I was hairy. I was a white person. It reminded me of first grade in Korea. Me: gigantic, grotesque, and manly next to all the tiny Korean girls. In this room we stood for an eternity, the ideal of Asian female beauty and me, whatever the fuck I was. There were billions of us. An eternity of us, over and over again. We had been there since the beginning of time. We stand there still. Alone.

We kissed.

We stumbled out of our eternity room and into her apartment two doors down. She took her clothes off to reveal large Asian-y tattoos covering her entire body, like, you know, lotus flowers and dragons. She pushed me onto the bed and started violently giving me head. She finger-fucked me hard but not like in that "frat guy who's actually fucking the side of your leg" way—like in an extremely talented way. I started coming and she slapped me across the face so hard that it snapped me out of it. She kept doing this until eventually my orgasm became so intense that even the most violent slaps couldn't stop it. She fucked me with a fury that no one has ever even come close to replicating. As I came, she yelled at me that I was a dirty whore bitch or something? I have no idea, but she was humiliating me for losing control and I agreed, it was humiliating. At one point she stopped because she heard someone coming in the front door. She put her finger to her mouth.

"Shh! It's Henry."

"What do you mean, it's Henry??" I whispered.

"Henry's my roommate. We literally talked about this all night last night!" she whispered back.

"Fuck my life. I told Henry I would have sex with him!"

Her eyes got wide. She slapped me across the face hard. We both started laughing, trying in vain to muffle our voices. We started fucking again. It was really loud. But not loud enough to drown out the sound of Henry's depressed sloshing around in the living room. I felt like I could hear every single depressed thing he was doing. He put a snack in the microwave. It was probably something sad like a pepperoni Hot Pocket or pizza rolls. He ate his snack on the couch—I could hear him slumped over. He brushed his teeth melancholically. He went to his room and closed the door.

The next morning, I was putting lipstick on in an attempt to draw attention away from the one side of my face that was swollen from all the slapping. I looked at Sam. She was rubbing her eyes. She looked cute. I turned back to the mirror and I could feel my brain recovering consciousness. In a moment of clarity, I turned to her again and gasped.

"Oh no!! I told Henry I would have sex with him!!"

Sam had lost all of the rage that had filled her the night before and had returned to a sweet, quiet comic nerd.

"Oh no!" she whispered.

We snuck out quietly and said goodbye and hugged by the entrance to the subway station. This was the last time I went out for nearly a year because the next day was March 14, 2020.

*   *   *

THE MAN

THERE'S NOTHING REALLY TO WRITE about the COVID-19 lockdown. All I'll say is that the first time I went out of my house with my son to get groceries a few days in, I had a scary encounter with a man on the street. He screamed, "Why aren't you people in hiding? You think we don't know it's your fault?!" while walking toward us at a quick, angry pace. I was holding my son's hand with one hand and holding three bags of groceries with the other. I let go of the bags in preparation to fight him, but I was too afraid to let go of my son's hand because he was still very young and I feared he would wander into the street. The man got so close to me that I pulled my balled-up fist up. He paused inches from my face and then angrily shoulder-checked me and walked away. After that, I only left the apartment when my son was at his dad's. I wanted to make sure that if I had to fight, I would have both hands free. I dyed my hair blue a month into lockdown partially to mask the fact that I was Asian.

Back to the dating, though. As soon as the lockdown began, I received a flurry of DMs from men who were alone at home or with their spouses. I got a DM from someone I knew in San Francisco confessing that he had been in love with me the whole time. He had been an excruciatingly handsome man, but I went to his profile and the years of binge drinking and cocaine had taken their toll. I sent him some nudes, though. Who cares. I got into long-distance text relationships with multiple people. I had late-night conversations with people I will never meet, confessing things I had never confessed before, listening to their confessions too. I never met up with anyone because I was filled with terror about the new virus that was sending ambulances screaming down First Avenue, where I lived at the time, all throughout the day and night. A few months in, Sam texted me that she was being deported. She came over. There was no talk. My son was there. We ordered sushi. I can't remember how. Did they deliver sushi during the height of the pandemic? We ate it standing up in the kitchen. We sat in the living room. She asked me, "What do you want from me?"

Maybe she meant it in a kinky way. Maybe she was trying to get some sexy sex talk in while my son watched his iPad in the other room. But I could not understand in what way she meant it, so I answered it the only way I knew how as an Asian woman who found herself in love with another Asian woman. "I don't know."

We were raised to think that our value and our identity came from the men we were with. But what if there is no man? What then? I think Sam was asking me to be the man. But I wasn't. I would never be the man. For some reason on my first birthday, a birthday thought of as extremely important for Koreans, my mother decided to dress me in a hanbok meant for a boy. For years after that, I was terrified that I had actually been born a boy and that no one told me. When I was on the playground as a young girl, the Korean girls in my class would tease me about my "boy hands." They would accuse me of having been born a boy. My little Asian mother wished for me to be a man, my little Asian classmates were convinced of it, and now Sam was wanting it. I didn't know what I wanted from Sam, but what she wanted was for me to be a man, because then our relationship would make sense.

"What do you want from me?"

"I don't know."

She flew out the week after.

My year of being single turned out to be close to two years because of COVID. My goal for this time was to relearn how to serve left-handed. My goal was to unlearn the idea that I needed a man. I did end up learning that but in a way I had not anticipated. The truth was we all need a man. My mother, Sam, all women, even all men. We all need a protector, an advocate, someone to stand up for us. We are all so small and weak and alone. We all need someone to give us value. What I learned was that I was the one who did that for other people and had been my entire life. All my life I had been searching for this man, and the entire time it had been me all along.

I was the man. A left-handed one, secretly the strongest one of them all.

*   *   *

FEELING ASIAN

WE REOPENED THE MISSION CHINESE on East Broadway briefly in the summer of 2020. It was a great time. I worked at the take-out window and Danny worked in the kitchen along with a skeleton crew of the staff. It felt like the old days when we first started Mission in San Francisco back in 2010. How things had changed in ten years. The restaurant ended up closing in the fall of that year, a victim of COVID-19. Danny thought I would be upset when we had to close it, but I was fine. All those years together and he still had not learned that I was not afraid of failure. But for a brief moment, it was what it had been so many years ago: a beautiful, glimmering success.

At this time, I had a popular Asian culture podcast called *Feeling Asian* with a fellow Korean stand-up comedian, Brian Park. We invited Danny onto the podcast to tell his story. Danny discussed his troubled past as a victim of narcissistic abuse, and how that abuse set him up for a life in the restaurant world. Danny is not a nice person to many people. I've seen tiny bits of his other persona when at work. I can understand why he is a polarizing figure. To me, though, he was always gentle and sweet but a little lost. An abandoned child, forever looking. Looking for what, I don't know. I feel like he's found everything one could find in life. But he still seems to be looking.

At the end of the podcast, we had a ritual where we asked each guest to state something they are proud of. Danny surprised me by saying he was proud of us. He looked at me and he had tears in his eyes. I, too, started crying. I had not been expecting him to say this. This was my standing-in-tall-grass moment. I thought a lion was going to jump out and kill me, but the wind blew and it was just my ex-husband saying something nice. Instead of laughing from relief, I cried.

These COVID times were an eternity. An eternity made up of moments.

CHAPTER 12

A Moment

> Eventlessness has no posts to drape duration on. From
> nothing to nothing is no time at all.
>
> —John Steinbeck, *East of Eden*

(Sorry, I really wanted to do that thing where a chapter starts with a
quote like I see in other books.)

NOTHING

EVEN THOUGH I HAVE A lot of difficult memories of my father, for the
most part he is a really interesting and good-natured person. He is also
extremely intelligent and well read. He told me he studied journalism at UC Berkeley and dropped out because he hated it, but then I
found his résumé on the family computer when I was a kid and saw
that he went to some community college in Redwood City. It fasci-
nates me that he lied about this my entire life. Part of the charade
was doing things he thought someone who studied journalism at UC
Berkeley would do. That included making me read books that were
at the high school and college levels when I was a small child. I read
books by Hemingway, Nabokov, Steinbeck, Fitzgerald—you know,
The Men™—all before my tenth birthday. This was really formative

for me because it made me a pompous asshole and also caused some severe anxiety. I remember reading *Animal Farm* when I was like eight and staying up for days, deeply disturbed by the death of Boxer, the hardworking horse sent to the glue factory as a reward for being a true believer. These books did to me what selling at the lemonade stand did to rich kids: they made me think I was better than other people because I did something at a young age that most people do later in life. By the time I was in high school, I suffered from romantic ennui, utterly unimpressed by the literature that moved my peers. I thought people being blown away by *The Catcher in the Rye* were idiots. I would roll my eyes exasperatedly like a fifty-year-old Gen Xer when someone mentions the Pixies.

"Oh, you mean the Pixies? Yeah, I know who they are. I used to go to college with the brother of the neighbor of the woman married to the drummer."

I read *East of Eden* as a young child and for some reason that quote has stuck with me all these years. It's strange because I barely remember anything else from the book or my life when I read it. I don't even remember how old I was, just that I was a child. If I were to guess, I think I read this book during one of the summers our house had no power and I rode my bike outside all day long and read by candlelight all night long. I remember nothing from this time because it was an eventless time between nothing and nothing and it was no time at all. The quote pierced through the nothing by naming exactly what I was going through. Even as a child, I was able to recognize it.

In the years I was married, this quote would pop into my head during birthdays, anniversaries, Mino's birthdays, New Year's. I remember feeling the passage of time, but it felt like it was no time at all. I remember seeing the number of years grow: my age, the years I was married, the years I lived in New York, the years since I quit smoking, the years since I started smoking, the years since Miley Cyrus stuck her tongue out at the VMAs, but the number didn't feel like anything. Because it was time between nothing and nothing. I was married for ten years (twelve if I'm counting from the secret city hall marriage) and it could've been a day. A moment.

* * *

HELL

ONE OTHER THING I READ has stuck with me all these years. It was in high school, in the class taught by Florida Santa, the villain from a few chapters ago who took away my dream of becoming a writer. Florida Santa was a lot like my father in that he was very well read and he loved discussing the Bible, not as a religious text but as a piece of fictional literature or, at best, a heavily biased account of history. I liked that he discussed it like a book written by The Men™ instead of the word of God. I remember one story vividly: the story of Lucifer.

Apparently, there are many iterations of the books of the Bible from surrounding cultures around that region. One version of the story is a Persian iteration, which states that Lucifer and God were in a romantic relationship (GAAAAYYY). Anyway, Florida Santa gave us this article to read that was written by a theologian who discussed how the Bible's version might've been heavily influenced by the Persian story, except they took out the romantic love part because, well, it was gay. Gay as hell. Literally. I vaguely remember that the modern Bible does state that Lucifer "loved" God, but Christians will say they meant it like love between two bro dudes. Like they said, "I love you, man!" to each other after a few beers and that was it. But if you think about it, if Lucifer and God were romantic partners, then the Lucifer story would make sense because the Bible version absolutely does not. In the Bible, it states that God made Lucifer the ruler of hell for the sins of pride and disobedience because Lucifer

220

refused to serve humans as his master. Why would God give him an entire world to rule for the sin of pride? That's like if he sent him to an all-you-can-eat buffet for the sin of loving Alaskan king crab legs. Plus the Bible says hell was the one place God didn't exist. But they made it sound like Lucifer was sick of God's controlling ass, so wouldn't being away from God also be a reward?

If you think of Lucifer and God as lovers, though, it all fits. Think of Lucifer as a first wife and God as a husband. God gets a second wife, humans, and tells Lucifer that humans are now above him in the hierarchy of the household. Lucifer is pissed but also sad because he loves God and wants to be God's only wife. Lucifer refuses, so God gets pissed and sends him out of his house. This completely makes sense as a punishment because Lucifer now lives in the one place where God doesn't exist. The one place love doesn't exist. For someone in love, being without their lover is hell.

I feel like this story was written by some stupid men two thousand years ago about their wives getting mad that they were going to marry their fourteen-year-old cousin. But they pretended God said all this so they could get away with it and pretend it was their wives who were sinning.

Who cares. The Bible is so fucking stupid. What I want to talk about is the fact that ancient humans thought of the worst feeling possible when inventing the idea of hell. And they were trying to tell us that their idea of hell was being in love with someone who didn't want anything to do with your ass. It's touching to understand that people thousands of years ago were petty and jealous and got their hearts broken too. I love their message because none of us can really conceptualize the pain of burning in a lake of fire for eternity, but we all deeply understand the pain of heartbreak. The pain of someone cheating on us. The pain of unrequited love. We know that an eternity of that would be, in fact, hell.

I had never been in love until this period of my life because I knew inherently that the loss of that love would be hell. I was too afraid of that pain. In this aspect, I was, in fact, afraid of failure. Terrified of it. So I waited around for other people who desired me and got into relationships with them. It was a cruel control tactic, but it's important to note I did it without knowing. It was a self-defense mechanism I was unaware of. However, I was the one who lost the most in these relationships because the people who were vulnerable enough to be in love with me were rewarded with true love, even at the expense of hell when the relationships ended. But I never felt anything. It's true I never got hurt, but I never felt the joys of being deeply in love. It wasn't until I let myself really love that I was able to experience what ancient Persians thought was hell, and that in turn made me realize that it wasn't hell at all. Nothing was.

*   *   *

NOTHING VS. HELL

WHAT I DISCOVERED WAS THAT hell wasn't the pain of truly living and then failing. Hell was where I came from. Hell was nothing. An eternity of eventlessness. The time between me riding my bike on Saipan as a small kid whose TV wasn't working and the first open mic I went to at the age of thirty-three was a moment. An eternity.

The year I spent being single was the year I spent trying to fall in love. I succeeded. And failed. It hurt a lot. But it was not hell.

Whenever you see depictions of Lucifer, he looks happy as hell. It's because he got sent to hell, only to discover what I did—that it wasn't the thing to fear. The thing to fear was feeling nothing and dying after a life of nothing. Lucifer told me the truth. I ran away with him to dance naked under the moonlight with a goat for some reason. I know that what I signed up for is an eternity of suffering, but it's OK because it means I get to live deliciously moment by moment. I am free from hell now, free from nothing. Free to fail.

I was never afraid of failure in my career. I am now no longer afraid of failure in love.

But I am terrified now. Because I'm succeeding.

CHAPTER 13
Death

BITCH

WHEN I WAS PREGNANT, I noticed something strange about how people who had already given birth would talk to me. They would congratulate me like everyone else, but then they would pause and stare silently into my eyes for a moment too long. I started calling it the "pregnant pause" and would point it out to Danny whenever it would happen. They all had the same look, blank yet intense, full of some sort of emotion. It's like they were trying to warn me or something. But what the hell were they trying to tell me? After giving birth, I understood exactly what it was, and I realized there is actually no way to explain it with words. They were communicating it the only way they knew how; the PTSD stare of a war vet whenever someone says they enlisted in the army.

I was never the kind of person who was dying to have a baby. In fact, I wasn't even sure I wanted to have a kid. The only reason I ultimately decided to do it was because I couldn't understand what it felt like. I noticed that people were really vague when explaining how it *feels* to have a kid. A common thing a parent will say to someone who isn't a parent is "It's the greatest love there is, and you won't understand it until you have one yourself." I felt the need to experience this thing that everyone was at a loss for words to describe. I didn't want to regret not knowing how it felt at the end of my life. I wanted to give birth before I died.

I think for a lot of people who really want kids and can't have them, this is one of the more painful parts of their loss. The idea that they don't even know what it is they lost. I wish there was a way to communicate that it is a profound loss, but also a profound gift to never be a parent. Yes, it's true. Not having a kid means missing out on a type of love that I, like every other parent, consider the deepest love of all, but it also means missing out on the most terrifying fear: the fear of death. Not your death, but something way worse: the death of your child. This is a disgusting feeling. It tethers humans to existence in a torturous way. It turns cool, sarcastic people into earnest try-hards. It makes hard people soft. It makes people cry at TV commercials. Not knowing this fear is worth never having a child. Having a kid is being hit by the truck that is life. Watching this truck pass you by might seem sad, but then again, you're not getting hit by a fucking truck.

The horror of imagining that your child might die is followed closely by another horror: breastfeeding. There is a good reason we are referred to as mammals, because breastfeeding makes you realize that's all your body was created to do, like other mammals. You realize there is nothing that differentiates you from a fucking kangaroo. When Mino was born, I turned into a boxing kangaroo. It felt as though a switch went off in my head. A switch that was in me since before any of us were human. I don't think I would describe the feeling I had after giving birth as love; it's more like a feeling that existed before we had emotions. I didn't feel love, I felt what a polar bear feels. I felt cow emotions. I felt whatever a hyena feels. I only had one thought in my mind: *BABY, LIVE*. I returned to this. I returned to what I really was. A mammal.

Before I gave birth, I read about the first week of breastfeeding. In case you haven't read about it, this is the basic info: On average it takes about two to five days for milk to come down or whatever. Newborns are desperately hungry during this time and will frantically attempt to nurse for the first few days of their lives. The repeated suckling action is the stimulus that sends the message to the mother's brain to start creating milk. The frequency of the suckling tells your body exactly how much milk it needs to make. During the days before milk flow, the breasts expel a tiny amount of a nutrient-rich oily substance called colostrum. It's a very small amount, so the newborn will naturally lose weight in the first week of life. Infant weight loss during this time is supposedly not dangerous since they're getting their nutritional needs met by the colostrum. Doctors have differing opinions but usually seem to be comfortable with a baby losing up to a pound (!) of weight during the first week.

None of that describes the absolute terror of the experience. The fucking baby thinks it's starving to death and screams and cries for twenty-four hours a day until enough milk comes through, meaning the first few days of having a baby, you go from not having a baby to having an angry, squirming larval thing scream-crying at you twenty-four hours a day. The pain of starting to breastfeed was nothing short of unbearable. Each person has a different experience but for me, breastfeeding felt like getting ten thousand paper cuts on my nipples for the duration my baby was latched on (usually thirty minutes to an hour). It took months for the skin on my nipples to harden enough for it to not feel like that. I developed a psychosomatic response to the pain called Raynaud's disease, where my body refused to send blood to my nipples. My nipples turned the color of a popsicle after you suck all the juice out. After nursing, I had extreme pins and needles in my entire torso for an hour. The pain was so unbearable, I couldn't get up. And then when the throbbing finally stopped, the baby was crying to nurse again. This went on every hour and a half to two hours night and day. I developed mastitis so bad that I needed to have "surgery," which was just the surgeon cutting my breast open to the muscle and squeezing green pus out while I was still awake. The doctor very matter-of-factly told me I would have to be awake because I had decided to keep nursing. I also wasn't able to take any of the Percocet he gave me, even though I wouldn't have anyway because Percocet was an opioid and would cause me to projectile-vomit. There was a hole in my breast from the nipple to the end of the breast meat. I had to change the gauze inside the hole by opening up the skin to see my breast muscle and fill it with a two-inch roll of medicated gauze every day. One day, I noticed that the bottom of my breast came to a head, like a giant pimple. I squeezed it because I thought it was excess pus that he missed from the surgery, and part of the gauze came out. The infection cavity had created a flesh tunnel. It was so fucking metal.

I couldn't nurse from the infected boob, so I continued to breast-feed from one breast so that it ballooned up with up to eight to twelve ounces of milk at a time. Sometimes Mino would nap too long, so I would have to pump and easily fill two bottles. I walked around with one giant breast for the fourteen months I continued to nurse. The reason I survived all this and was able to continue breastfeeding was that I was in kangaroo mode. I am a mammal and my body was created just to do this. I survived because I am nothing more than an animal. I survived because I became a bitch.

It's weird that *bitch* is a slur in most cultures of the world. I think this stems from the idea that ancient people had that the bond between mother and child was holy. I think *bitch* is a slur for so many cultures for the same reason so many of them worship mother-and-child imagery. They needed to knock bitches down a peg because they knew we were too powerful. In Korea, the word 새끼 (sekki; animal baby) is used interchangeably with 개새끼 (gae-sekki; dog baby). The interesting thing about the word *sekki*, though, is that it's also a term of endearment that a lot of Koreans use for their own children. For a non-Korean speaker, it might seem strange that Koreans refer to their own children with the derogatory term for child of a beast, but there's two meanings in how Koreans use *sekki* for their child. They are being

227

derogatory by admitting we are nothing but animals, but they are also saying that being nothing but an animal is the highest honor of all. The most sophisticated and profound emotion a human can feel is the most common and bonds us to everything that has ever lived and reproduced: love of child.

People who have kids like to say there's no way to describe what it feels like to have a child to someone who doesn't have a child. I feel the same way, but I also don't. Having a baby is strange in that it is something you've never felt before, but it's also the only thing you've ever felt before. Having a baby makes you feel love and fear death, but it's not because those things are taught to you—they're reactivated in you. Having a baby isn't learning; it's realizing you've already known everything all along. It feels like you're being made to do something and you have no idea how to do it, but then you are doing it and realize it's literally the one thing you naturally know how to do. Before giving birth, I was convinced I had no idea what it felt like, and only after I gave birth did I understand that I had known all along.

I know I've been hard on Japanese people in this book, but I never meant actual Japanese people; I meant the small handful of Japanese men who ran the government of that nation over one hundred years ago. The Japanese people who committed violent acts against Koreans and other Asians had no choice. Just like Japanese Americans had no choice when they were placed in concentration camps. On Saipan, the most popular tourist destinations are Banzai Cliff and Suicide Cliff. They are the most spectacularly beautiful, scenic parts of the island, but they're also visit-worthy because of their historical significance. When the Americans invaded Japanese-occupied Saipan during WWII, the Japanese civilians went to these cliffs and engaged in mass suicide. Most of them were the wives and children of men who were sent off to war. Wives and children, the people whose deaths meant nothing in "Heungbu and Nolbu." The women were told propaganda by their own government that American soldiers would boil their babies alive and rape the women to death, and if Americans ever invaded, they should kill themselves because it would be far less painful. Ancient black-and-white film footage remains of this event. In the footage Japanese women are seen throwing their babies off the cliffs before jumping off themselves. My mother, who grew up in the devastating aftermath caused by Japanese imperialism and the Korean War and who should've been the one angriest at the Japanese, was so moved by these images of women who looked exactly like her, killing their own sekki-dul (plural for *sekki*), that she forgot all her anger. She never spoke poorly of the Japanese after that. She realized that if we are all the same as bitches for our shared love of our sekki, then we are also the same as the Japanese.

One of the things that angers Koreans most about the war crimes committed by the Japanese was their practice of kidnapping Korean girls and women for use as comfort women. *Comfort women* was the term for Korean prisoners of war taken to be raped by Japanese soldiers during active duty. They were raped from sunup to sundown every day, many of them to death. Although many women from other countries were taken to be comfort girls, allegedly Koreans were said to be favored for this position because the Japanese government thought they most closely resembled the Japanese, and therefore would be most pleasing to the soldiers. It's interesting that the reason the Japanese government wanted to harm Korean women was the same reason my mom felt love for Japanese women. Because they looked the same.

What Koreans seem to not ever want to mention is that a lot of the Korean comfort women were brought into this role by Korean men. Korean men, often from poor backgrounds, would help procure these women for the Japanese for financial or political incentives. It's hard to hold people under imperialistic rule accountable because we don't know how much autonomy they had, but I feel like it's safe to say that some of them did it to make money and not because they were forced. Another thing often left out of the conversation is that a lot of the comfort women were Japanese. Japanese women made up at least 10 percent of them. It's easier for Korean people to say Japanese people victimized the Koreans, instead of going into the nuance that both Japanese and Koreans were partially victim and perpetrator. Sometimes I feel like the men who control Korea today see the suffering of the comfort women as a pawn in a political game, since they don't seem to care about Korean women who are raped and killed by Korean men. They don't even care about the imaginary women who died in their folktales enough to give them names. Japan and Korea are the two brothers, the main characters. Their women and children suffer, die, and are replaced without any change in the plot.

Years ago, I saw a collection of short films that deeply moved me by the famed Japanese director Akira Kurosawa entitled *Dreams*. One of the films is called *The Tunnel* and portrays a conversation between two Japanese soldiers returning home from war, and it takes place on the country road leading into their hometown. The first soldier says he went home already, but he cannot stay and explains why. When he arrived home after a long journey, he found the house empty. He was starving because he had not eaten in days. He sees a ceremonial offering table full of food for the dead. In Korea, this table is called a Jesa. Jesa is displayed for major holidays and anniversaries of any family member's death, and it is not uncommon to see one in a home at any time. Koreans and Japanese are the same in that we are all taught as children that the food on the table is forbidden. There is a running joke in both cultures that eating the food off the dead-people food table is the worst ass-whooping you can get as a kid. In Japan, they have a practice of placing chopsticks sticking out of the ceremonial bowl of rice in the center of the Jesa and are so superstitious about this that they won't ever leave a pair of chopsticks in any food they are eating. Most Koreans don't really adhere to this superstition, but "chopsticks in food are taboo" blew up on TikTok in the US and I noticed that a lot of Korean Americans now mistakenly think it is also

230

a Korean tradition. But it's not really that common there. That's how intertwined our cultures are. The little nuances between the two are not even known to Koreans or Japanese who live in America.

Anyway, back to the story. So, this Japanese soldier returned home and was starving, so he just started eating the Jesa food. All of a sudden, he hears his mom behind him and he starts apologizing, but he turns around to realize that she is just watching him, crying silently. This is how he realizes he is dead. This film terrified me because I know this is also how I will realize I am dead. This is how all Japanese and Korean people will realize they are dead: when your mom sees you eating the food off the Jesa, and instead of whooping your ass, she cries.

How can I be upset with Japanese people? We are the same people.

I read a little bit about this film, and apparently this was Kurosawa's way of explaining how pointless and cruel he thought war was. The way he chose to communicate this was to tap into the shared fear of the breaking of the bond between mother and child. Comparing anything to that monumental pain puts it into perspective. Nothing is worth the pain of a bitch losing her sekki. No war. No land. Nothing.

Having a kid means understanding we are all the same because we fear the same thing. It means understanding war is worthless because it causes the one thing we all fear. Having a kid means becoming a bitch, the most sacred being. But even someone who doesn't have a kid can be a bitch. Because every single one of us is a sekki, and there is no difference between a bitch and the baby of the bitch.

* * *

NE SEKKI (MY SEKKI)

I CALL MINO "NE SEKKI" all the time. He calls me a bitch all the time. As a joke. He does this funny thing where he self-bleeps himself when

231

using words he's not "allowed" to say. I'll tell him to turn off his iPad, and he will reply, "Stop being a b—!" It makes me laugh every time he does it. One time my friend heard him call me that and told me they thought it was disrespectful. I realized that I had to explain to Mino the definition of the word *bitch* as it had left the realm of the holy and entered the world of men. I had a talk with him and explained that a lot of men who hate women use that word to make women feel bad. He cried and said he didn't mean it in that way. I told him I know he didn't mean it in that way. I know what way he meant it. He meant it in the same way I call him "ne sekki." It is our admission to the universe that we know we are nothing more than a bitch and her sekki. It's our admission that we know we are sacred.

*   *   *

BLACK BEAR

Before I knew I was pregnant, I had a dream. I was with a large group of people who I instinctively knew were my entire family. Some of them were dead and some of them alive. They were not all old. Some were the ghosts of children who died long before I was born; some of them were children born recently, still alive. We were walking through a haunted, eerie, decaying jungle. The journey was so treacherous, many of my family members broke down in violent despair and had to be dragged or carried. All I felt was desperation to get away. I was caged in by the rotting trees, the suffocating heat, and the painful shrieking of my family members. Then, out of nowhere, the jungle cleared, and we stood at the far shore of a glacial lake at the foot of a frozen mountain. In our sweaty, painful misery, we thoughtlessly jumped into the cold blue water. There I swam happily with my entire family, living and dead.

I swam farther out than anyone else, way out into the center of the lake. I was so overcome with the exuberance of life that I failed to see a black bear slowly descend the mountain on the far shore and enter the lake. The black bear swam slowly yet steadily toward us. Everyone in my family rushed out quickly in a panic, without alerting me. I was laughing and splashing when suddenly I noticed my family all standing on the shore, staring in silence. I could see they were not staring at me but at something behind me. I turned and saw the black bear. The bear was almost to me now. I knew it was far too late for me to even attempt to swim to safety. My family had abandoned me. I tried to cry out in despair and rage, but when I opened my mouth, the cold water rushed into my lungs. I was drowning. With this realization, I stopped fighting. I floated, my face barely above the surface of the water, drowning in the anguish of knowing that my family had let this happen to me. I closed my eyes and waited for the bear to kill me. But it never did. After a long time, I opened my eyes to find it quietly swimming alongside me.

Suddenly, I was aware that I was drowning still. No longer afraid, I placed my hands on the bear's shoulders, and he started slowly swimming away from my family.

I looked behind me at the faces of my family. They were not sad or happy. They were nothing. They were everything. In that moment I realized that my family had not left me in the lake to watch me die; they had come with me on a treacherous and terrifying journey so that I would not be alone while going to meet the spirit of my son, their descendant. They had not abandoned me but had taken me as far as they possibly could. They went through millennia of pain and suffering so that I could arrive at the ancient lake at the foot of the heavens. When they saw the spirit of my son, they knew their work was over. The great black bear had descended at that exact moment. He too had had a long journey through the universe since the beginning of time. He was life. But I was terrified because life looks exactly like death.

I had been angry at my family because I thought they had handed me over to death, but they had brought me to life.

My hands felt warm on the fur of the bear, and I relaxed as I felt him easily support my weight. I didn't know where we were going, but I felt safe even though it was somewhere new. Somewhere unknown to my family who were still watching ashore. They didn't want their journey to end; they wanted to continue with us too. But they knew the black bear was there to take only me. The only thing that made the sadness of leaving them behind disappear was to go forward into the unknown with my son.

I woke up the next morning knowing that this was a taemong. I was pregnant and I had met the spirit of my baby.

Mino has always run hot all his life. In the icy winter, walking along the streets of New York City, we will walk side by side, my hands buried in his pockets or under his elbow, since my hands are always cold. Sometimes he will grab my hands and say, "I have heater hands!" Then, while holding them, he confidently leads the way to somewhere I've never been before, somewhere far away from the pain our family has suffered before us. He doesn't know I was drowning in anger at our ancestors before he came.

CHAPTER 14

Life

HATE

A COMMON THING I HEAR Asian American women say on social media about why they don't date Asian American men is that Asian men look like their brothers. The women who say this say it right in the faces of Asian men, the men who look so much like them that it's like they're saying it to their own reflections. They say it to cut them down into a million pieces using a weapon that was handed to them by the whites.

I do not understand it at all because I don't have a brother. I don't know what it feels like to look out at a sea of people and see someone who is in my family because I have no family. I am a part of no tribe because I come from a combination of two. My mother and father come from two races that I am not a part of. My own parents are for-eigners to me. My parents thought I would come out one race or the other, but I came out a secret third thing. I have never seen my brother on the street. Although there are millions of biracial people, we do not see one another because we are fractured into little boats dotting the human race with no established way to meet each other. There is no biracial community made up of biracials speaking their own biracial language in every major city like there are for other ethnic groups. We just have to hang with the Koreans, or pretend we love white water rafting with the whites. This is why we always end up thinking we are the only one. With the exception of siblings, we are alone in our race even in our own families. It's fucking lonely. Even when we see each other in public, we miss each other because we've spent our entire lives in hiding. We've spent our lives shrinking ourselves to fit in with the Koreans or taking up more space to fit in with the whites. Walking past each other without recognition like that heartbreaking Shel Silverstein poem about the two people who had blue skin but didn't recognize each other behind flesh-colored masks.

Is it really that bad to see your brother in the face of someone you don't know?

When one of my mother's many brothers was in grade school, the students were forbidden to speak Korean by their Japanese teachers (I swear to god this is the last time I'm bringing this up, I'm so fucking sorry). If any of the children did, they would be punished but not by the Japanese teacher. They would be slapped across the face by their best friend. The teacher would call the child who spoke Korean up to the front of the class along with their best friend. The best friend was made to slap the child as hard as possible across the face, and if they showed any mercy, the teacher would make the entire class pair up and slap each other until they were satisfied. One day when he was around nine or ten years old, my uncle spoke Korean and was called up to the front of the class along with his best friend. His friend had no choice but to hit him so hard that my uncle fell over. The teacher was satisfied and made them sit back down. After class, my uncle and his friend cried together. They understood that although the hand belonged to one of them, the slap had not. The slap had come from the teacher.

My uncle remained close to this friend until he died. He thought of him as his brother. My mother told me this story to explain to me why the rest of my Korean family could not forgive the Japanese in the way that she had. For her, peace was found through relating to them like they were her own people, but to the rest of her family, they only saw them as a force separating them from one another. My uncle saw that what the Japanese teacher was trying to do that day was make him turn against his friend, his brother. He wouldn't allow this. He wouldn't let the teacher convince him his brother was his enemy.

I know I said I don't understand why Asian American women say that about Asian American men, but I also do understand it. I understand looking in the mirror and hating what you see in it. I also do think that a lot of Asian men are the fucking worst. My short career as someone who is visible on social media has brought the most deranged Asian men my way. The worst, most terrifying hate mail I've received is from them. The levels of depravity they seem to easily access scare me. Asian men hate Asian women with a ferocity that is only matched by how much Asian women hate Asian men. There is so much slapping going on between these two groups that they seem to not notice the teacher is no longer there. This is what the teacher had wanted all along. For us to remain in this room, slapping each other until all of us are destroyed.

There are so many emotions that circle around the idea of "our people." My mother forgave the Japanese because they reminded her so much of herself and "her people," and my uncle hated them because they tried to harm him and "his people." Asian American women hate fucking "our people," but Asian American men think they own "our people." After a while, it gets blurry and confusing. Whose side am I on? Whose side is anyone on? Who are we fighting? One another? I can't find the point I want to make here. Weirdly enough, this is my point. Because this is exactly what my entire life has felt like as a biracial person.

This entire book has been full of repetitive ideas that go around in circles and come out without an answer. This is how the inside of my mind feels. All my life, I have been going around and around without an answer. Maybe there is no answer; maybe life is just about going around the circle over and over again. I thought I would get to the answer of who I was at the end, like gold at the end of a rainbow, but a rainbow is a circle too—it's just that from my perspective, only half of it is visible. When something is a circle, there is no end.

*   *   *

LOVE

MY MOTHER'S BROTHER DIED SUDDENLY of a heart attack when I was five years old. The only things I know about him is that story about getting slapped by his best friend and the fact that (according to my mom) he was the most handsome, funniest man in their town and extremely popular with the ladies for that reason. By the time he died, he was married and had three children and had recently come into a lot of money because of a window factory he had opened that provided all the windows for high-rise apartment buildings that were springing up around the neighborhood during that time. After his funeral, we all met up at his brand-new two-story house in downtown Cheonan. The dark red brick house sat behind a manicured garden and high brick wall, hiding it from the city street. The interior was furnished with chairs and seats made of elaborately carved dark wood and embroidered floral upholstery. The furniture matched the dark wood of the walls. Glitter-speckled linoleum lined the floors. Linoleum, especially glitter linoleum, was coveted as a floor covering in Korea for its clean-feeling properties and the ability to distribute ondol heat evenly. This was the first time in my short life that I had ever been inside a two-story house. The garden and the interior gave it the look of a royal palace. In my mind, my uncle was a king.

That day, the house was full of relatives and extended family crying loudly and pounding their chests. It seemed every corner was taken up by a devastated grandma or old aunt rolling around the floor in anguish. In the living room was the Jesa. A black-and-white photo of my handsome uncle sat at the center of it, surrounded by mountains of autumnal fruit and rice cakes of every shape and size. The relatives would sit in front of it, wailing while looking at his handsome face, surrounded by incense smoke. I remember thinking that they all loved him so much because they were acting so violent and sad. My mother wasn't crying, though. She was acting like nothing was wrong at all. Since she was the only one not consumed by grief, she spent the entire day buzzing around the home, cooking and cleaning, stopping only to wipe the tears off the face of a devastated relative or help another who had fallen down in a fit of tortured crying. I remember thinking my mother didn't love her brother as much as everyone else did.

Later that night, I woke up and my mom wasn't sleeping next to me like usual. I went looking for her through the terrifyingly dark house, full of dark wood, glittering surfaces, ancient-looking floral prints, and ghosts. I found her in the living room, sitting in front of the Jesa. It was empty now and all the lights were off. The visual of her sitting rigidly on the floor in the center of the dark room haunts me to this day. My mother sat in front of the altar of her dead brother, crying silently. She wasn't alone.

My uncle stood in front of her with his back turned, ravenously eating the food meant for him and only him. He turned around mid-bite and realized she was there. He said with a chuckle, "엄마안태일르지마!" (Don't tell Mom!)

My uncle studied my mother's face. She wasn't laughing at his joke, a throwback from a time when they were both children and could get in trouble for eating the food meant for the dead. But they were both adults now, and no one would whoop their asses for something like that. Why wasn't she laughing? She always laughed. Little sister with a mistake for a name, Ippun-i. Why was she crying? Was it because his joke mentioned their mother who had died only three years ago? Was she crying because he had taken the joke too far like he did on so many occasions? No. It was something else. Something else was making her sad. Something was very wrong. When my mom didn't respond to his joke, he slowly turned back to the Jesa, where he saw the black-and-white photo of someone who looked just like him.

This was how my uncle, my mom's brother, realized he was dead.

At that moment from behind her, I whispered, "엄마 나 무서워." (Mom, I'm scared.) My mother wiped her face silently. She got up, picked me up in her arms, and carried me back to the room, where she sat next to me until I fell asleep. She sang the only Korean lullaby, the song every Korean mother sings to every Korean child, the song my grandmother sang to her and all of her countless brothers: 자장자장자장자장 (jajang jajang jajang jajang; [go to] sleep). After I fell back asleep, she went back to help her dead brother realize he was dead.

The thing about being afraid of the death of your child is that it is so terrifying that it makes you immensely strong. The possible loss of my sekki has made every other fear I used to have mean absolutely nothing in comparison. If I was told to kill myself to save my child, I would do it without hesitation. My own death no longer means anything to me. But I am still terrified of one thing: the death of my mother. Before I had Mino, I decided that if my mother died, I would kill myself. I could not imagine living without her. I know I have been harsh on her in the telling of my past, but it's because I consider her and me the same. I am like the cruel Japanese soldiers in the way that I feel the need to harm the people who look just like me. My mother is the only person I have truly ever loved besides my child. When I told my mother the fear I had of her death, she spoke about the death of her own mother for the first and only time. She said that it was just as bad as she had ever feared. But one thing made it feel OK, and that was knowing that her children were still alive. She said the only thing that made her feel better was being around her kids. My mother was trying to teach me that in order to survive her death, I needed a sekki of my own. She wanted me to have a kid so I could experience being the most powerful being in existence: a bitch. A bitch is only afraid of one thing: the loss of her sekki. Therefore, she is not afraid of anything else, not even the death of her own mother.

The gift that children give their mothers is the ability to survive the death of their own mothers.

* * *

LIFE

TEN YEARS LATER, MY UNCLE'S WIDOW came to visit our house. She sat on the floor with my mom, and they ate and drank soju. It was like one in the afternoon. My aunt is one of the most amazing people I've ever met in my life. She is vibrant, clever, funny, and exceedingly beautiful. However, she is considered fat by Korean standards (130 pounds), so no one in Korea has ever told her how beautiful she is. She is one of the most dynamic and fascinating people I've ever met. When she bust out the soju, my mom just went along with it. My mom never drank back then, but she never would refuse a drink because she didn't want to ruin anyone's good time. I was sitting in the living room a few feet away. My aunt drunkenly started telling this story of how she found out her late husband had cheated on her while he was still alive, early on in their marriage. I'm going to paraphrase her story below, keeping the energy intact. She said:

"We were married less than a year, and your fucking useless, lazy brother was already fucking other rags [Korean slang for sluts]. He thought I was fucking stupid and didn't even try to hide it, that ugly, dark motherfucker. He would just leave all night long and come back in the morning, and even if I hit him and screamed at him, he would just sit there quietly like a fucking babo idiot son of a bitch! Then finally I got fed up and followed him one night secretly in the other car, and he was so stupid he didn't even notice I was following him, that stupid, crazy son of a bitch!"

During the story, my mom was interjecting with approving little nods and noises while softly disagreeing with the insults hurled at her beloved late brother. "Yes...I remember...I remember. Oh, no, but he wasn't lazy, he was hardworking...Yes, but he was stupid for doing that...He was dark BUT he was handsome! But yes, he was dark...I remember you followed him in the car! Good for you!"

My aunt continued, "How is anyone so stupid they can't see someone following them on a country road with no other cars? He was probably so fucking horny, that dirty son of a bitch! Imagine being too horny to even see a car following you? He was that excited?? I followed him so I could catch him in the act. Then I followed him to that stupid bitch's house, the one who went to school in Seoul, remember? She thought she was better than us? Fucking crazy bitch!! I saw him go into the house! Then I sat there waiting. My fucking heart was going to fucking explode, I swear, but I waited!! So they would be in the middle of doing it! Then I ran out and I screamed at the window for him to come out, remember? I screamed??"

My mom replied, "Yes. I remember!"

By this point, my aunt was so angry she was almost delirious and was screaming at the top of her lungs. I could barely understand what she was spit-screaming, but from what I could piece together in between violent inhaling and cuss words was that my aunt tried to climb into their window, at which point my uncle climbed up to the roof of the woman's house. My aunt couldn't climb up that high, so she was left outside screaming at him for hours.

Finally she said, "I kept screaming at him, 'Get down! I'm going to fucking kill you! Get down here, you fucking crazy son of a bitch! You're dead!! YOU'RE DEAD!'"

Her red face and neck were pulsing and swollen, full of K-rage and soju. Her bloodshot eyes were laser-focused on my mom's soft, understanding face, nodding quietly in agreement still.

My aunt screamed over and over again, "YOU'RE DEAD!"

"너 죽었어! 너 죽었어!" (Nuh jukeoseo! Nuh jukeoseo!)

When she paused to catch her breath, she broke eye contact, seemingly confused at her own anger. She grabbed her soju glass and took a shot. My mom quietly said, "근대 이재 죽었내." (Gundae Ije jugeone; Well, now he is dead.)

My aunt suddenly looked at my mother, and all the color immediately left her face. I saw the realization flash across my aunt's face that he *was* dead. He had been dead for ten years. She had been so angry at him for cheating on her nearly thirty years ago that she had forgotten. In a split second, I saw her expression turn from angry to confused, then hurt, and then she closed her eyes very, very hard. I thought she was going to burst out crying, but instead she let out the strongest, loudest laugh. The laughter filled the room and bounced off the walls. The laughter coated all the food laid out in little plates on the table. It fell like heavy summer rain onto all the inanimate objects in the room, making them come alive with the vibration. These items that were never alive and would never die danced with the life injected through them from my aunt. My mom started laughing just as hard, and they fell into a violent fit of cry-laughing and slapping each other on the knee. The sound of their laughing penetrated the floors, through the ondol, and through the earth. The Korean dirt that they had both come from and where they would both return one day. The dirt my uncle had returned to ten years ago. Somewhere a few kilometers away, his body danced with the trembling of their laughter. Their laughter soon turned to violent, ravenous sobbing. The hungry sobbing of longing. Their loud cries reached my dead uncle too. The cries surrounded him and tried to pull him out in vain. They wanted so badly for him to join them again for one last laugh and one last cry.

In between laughter and sobs, my aunt and mom kept repeating, "죽었내." (He is dead.)

My mom and aunt were sad and happy that he was dead.

Because when someone is dead, they cannot laugh and that is bad, but they also cannot cry, which is good.

To live is to laugh and cry.

To love is to make people laugh and cry.

Even ten years after you've died.

Acknowledgments

Although this is a book about my life, a lot of what I understand about myself was meticulously unearthed by the brilliant Ariel Flavin. I can say without any doubt that this book would not have existed without her work, and I am forever grateful.

Professionally, I would like to thank my editor Vivian Lee, my agent Kim Witherspoon, and Jessica Mileo. All of these women believed in my work and championed for my voice to be heard, even before I felt the confidence to do so for myself. I would also like to acknowledge the hard work of all the people involved with the creation of this book at Little, Brown. I also want to thank Brian Park, a brilliant comedian and my esteemed former podcast cohost.

Personally, I would like to thank all of the friends who were there for me during the difficult period of writing this book: Chansophalla Nop, Oak Laokwansathitaya, John deBary, Alex Pemoulie, Guang Xu, Helen Cho, Anne Ishii, Chris Crawford, and David Cabello.

Lastly, I would like to thank my son, Mino Bowien, his dad, Danny Bowien, and Sara Hiromi Skinner.

About the Author

Youngmi Mayer is a stand-up comedian and host of the podcasts *Feeling Asian* and *Hairy Butthole*. She has been on *Today*, ABC News, *Rolling Stone*, CNN, Munchies, *Eater's Guide to the World*, and *The Mind of a Chef*. Her work has been featured in *Netflix Is a Joke*, Comedy Central, and the BBC. She has written for *Lucky Peach*, *Cherry Bombe*, *InStyle*, and *Women's Health*. She is one of the rare comedians working today who has obtained success both on online platforms and in the mainstream. She lives in New York City with her son, Mino Bowien.